# Warrior Ghost Plays
# from the Japanese Noh Theater

# Warrior Ghost Plays from the Japanese Noh Theater

## Parallel Translations
## with Running Commentary

Chifumi Shimazaki

East Asia Program
Cornell University
Ithaca, New York 14853

The *Cornell East Asia Series* publishes manuscripts on a wide variety of scholarly topics pertaining to East Asia. Manuscripts are published on the basis of camera-ready copy provided by the volume author or editor.

Inquiries should be addressed to Editorial Board, Cornell East Asia Series, East Asia Program, Cornell University, 140 Uris Hall, Ithaca, New York 14853.

To Dr. Howard B. Hamilton

in thanks for his wholehearted collaboration
in the making of this book

# TABLE OF CONTENTS

# PREFACE

Some two hundred Noh currently performed are classified into five categories so that a formal five-Noh program, or a less formal one with fewer Noh, can be made with proper choice and arrangement. The Noh in the first category are ceremonial and congratulatory, whose *shite* (leading character) is a deity. The usually pathetic second category is *shura* (*Asura*'s Hell/battle)-Noh, with a warrior ghost as *shite*. Typically the *shite* of graceful third-category Noh is an elegant woman, ghost or living. The fourth and fifth categories are of miscellaneous types, which can be further broken down into sub-groups.

In addition to the type of *shite* and dominant mood, a number of other characteristics at various dramatic levels distinguish the five categories. Such characteristics regarding the first three categories are explained in some detail by this author in previous publications devoted to these categories. Since this is the second book on *shura*-Noh, only a brief explanation is give here about this genre. For details, the reader is invited to refer to the introduction to the first book.*

There are today sixteen *shura*-Noh (seventeen in the Kanze school) in the repertories of the different Noh schools. The *shite* of *shura*-Noh are ghosts of warriors. With once exception, *Tamura*, they belonged to either of the two rival clans, Heike and Genji. Most *shura*-Noh are based on *Heike Monogatari*, which tells about the rise and fall of Heike. As *mugen* (visional) Noh, typically a *shura*-Noh is made up of two scenes. In the first scene, the *waki* (supporting actor), a traveling monk, comes to a place where a battle was fought in the past. A villager tells him about the battle and disappears. In the second scene, the villager, who is actually the ghost of warrior, reappears in full battle attire and describes in song and mime the battle in which he fought, then disappears, having begged the monk to pray for his soul condemned to eternal fighting in Asura's hell, like all warrior ghosts. In a number of *shura*-Noh the *shite* performs *kakeri*, a short dance which describes his anger and anguish in Asura's Hell. Depending on the definition of the term, six or seven *shura*-Noh have *katari*, a long narration of spoken lines, often ending in singing. Only about thirty Noh out of some two hundred now performed have *katari*. Thus, the frequency of *katari* among *shura*-Noh is extremely high, a reflection of the influence of their sources, *Heike Monogatari* and other military stories, which were chanted and narrated by professional singers and narrators.

*Shura*-Noh can be classified by a number of criteria. For example, in three of them the *shite* is a ghost of victorious warrior. These Noh are referred to as *kachi* (victorious)-shura. The rest are *make* (defeated)-shura, the dominant mood of which is pathos. *Shura*-Noh are also classified into four groups by the *shite*'s age and sex:

1. Seven *kindachi-mono* (young nobleman-pieces)
2. Four *heida-mono* (*Heida* is a mask for a brave warrior.)
3. Two *rô-musha-mono* (old warrior pieces)
4. One *onna-musha-mono* (female warrior-piece)

The first book on *shura*-Noh in The Noh series deals with five *make-shura* whose *shite* is a *kindachi*. Of these, Tomonaga is Genji, and the rest are Heike. This book contains:

| | | | |
|---|---|---|---|
| *Yashima* | Genji | Victorious | *Heida* |
| *Michimori* | Heike | Defeated | Young nobleman |
| *Tomoakira* | " | " | " |
| *Yorimasa* | Genji | " | Old warrior |
| *Kanehira* | " | " | *Heida* |
| *Tomoe* | " | " | Female warrior |

The translations, based on the Taisei Edition of the Kanze school published by Hinoki Shoten, Tokyo, are rendered line by line, in parallel with romanized Japanese texts, in an attempt to be faithful to the original, even in regard to the length of each line, the word order, pivot words and other rhetorical subtleties. The term *mae-shite*, *nochi-shite*, *mae-tsure*, *nochi-tsure* and *waki-tsure* instead of *mae-zite* etc. are used in accordance with the practice of the Kanze school.

I am most grateful for kind support and assistance of many friends, among them especially Dr. Howard B. Hamilton, Noh expert and demonstrator, Falls Church, Virginia, Professor Mae Smethurst and Professor J. Thomas Rimer of Pittsburgh University and Mrs. Darlene King of the University of Maryland, Dr. Dale Preston, Radiation Effects Research Foundation, Hiroshima, Mr. John W. Dunbar, Falls Church Virginia and Mr. Shawn Helm of Washington, D.C. for their advice and help in preparing this book for publication. I thank Professor Haruo Nishino of Hosei University and the Nogami Kinen Kenkyujo (Nogami Memorial Noh Research Institute) for his technical advice.

Among references, I am much indebted to the following, particularly for the sources of quotations and allusions made in the Noh texts: *Yôkyoku-shû*, 2 vols, by Hiroshi Koyama, Nihon Koten Bungaku Zenshû series; *Yôkyoku-shû*, 2 vols, by Akira Omote and Mario Yokomichi, Nihon Koten Bungaku Taikei series; *Yôkyoku Taikan*, 7 vols, by Kentarô Sanari.

* Previous publications of The Noh series by Chifumi Shimazaki, published by Hinoki Shoten, Tokyo:

Volume 1. *Kami* (god)-Noh
  *Takasago, Oimatsu, Yôrô, Ema, Kamo, Seiôbo*, with an introduction to Noh and an introduction to *kami*-Noh. 1972.
Volume 2. *Shura* (*Asura*'s Hell/battle)-Noh
  Book 1: *Tsunemasa, Atsumori, Tadanori, Kiyotsune, Tomonaga*, with an introduction to *shura*-Noh. 1987.
Volume 3. *Sanbanme-mono* (woman Noh)
  Book 1. *No-no-miya, Yûgao, Hajitomi, Kochô*, with an introduction to woman Noh. 1976.
  Book 2: *Eguchi, Izutsu, Kakitsubata, Obasute, Matsukaze*. 1977.
  Book 3: *Hotoke-no-hara, Futari Shizuka, Senju, Yuya, Ohara Gokô*. 1981.

Chifumi Shimazaki

# NOTES ON THE PRONUNCIATION
# OF NOH LANGUAGE


The Japanese version of the Noh libretti in *the Noh* is romanized according to the system used in Kenkyū-sha's *New Japanese-English Dictionary*.

Unless marked with a macron the vowels *a, e, i, o* and *u* are all short:
*a* as *a* in *star*: *hana* (flower), *yama* (mountain), *mata* (again)
*e* as *e* in *nest*: *take* (bamboo), *tera* (temple), *ware* (I)
*i* as *e* in *below*: *ima* (now), *aki* (autumn), *kami* (deity)
*o* as *o* in *obey*: *hito* (person), *kono* (this), *tokoro* (place)
*u* as *oo* in *rude*, but shorter: *uta* (song), *mizu* (water), *yuki* (snow)

There are no double vowels, each vowel forms a separate syllable, pronounced separately:
*mai* (dance) *ma-i, ao* (blue) *a-o, koe* (voice) *ko-e, oi* (old age) *o-i,*
*sue* (the end) *su-e, kie* (to vanish) *ki-e, ei* (prosperity) *e-i*

All vowels are pronounced. In the texts, there is no accent over an *e* to indicate that it should be pronounced:
*tae* (exquisite) *ta-e, aware* (pathos) *awa-re, shite* (protagonist) *shi-te,*
*mare* (rare) *ma-re, tera* (temple) *te-ra, seki* (barrier) *se-ki*

Macrons are used over long vowels in spoken lines, and hyphens are used in lines that are sung: *sō* or *so-o* (monk), *kokyō* or *kokyo-o* (native place), *nyoshō* or *nyosho-o* (lady)

Of the consonants, the following have approximately the same sounds as in English:
*b, d, h, j, k, m, n, p, r, s, t, w* and *y.*
*ch* as *ch* in *church*: *michi* (way), *uchi* (within), *chō* (butterfly)
*fu* as *hoo* in *hoof* but shorter: *fune* (boat), *fushigi* (strange), *fūfu* (man and wife)

*g* is pronounced hard, as in *god*, when it comes at the head of a word: *Genpei* (combined word for *Genji* and *Heike*), *Gojo* (fifth street).

Otherwise *g* is soft as in *singer*: *kage* (shade), *gaga* (steep). *g* is often pronounced softly even when it comes at the head of a word: *gotoku* (like), *kimi ga yo* (my lord's reign), *warawa ga iori* (my hut).

Because Noh was mostly written during the Muromachi period (1336-1573), based on the language in use since the preceding periods, there are certain words in the Noh texts with pronunciations peculiar to those times. Some of the peculiarities are literary, some colloquial; a number of others are technical terms, such as Buddhist terms. Following are some of the most important examples of special pronunciations that are found in the Noh texts included in this book, some common to all five schools, others peculiar to one or more. (For details, see "Pronunciation of Noh Language" in *The Noh* Vol 1, *God Noh*.)

At the beginning of certain words, and when followed by an *m*, *u* is pronounced like *n* in *and*, instead of the usual *oo* sound as in *rude*.
*uma* (horse) -- > *nma, ume* (plum tree or blossom) -- > *nme*
The monosyllabic long *yū* sound is pronounced in two syllabic *i-u:* *yū* (to say) -- > *i-u, mōshū* (attachment) -- > *mōshi-u*,
*kyūjo* (court lady) -- > *ki-ujo, ryūsui* (running water) -- > *ri-usui*

The use of hyphens in the Japanese romanization in *The Noh* series is not always consistent. Often, especially, in notes, they are used to clarify the meaning of elements making up a word.

The romanization of the Japanese version is based on the pronunciation of the Kanze school.

# PLAN OF A NOH STAGE
## (Based on the Kanze Noh Theater)

The Stage area, defined by the four pillars, is roughly 19 feet square. The *hashigakari* (bridgeway) is about 25 feet long. The stage floor is made of long thick planks of unpainted but highly polished cryptomeria wood. Many Noh stages have several reverberating earthenware jars suspended under the floor to intensify the actor's stamps while dancing.

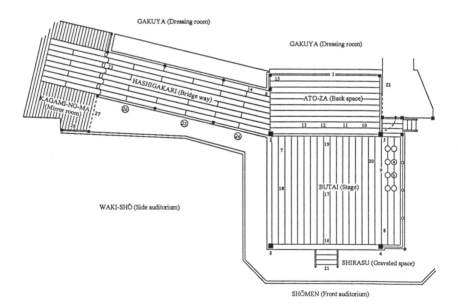

1. *Kagamiita*, the back panel, with a painting of an old pine tree.
2. *Shite-bashira* (*shite* pillar)
3. *Metsuke-bashira* (eye-setting pillar), serves as a guide post for actors wearing masks whose range of vision is limited by the small eye holes.
4. *Waki-bashira* (supporting actor's pillar)
5. *Fue-bashira* (flute pillar)

6. *Kyōgen-bashira* (*kyōgen* actor's pillar)
7. *Shite-za* (*shite*'s place), or *jō-za* (fixed place), the *shite*'s home place, also called *nanori-za* (naming place), where characters on entering the stage tell their names.
8. *Waki-za* (Supporting actor's place), where the *waki* sits while not in action.
9. *Jiuta-za* (chorus' place) a̱ is the chorus leader's place in Hosho, Kongo and Komparu Schools of Noh; ḇ is that for Kanze and Kita.
10-13. *Hayashi-za* (musicians' place)
10. *Fue* (flute)
11. *Kotsuzumi* (small hand drum)
12. *Ōtsuzumi*, also called *ōkawa* (large hand drum)
13. *Taiko-za* (stick drum)
14. *Kyōgen-za* (comedian's place) In many Noh, a *kyōgen* player, who performs during the interlude, enters late in the first act to sit there until his turn comes, as well as returning there when not in action at other times.
15. *Kōken-za* (stage assistants' place) Occupied by two, sometimes three stage assistants helping actors with change of costumes, providing stage props, prompting and so on.
16. *Shōsaki* (stage front)
17. *Wakishō* (stage center)
18. *Wakishō* (side front)
19. *Daishō-mae* (in front of large and small hand drums)
20. *Jiutai-mae* (in front of chorus), also, *fue-za-mae* (in front of the flute) Minor characters sit there when not in action. The *waki* also sits there when the *waki-za* is occupied.
21. *Shirasu-bashigo* (stairs to the gravelled space) During the Tokugawa era, actors descended from the stage by these stairs to receive gifts from dignitaries; a vestige of those times, no longer used.
22. *Kirido* ("hurry" door, a small, low, sliding door) Chorus and stage assistants enter and exit here as well as minor and "dead" characters.
23. *Agemaku* (lift curtain) The *hashigakari* is separated from the *kagami no ma* by two bamboo rods attached to its lower corners.
24. *Ichi no matsu* (the first pine) Three small pine trees beside the bridgeway serve as guide posts, similar to the *metsuke bashira* described for 3. In some Noh, significant action occurs on the bridgeway near these pines.
25. *Ni no matsu* (second pine)
26. *San no matsu* (third pine)
27. *Bugyō-mado*, also *arashi-mado* and *monomi-mado* (lookout window)
28. *Kagami* (mirror) A *shite* actor in costume, ready to put on a mask, sits for a while in front of the mirror in quiet contemplation, to identify himself with the character he is going to impersonate.

屋

嶋

# YASHIMA

ふたたび一葉に　くだけて二三一。
空川くもまれ雲の波のよ

The sky rolling with clouds, a sea of
    billowing waves

Sora yuku no mata kumo no nami no

                -Line 290

# INTRODUCTION

Minamoto no Yoshitsune (1159--1189), the hero of *Yashima*, was a son of Yoshitomo, the head of the Genji clan, by his mistress Tokiwa. When Yoshitomo was assassinated after his defeat in the Heiji rebellion in 1159, Yoshitsune, still a young baby, was captured with his mother and two elder brothers. Taira no Kiyomori, the head of the Heike clan and the leader of the Imperial army, spared their lives on condition that the mother become his mistress. (See the Introduction to *Tomonaga, Shura*-Noh, Book 1, p. 167.) The boys were sent to different temples to become monks when they grew up. When he was fifteen years old, Yoshitsune escaped from his temple and went to Hiraizumi in Mutsu, the northernmost province of Japan's mainland. There he lived under the protection of Fujiwara no Hidehira, the head of the most powerful family of the province. Then his exiled elder brother Yoritomo raised an army against their cousin, Minamoto no Yoshinaka, also called Kiso Yoshinaka, after the name of his home province. Having driven the Heike out of Kyoto, Yoshinaka had occupied the city and thrown the place into confusion with his unruly actions. Yoshitsune left Hiraizumi to join Yoritomo. He and Noriyori, another brother, marched to Kyoto as commanders of the Genji army, while Yoritomo remained at his headquarters in Kamakura. Yoshitsune and Noriyori defeated Yoshinaka, then fought against the Heike, finally destroying them at Dan-no-Ura off the northern coast of Kyushu. Yoshitsune's promotion by the Imperial court in reward for his services incurred Yoritomo's anger, and Yoshitsune had to leave Kyoto as a fugitive. Finally he made his escape to Hiraizumi, where he lived in peace until his protector Hidehira's death. Then the latter's son Yasuhira attacked Yoshitsune with Yoritomo's force. Yoshitsune killed himself. His wife and children, as well as his retainers all perished.

Yoshitsune first appears in *Heike Monogatari* in "Battle at Hōjū Temple" chapter in Vol. 8, as the commander of the Genji army on his way to Kyoto to attack his cousin Yoshinaka. In the succeeding volumes, we see him winning every battle against the Heike, until he destroys them, but finally, persecuted by his brother, fleeing from Kyoto. Following is an outline of the passages in *Heike Monogatari* which provide material for *Yashima*.

The Heike, driven out of Kyoto by Kiso Yoshinaka, wandered about remote western provinces, finally returning to Ichinotani (near present Kobe) after Yoshinaka's fall.  In February 1184 they were attacked by Yoshitsune and fled by sea to Yashima in Shikoku, having suffered heavy casualties.  Atsumori, Tsunemasa, Tadanori, Michimori and Tomoakira, the heroes of *Shura*-Noh named after them, were among the Heike noblemen who fell in the battle.  In February 1185 Yoshitsune left Kyoto to attack the Heike at Yashima.  He was detained at the seaport Watanabe near present Osaka, while the ships damaged by a typhoon were repaired.  Kajiwara no Kagetoki, a retainer of Yoritomo, suggested to Yoshitsune that he equip the ships with "back-rudders," which would enable them to make a swift retreat.  Yoshitsune at once rejected the proposal, saying that only a coward resorted to such means.  In retort Kagetoki called Yoshitune a foolhardy man.  They confronted each other, their hands on their swords, but were held back by those present.  This incident eventually led Kajiwara to malign Yoshitsune to Yoritomo.  When the ships were repaired, Yoshitsune, defying the protests of the ships' captains, immediately set out in the midst of the still raging storm.  Only four out of two hundred Genji ships followed their leader.  Sailing swiftly before a tail wind, and arriving at the opposite shore in a few hours instead of the normally required three days, Yoshitsune and his followers headed towards Yashima for a surprise attack. . . . ("Back-rudder," Vol. 10) Defeating remnants of Heike troops on the way, and adding the surrenderers to his force, Yoshitsune marched on quickly.  The Heike forsook their Yashima Front and, having escaped to the sea by ships, confronted Yoshitsune's forces on the beach.  On that day, Yoshitsune was attired in a bright-colored brocade robe under armor threaded with strings of graded shades of purple and white, a gold-mounted sword on his belt and arrows with dappled feathers in his quiver.  Holding the middle of a bow thickly covered with rattan, his glaring eyes fixed on the enemies on the sea, he called aloud, "I am the delegate of the First Ex-emperor, the Third Officer of the Police and Justice Office in the Fifth Court Rank, Minamoto no Yoshitsune."  A number of small Heike boats led by Noto-no-kami Noritsune[1] came toward the land and took their position near the beach.  One after another, the men on both sides jeered at each other, until the verbal attacks came to an end, as a Genji archer shot a Heike man who was throwing insults at Yoshitsune. (110-122)[2]

Noto-no-kami, Heike's mightiest archer, took aim at Yoshitsune. Hindered by Yoshitsune's followers who exposed themselves to Noritsune's arrows in defence of their leader, Noritsune quickly struck down a dozen of them with his mighty arrows.  One of the arrows pierced through the

---

[1]Noto-no-kami (Lord of Noto Province):  A brave Heike general, son of Kiyomori's younger brother Norimori.
[2]The number refers to the line in the libretto.

breast of the man in the forefront, Satō Tsuginobu.[3] Noritsune's page Kikuōmaru ran toward Tsuginobu and was about to cut his head off, but fell on all fours, hit by an arrow shot by Tsuginobu's younger brother Tadanobu.[3]

Noritsune jumped off his boat, and picking up Kikuōmaru, threw him into the boat, preventing his head from being taken by the enemy. However, mortally wounded, Kikuōmaru expired. Yoshitsune, deeply grieving over Tsuginobu's death, had funeral rites performed for him by a priest in the neighborhood, giving him one of his prized horses. Those who saw this said that they would die willingly for such a lord. (144--148)

Three Heike warriors landed on the beach, one of them carrying a shield, another a bow, and the third a halberd, shouting challenges at their enemy. At this, five Genji horsemen charged at them. Mionoya no Jūrō, who was at their head, had his horse shot by an arrow, so he leaped to the ground and drew his sword. One of the Heike men rushed at him, brandishing his halberd. Armed as he was with only a small sword, Mionoya quickly took to his heels. The enemy ran after him and, instead of slashing with his halberd, tried to grasp the neck plate of Mionoya's helmet with his right hand, Mionoya ran off, the enemy running after him. Three times Mionoya escaped, but then the enemy at last took hold of the neck plate. For a moment they stood still, each pulling with all his might till the neck piece came off and Mionoya made his escape. This Heike warrior shouted that his name was Aku-Shichibyōe Kagekiyo. (121--141)

Plucking courage at this, about two hundred Heike landed on the beach and challenged their enemy from behind a row of shields which they set upright on the sand. Yoshitsune with eighty horsemen sallied out towards them, leaping into the seawater after the enemy who fled back to their ships. With rakes they hooked Yoshitsune's helmet two or three times, but every time his men struck them off with their swords and halberds. Then Yoshitsune had his bow knocked off by a rake. As he tried to retrieve it with his horse whip, his men told him to give up, but finally he picked it up and returned with a smile on his face. Veteran warriors snapped their fingers,[4] saying to him, "Your conduct was most regrettable. Even if your bow were worth a thousand pieces of gold, why should you risk your life for it?" To this Yoshitsune answered, "It was not because I was sorry to lose it that I retrieved it. If my bow were like my uncle Tametomo's,[5] which took two or three men to string, then I would drop it deliberately and let them take it. However, I should hate to have the enemy, having taken hold of my poor bow, laugh at me, saying that such was the bow of the

---

[3]They left their home in Mutsu Province to accompany Yoshitsune. Tadanobu is the *Shite* of the Noh by the same name and the *Waki* in *Yoshino Shizuka*.

[4]Snapping fingers is a gesture expressing reproach.

[5]Tametomo: The eighth son of Tameyoshi and a younger brother of Yoshitsune's father Yoshitomo, was an archer of supernatural power.

Genji's commander. So I retrieved it at the risk of my life." All who heard this were deeply moved. (226--265) When it grew dark, they made a retreat and encamped in the fields and on the hills of Mure and Takamatsu. ("Dropping of the Bow." Volume 10)

The Noh *Yashima* closely follows the original story. The neckpiece-pulling episode is told in the *katari* in the first act, that of bow-dropping in *sashi* and *kuse* in the second act. The Noh faithfully presents the imagery of Yoshitsune portrayed in *Heike Monogatari*, a brave warrior, a winner of every battle through bold and shrewd tactics, who captivated people's hearts with his human touches, personal traits which have made him the most sympathetic hero figure in the folklore of Japan. His tenderness toward his followers is hinted in a brief reference to Tsuginobu's death. His break-neck bravery which led to Kajiwara's calumniation of him to Yoritomo, is briefly referred to in the *sashi* coming just before the *kuse*. The Noh develops as follows:

The *Waki*, a traveling monk, comes to the coast of Yashima with *Waki-tsure*, the attendant monks. To obtain a night's lodging, he waits by a fisherman's hut for its owner's return. Two fishermen, one aged, the other young, the *Shite* and *Tsure*, enter, each carrying a fishing rod on his shoulder. They sing songs that describe the evening seascape in spring. When they come home, the monk asks them for a night's shelter. The old man refuses at first because of the shabbiness of his hut, but, hearing that the travelers are from Kyoto, his heart warms towards them and invites them to stay. The fishermen, the old man says, are also from Kyoto. They are moved to tears as the visitors remind them of the past days. Then, at the monk's request, the old fisherman tells about the battle fought long ago at this place between the Genji and Heike. First he gives a description of the brilliant young commander of the Genji, Minomoto no Yoshitsune in his splendid military attire, then he relates the "neck-plate pulling" episode, and how the day's fighting came to an end when Yoshitsune's retainer Satō Tsuginobu and Kikuōmaru, an attendant of Noto-no-kami Noritsune, the Heike commander, lost their lives. To the monk wonder-struck at the detailed narration told by an old fisherman, the old man hints at his name, and disappears with a promise that he will return and reveal his identity when the time for fighting in Asura's Hell arrives.

When the night is about to pass, as the monk lies on a mat of moss, a figure in full battle attire appears, saying his name is Yoshitsune. Because of his earthly attachment, he is condemned to eternal fighting in hell, and his spirit hovers between the boundary of life and death, now appearing to the monk in a dream to tell his story. First, the story about retrieving the bow is told in the *kuri-sashi-kuse*. Then the *Shite* performs a *kakeri*, a brief dance expressing the fury and agitation in battle. In the final song in *shura-nori*, the ghost describes by dancing mime his fighting with Noto-no-kami Noritsune in the midst of war cries and white flashing swords in the moonlit seascape, but all vanishes with the first light of the day.

As a *shura*-Noh, *Yashima* has certain features which characterize the Noh of this type, such as the special costume representing battle attire; the *kakeri* which describes the warrior's burning anger in battle; *shite*'s reference to *shura-dō* (fighting hell), to which all warriors are condemned;[6] description of fighting, accompanied by miming and songs in *shura* rhythm. With these characteristics common to *shura*-Noh, *Yashima*, along with two others, *Tamura* and *Ebira* (The Quiver), is different from the rest of *shura*-Noh. Whereas typically the hero of a *shura*-Noh is a defeated warrior, the *Shite* of these three *shura*-Noh are victors. The two types of *shura*-Noh are respectively called *kachi* (victorious)-*shura* and *make* (defeated)-*shura*. *Kachi-shura* distinguish themselves from *make-shura* not so much in structure as in the general atmosphere, which is pervaded by high spirit, in contrast to the pathetic mood dominant in *make-shura*. This is symbolized by the *shura* fan carried by the warrior ghost. A *kachi-shura* fan depicts a large bright red rising sun in the center, whereas a *make-shura* fan has a large setting sun sinking onto sea waves. In *Ebira*, the warrior fights with a branch of plum blossom in his quiver, a harbinger of spring and the symbol of blooming youth. *Yashima* ends with a description of refreshing morning seascape which greets the monk awakening from his dream.

*Shura*-Noh can also be classified, though not very precisely, into the following three groups by the degree of dominance of dance and song versus narrative elements: (1) song and dance type, (2) narrative type, (3) those standing between (1) and (2). (See pp. 18-21, *Shura*-Noh 1.) The second type is closer to the original than the rest in that the original stories, such as *Heiji Monogatari* and *Heike Monogatari*, are *katari-mono* (narrative stories chanted or narrated). Most of *shura*-Noh in this group have *katari* (narration), in which a character tells a story to other character(s) in spoken lines. Unlike the dance-and-song type *shura*-Noh, none of these has dance in the *kuse*. In *Yashima*, which belongs to the second group, the episodes of neck-plate pulling and of Tsuginobu's and Kikuômaru's deaths, told in a long *katari* by the *Mae-Shite*, Yoshitsune's ghost in the guise of an aged fisherman, are the major features of the first act, while the entire *kuri-sashi-kuse* in the second act, unaccompanied by a dance, is devoted to the "dropping of the bow" episode.

Appropriately for a victorious battle Noh having a great national hero for its protagonist, *Yashima* is conceived as a large-scale major opus. For example, the *Mae-shite* makes his entrance with a *tsure*, to the accompaniment of *issei* music. They sing a series of songs in *sashi*, *issei* and another *sashi*, and enter the main stage accompanied by *ashirai* music. This elaborate and dignified style of *Mae-shite*'s entrance is comparable to that of any *waki*-(god) Noh, and is rare among *shura*-Noh. Among other

---

[6]In *Tamura* there is no allusion to Asura's Hell. The Noh is exceptional as a *shura* piece, based on sources other than *gunki-mono* (military story), and is a hymn to Kanzeon Bosatsu (Avalokitesvara). See p. 10, *Shura*-Noh Book 1.

categories, a similar dignified entrance of *Mae-shite* accompanied by a *tsure* is made in *Matsukaze*, a *sanban-me-mono* of a grand scale, rich in *yūgen*. Besides the *Mae-shite*'s entrance, there are certain similarities between the two Noh. In both, the owner of the hut gives a night's shelter to a monk after they have refused it because of the shabbiness of their dwellings. Both the fisherwomen and fishermen are moved to tears as the monk's words remind them of their past. Then they proceed to tell their stories. The first act of *Yashima* is rich in poetic passages describing the lonely seascape and desolate life of fishermen, which again strikes a close resemblance between the two Noh. With an assortment of colorful episodes told in a series of a well-structured, fast-moving narratives against a background rich in poetic imagery, *Yashima* can be counted as one of the great Noh of all categories.

Scene    Yashima on the northeastern coast of Shikotu.

Season    Spring

Characters and costumes

> *Waki*    A traveling monk in *sumi-bōshi* head covering, *mizugoromo* robe over plain *noshime kitsuke* worn in the *kinagashi* style, a rosary in hand.
>
> *Waki-tsure*    Two or three attendant monks, similarly attired as *Waki*, with some difference in materials, colors and accessories.
>
> *Mae-shite*    The ghost of Minamoto no Yoshitsune in the guise of an old fisherman, in a mask of a humble old man, such as *warai-jō* or *asakura-jō*, *mizugoromo* robe over a plain *noshime* or plaited *atsuita kitsuke*, with or without a fisherman's straw mat around his waist, carrying a fishing rod.
>
> *Nochi-shite*    The ghost of Yoshitsune in a *heida* mask, attired in a military costume consisting of a *nashiuchi-eboshi* hat, *happi* robe over a colorful *dan-atsuita* or *atsuita karaori kitsuke*, a *hangire* divided skirt and a long sword.
>
> *Tsure*    A fisherman, in the first act only in most schools, without a mask, a *mizugoromo* robe over a plain *noshime kitsuke*, with or without a straw mat around his waist, carrying a fishing rod.
>
> *Ai-kyōgen*.    A local man.

*A kakeri* by the *Shite*.

Author:    Attributed to Ze-ami Motokiyo.

*Kogaki*    *Yumi-nagashi* (bow-dropping) in the Kanze and Kita schools: During the "dropping of the bow" section, the <u>Shite</u>, who has been sitting on a stool, rises and makes a gesture of dropping a bow. In the Kanze school, it is preceded by an *iroe* and after dropping the fan which represents the bow, the *Shite* mimes drifting in the waves.

# YASHIMA

| | |
|---|---|
| SHIDAI | *Waki and Waki-tsure enter and stand center stage, Waki on the right, Waki-tsure on the left, facing each other.* |

Shidai *au*

**WAKI and WAKI-TSURE**
The moon, too, sails southward over the sea waves,
The moon, too, sails southward over the sea waves,
To the coast of Yashima we make a tour.[1]

**JI**
Jidori *awazu*
The moon, too, sails southward over the sea waves,
to the coast of Yashima we make a tour.

Nanori *spoken*
**WAKI**
I am a monk from a place near the Capital.
As I have not yet visited the Shikoku Provinces,
I have decided to go on pilgrimages through the Western Provinces.

**WAKE and WAKI-TSURE**
Michiyuki *au*
Spring mist hovers o'er
The buoyant waves rolling to the far off ship,[2]
The buoyant waves rolling to the far off ship,
Sunset clouds shine with growing brilliance[3]
In the yonder sky the ship is heading for,
Till the long voyage at last comes to an end,
At the coast of Yashima we have arrived,
At the coast of Yashima we have arrived.

Tsuki-zerifu
*spoken*
**WAKI**
We have hurried and
Arrived at the coast of Yashima in Sanuki Province.
It has grown dark, so
Let us go into this salt-maker's hut and
Pass the night there.

**WAKI-TSURE**
Yes, let us do so.

*Waki goes to waki-za and sits down. Waki-tsure sit to his right.* ISSEI *Shite enters preceded by Tsure. Tsure stands by the first pine, and Shite by the third pine.*

Sashi *awazu*
**SHITE**
Such enchantment!   The moon floats on the sea and waves' crests shine like fishing fires.

---

[1]Yashima, a peninsula on the northern coast of Kagawa Prefecture in Shikoku, was an island at the time when the battle between the Genji and Heike was fought there.

[2]*Ukitatsu* (float and rise):   Related to the preceding *Haru-gasumi* (spring mist), and to *nami* (waves), also means "to be exhilarated, cheerful," and expresses spring mood. *nami no oki* (waves rise) --> *oki-tsu-bune* (far-from-coast boat).

Tsuki mo minami no unabara ya
Tsuki mo minami no unabara ya
Yashima no ura o tazunen.[1]

Tsuki mo minami no unabara ya
Yashima no ura o tazunen.      5

Kore wa miyako-gata yori idetaru sō nite sôrô.
Ware imada Shikoku o mizu sōrō hodoni
Konotabi omoitachi Saikoku angya to kokorozashi sōrō.

Haru-gasumi
Ukitatsu nami no oki-tsu-bune[2]      10
Ukitatsu nami no oki-tsu-bune
Irihi no kumo mo kage soite[3]
Sonata no sora to yuku hodo ni
Harubaru narishi funaji hete
Yashima no ura ni tsukinikeri,      15
Yashima no ura ni tsukinikeri.

Isogi sōrō hodoni
Kore wa haya Sanuki-no-Kuni Yashima no ura ni tsukite sōrō.
Hi no kurete sōraeba
Kore naru shioya ni tachiyori      20
Ichi-ya o akasabaya to omoi sōrō.

Shikaru-byō sōrō.

Omoshiro ya tsuki kaisho-o ni ukandewa hato-o yaka ni nitari.

---

[3]*Iri* (to go in) in *Iri-hi* (setting sun) is an *en-go* (associate word) of *-bune* (boat), with an implication of a boat entering a harbor.

*TSURE*

"An old fisherman passes the night by the western bank;[4]

*SHITE and TSURE*

"At dawn, drawing the Hsiang water, he kindles fire,
    burning Chu-land's bamboo,"
Like the old poem indeed.  The reed fire light's[5]
Flicker becomes dimly visible.
A desolate sight!

Issei *awazu*    Moonrise evening tide, out at sea, high surging waves,[6]
        *TSURE*
Dim in spring mist, boats[7]

Rowing, eager for shore.
    *SHITE*
Fishermen
Call to one another,
    *SHITE and TSURE*
A hamlet not far off.

*Accompanied by the ashirai music, Shite and Tsure enter the main
stage.  Shite stands at jō-za, Tsure in front of daishō.*

        *SHITE*
Sashi *awazu*    A leaf blown a thousand leagues, the skiff coursing her
        way,[8]
To a single sail's wind leaving all;

        *TSURE*
In the evening sky cloud billows
    *SHITE and TSURE*
From the moon's path fade away,
As if floating in the mist, pine groves loom,
Their reflections green on the sea water
Blur the coast line as far as Shiranui,[9]
To the Sea of Tsukushi
Endlessly stretching.

Sage-uta *au*    Here at Yashima along the beach path
Fishermen's cottages lie here and there.

---

[4]Lines 24-25.  From a poem by Liu Tsung-yuan (773--819).  Shō-sui (the River
Hsiang) flows into Lake Tsungting in the Land of Chu on the southern side of the
Yangtze River.
[5]Lines 26-27.  In *Hono* (faintly), *ho* in the sense of "tuft" is an *en-go* of *ashi* (reed)
in *ashi-bi* (reed fire).
[6]*Tsuki no de* (moon-rise) --> *de-jio* (rising tide).

"Gyo-o-o yoru seigan ni so-ote shukusu[4]

"Akatsuki Sho-osui o kunde sochiku o taku" mo                    25

Ima ni shirarete ashi-bi no kage[5]
Hono mie-somuru
Monosugo-sa yo.

Tsuki no dejio no oki-tsu-nami[6]

Kasumi no o-bune[7]                                               30

Kogare-kite

Ama no
Yobi-koe

Sato chikashi.


Ichi-yo-o ban-ri no fune no michi[8]                             35

Tada ippan no kaze ni makasu;

Iube no sora no kumo no nami

Tsuki no yukue ni tachi-kiete
Kasumi ni ukamu matsubara no
Kage wa midori ni utsuroite                                      40
Kaigan soko tomo Shiranui no[9]
Tsukushi no umi niya
Tsuzukuran.

Koko wa Yashinma no ura-zutai
Ama no iei mo kazukazu ni                                        45

---

[7]*Kasumi no* (Misty) is related to *nami* (waves) in 29 and *o-bune* (small boat) that follows. *Kogare-kite* (being rowed and coming) also means "to be yearning and coming."

[8]*Ichi-yō no fune* (a leaf boat): From Chinese legend about *Huo-ti* who is said to have invented a ship, inspired by a spider floating on a leaf.

[9]In *Kaigan soko tomo shiranu* (that the coastline is there is not known, undiscernable), *soko* (there) also means "bottom," an *en-go* of *kaigan* (coast). *shiranu* (unknown) --> *shiranu-(h)i* (unknown or mysterious fire), a pillow word to Tsukushi (Kyushu), from the mysterious fires seen at night in the offshore in northern Kyushu.

Age-uta *au*          Men busy with their fishing lines out on the waves,[10]
                               Men busy with their fishing lines out on the waves
                               Mist-draped far away on the horizon move on
                               Fishermen's tiny skiffs, the sails faintly white[11]
                               Still visible in the gathering dusk.
                               Sea breezes blow, peaceful, untroubled[12]
                               Now in spring that stirs a soul to longing,
                               Now in spring that stirs a soul to longing.

*Spoken*                *SHITE*
                               Let us return to the salt-hut and rest.

*Shite goes center stage and sits on a stool.  Tsure kneels in front of taiko-za.  Waki stands up.*

Mondō *spoken*       *WAKI*
                               The owner of the salt-hut has returned.
                               I will go there and ask for a night's lodging.
                               Excuse me, I should like to speak with someone in this
                                    salt-maker's hut.

*Tsure rises.*          *TSURE*
                               Who is it?

                               *WAKI*
                               We are monks on a pilgrimage through various provinces.
                               Would you give us a night's lodging?

                               *TSURE*
                               Please wait for a moment.
                               I will speak to the master.

*Kneeling to Shite.*   If you please,
                               There are monks on a pilgrimage
                               Who wish us to give them a night's lodging.

                               *SHITE*
                               That we can do easily, and yet,
                               As this is such a poor and humble place,
                               We cannot shelter them.  Tell them so.

*To Waki*           *TSURE*
                               I have spoken to the master, who says that,
                               As this is such a poor and humble place,
                               We cannot offer shelter to you.

---

[10]*Tsuri no ito* (fishing line) --> *itoma mo nami* (time none) --> *nami no ue* (waves on = on the waves).

[11]*o-bune no ho* (small ship's sail) --> *honobono to* (faintly).

Tsuri no itoma mo nami no ue[10]
Tsuri no itoma mo nami no ue
Kasumi-watarite oki yuku ya
Ama no o-bune no honobono to[11]
Miete nokoru iugure                                                    50
Ura-kaze made mo nodokanaru[12]
Haru ya kokoro o saso-oran,
Haru ya kokoro o saso-oran.

Mazu mazu shioya ni kaeri yasumōzuru nite sōrō.


Shioya no aruji no kaerite sōrō.                                       55
Tachikoe yado o karabaya to omoi sōrō.
Ikani kore naru shioya no uchi e annai mōshi sōrō.


Tare nite watari sōrō zō.

Shokoku ikken no sō nite sōrō.

Ichi-ya no yado o on-kashi sōrae.                                      60


Shibaraku on-machi sōrae.
Aruji ni sono yoshi mōshi sōrō-beshi.

Ikani moshi sōrō,
Shokoku ikken no o-sō no
Ichi-ya no o-yado to ōse sōrō.                                         65


Yasuki hodo no on-koto naredomo
Amarini migurushiku sōrō hodo ni
O-yado wa kanōmajiki yoshi mōshi sōrae.


O-yado no koto o mōshite sōraeba
Amarini migurushiku sōrō hodo ni                                       70
Kanō-majiki yoshi ōse sōrō.

---

[12]Lines 51-51. *nodokanaru* (peaceful, untroubled) modifies *Ura-kaze* (sea breezes) and *Haru* (spring).

**WAKI**
Oh, we do not mind the place's being poor and humble.
Besides, we have come from a place near the Capital
To see this coast for the first time,
But it has grown dark, so
Will you ask him again to give us shelter for the night?

**TSURE**
Yes, I will.

*To Shite*    I have told them what you said,
The travelers say that they are from the Capital,
And, as it has grown dark,
They repeated their urgent desire for a night's shelter.

**SHITE**
Oh, do you say that the travelers are from the  Capital?

**TSURE**
That is so.

**SHITE**
Ah, I am moved to pity.

*To Waki.*    Well, I will give you a night's shelter.

*Kakaru*    **TSURE**
As you see, this is a poor cottage, its roof thatched with
reed,[13]

*Spoken*    **SHITE**
It would be like sleeping in the field, pillowed on
grass.[14]

*Kakaru*    **TSURE**
And tonight the moon is not in her full brightness,[15]

**SHITE**
Nor is she quite dimmed in mist, this spring night of

**SHITE and TSURE**
Softly veiled moonlight matchless,[16]
not a mat in the fisherman's rush-thatched -

---

[13]In *ashi-no-ya* (reed hut), *ashi* (reed) also means "bad, poor."
[14]*kusa-makura* (grass pillow): In ancient times travelers slept in the open, binding grass for a pillow. Hence the phrase became *makura kotoba* (pillow word) of *tabi* (travel). *kusa* (grass) is an *en-go* (associate word) of *ashi* (reed) in 86.

Iya iya migurushiki wa kurushikarazu sōrō.
Kotoni kore wa Miyako-gata no mono nite
Kono ura hajimete ikken no koto nite sōrōga
Hi no kurete sōraeba                                          75
Hirani ichi-ya to kasanete on-mōshi sōrae.


Kokoroe-mōshi sōrō.

Tadaima no yoshi mōshite sōraeba
Tabibito wa Miyako no hito nite onniri sōrōga
Hi no kurete sōraeba                                          80
Hirani ichi-ya to kasanete ōse sōrō.


Nani tabibito wa Miyako no hito to mōsu ka.


San-zōrō.


Geni itawashiki on-koto kana.

Saraba o-yado o kashi-mōsan.                                  85


Motoyori sumika mo ashi no ya no[13]


Tada kusa-makura to oboshimese.[14]


Shikamo koyoi wa teri mo sezu[15]


Kumori mo hatenu haru no yo no


Oborozukiyo ni shiku mono mo naki ama no toma . . .[16]       90

---

[15]Lines 88-90. *teri mo...shiku mono mo naki*: From a poem by Ōe no Chisato (ca. end of 9c.) in *Shin-Kokin-shū*, which ends *Shiku mono zo naki* (its equal not to be found). *shiku mono* also means "a spreading thing = mat or sheet to spread for sitting or sleeping on." (*zo* is emphatic.) Thus the phrase refers: (a) to the unequaled beauty of spring night; (b) to the poor dwelling without a mat to sleep on.

[16]Lines 90-91. toma-Ya (rush hut) --> Yashima. taka-matsu (tall pine tree) is also the name of a place on the opposite coast, the present Takamatsu City, the site of the prefectural office.

| *Au* | *JI* |
|------|------|
| *The three sit down, Tsure before ji-utai.* | Hut...on the Hut Isle grow lofty Takamatsu pines[17] Moss-clad, a mat of moss for you, poor travelers! |

Age-uta au

Solace for lonely souls on this coast named . . .[18]
Solace for lonely souls on this coast named
"Flock," . . . Look at all those cranes in flocks there,
To the cloud-bound heaven, would they not return?[19]
Travelers, your home place is also
The Capital, we heard, with longing in our hearts.[20]
We, too, are from . . . as they spoke thus,
Words failing them, they wept, suffocated with tears.
Words failing them, they wept, suffocated with tears.

*Spoken*

**WAKI**
I say,
I have a request which may not become a monk,
We are told that, long ago, during the war between the
    Genji and Heike, this place became a battlefield.
Tell me all night long about the battle.

*Shite sits on the stool.*

**SHITE**
Certainly, I will tell you the story.

Katari *spoken*

It was in the first year of Genryaku, on the eighteenth[21]
    of the third month,
The Heike assembled their ships at some distance from
    the coast,
The Genji had marched as far as this beach.
The general was attired[22]
In a red brocade garment under[23]
Noble armor threaded in purple and white.
Standing up erect in the stirrups,
"The delegate of the First Ex-Emperor,[24]
The leader of the Genji army, the Third Officer of the
    Police and Justice in the Fifth Court Rank,
Minamoto no Yoshitsune,"

---

[17]Lines 91-91. *matsu no Koke* (pine moss) --> *Koke no mushiro* (moss mat), a metonymy for sleeping outdoors or in a humble place. Line 91 is an introductory phrase to *koke no mushiro*, which is an *en-go* of *kusa-makura* (grass pillow) in 87, and *toma* (rush) in 90.

[18]Lines 93-95. *Ura no na no Mure* (the coast's name Mure) --> *Mure-iru* (flocking). Mure is to the south of Yashima and east of Takamatsu.

[19]*kumoi* (cloud-sitting/bound place) means: (a) heaven; (b) Imperial palace, and hence, Capital city.
Yoshitsune was brought up in Kyoto and came back there as the leader of the Genji army. See Introduction.

Yashima ni tateru taka-matsu no[17]
Koke no mushiro wa itawashi ya.

Sate nagusami wa ura no na no[18]
Sate nagusami wa ura no na no
Mure-iru tazu o goranze yo                                    95
Nado ka kumoi ni kaerazaran[19]
Tabibito no furusato mo
Miyako to kikeba natsukashi ya[20]
Warera mo moto wa tote
Yagate namida ni musebikeri,                                 100
Yagate namida ni musebikeri,


Ikani mōshi sōrō,
Nanitoyaran niawanu shomō nite sōraedomo
Inishie kono tokoro wa Genpei no kasen no chimata to
   uketamawarite sōrō.
Yomosugara katatte on-kikase sōrae.                          105

Yasuki aida no koto katatte kikase mōshi sōrō-beshi.

Ide sono koro wa Genryaku gan-nen sangachi jiu-hachi-nichi[21]
   no koto narishini
Heike wa umi no omote itchō bakari ni fune o ukame

Genji wa kono migiwa ni uchi-ide-tamō.
Taishōgun no onnidetachi niwa[22]                            110
Aka-ji no nishiki no hitatare ni[23]
Murasaki susogo no on-kisenaga
Abumi funbari kurakasa ni tsuttachi-agari
Ichi-in no on-tsukai[24]
Genji no Taishō Kenpi-ishi Go-i no jō                        115

Minamoto no Yoshitsune to

---

[21]Genryaku: Era name. The date of the battle is actually Febrary 19 (18th according to *Heike Monogatari*), in the second year of Genryaku, that is, 1184.
[22]Lines 110-116. from "Battle of Yashima," *Heike Monogatari* Vol. 11. See Introduction.
[23]*Hitatare* is a kind of large-sleeved robe, but here the word means *yoroi-hitatare* (armor *hitatare*), a short sleeved one worn under armor. *Hitatare* made of *nishiki* (brocade) are for generals and high-ranking warriors.
[24]*Ichi-in* (the First *In*: *In* = retired Emperor): Goshirakawa. His son, the retired Emperor Takakura, was called *Shin-in* (the New *In*).

| | |
|---|---|
| *Kakaru* | He gave his name aloud, his dignified appearance<br>Worthy of a great general.<br>As if I see it now,<br>The memory comes back into my mind. |
| | **TSURE**<br>Then from among the Heike vessels,[25]<br>After an exchanges of challenges,<br>A boat manned with warriors came heading shoreward.<br>The men disembarked at water's edge.<br>To confront their enemy on the beach. |
| *Spoken* | **SHITE**<br>At this, Genji warriors, some fifty horsemen, sallied forth.<br>Among them, one, Mionoya no Shirō, who gave his name in loud voice,[26]<br>Was seen to dash out ahead of all. |
| *Kakaru* | **TSURE**<br>On the Heike's side, a man, announcing himself as Aku-Shichibyo-oe Kagekiyo,[27]<br>Aimed his attack at Mionoya. |
| *Spoken* | **SHITE**<br>Mionoya, at that moment,<br>His sword breaking in two, helplessly<br>Withdrew a little distance from the shore. |
| *Kakaru* | **TSURE**<br>Kagekiyo, running after Mionya, |
| *Spoken, Shite mimes action.* | **SHITE**<br>Grasped the neck-plate of his helmet |
| *Kakaru* | **TSURE**<br>And pulled him back. Mionoya[28] |
| | **SHITE**<br>Trying to free himself, jerked his head back. |
| | **TSURE**<br>The two men, yelling "Yo-ho," |

---

[25]Lines 121-142. from "the Dropping of the Bow," <u>ibid</u>. See Introduction.
[26]According to *Heike Monogatari*, the warrior Kagekiyo fought was not Shirō, but his brother, Jūrō.

Nanori-tamaishi on-kotsugara
Appare taisho-o ya to mieshi
Ima no yo-o ni
Omoi-iderarete so-oro-o.                                     120

Sono toki Heike no kata yori mo[25]
Kotoba-datakai koto owari
Hyo-osen isso-o kogi-yosete
Namiuchigiwa ni oritatte
Kuga no kataki o machikakeshini                              125

Genji no kata nimo tsuzuku tsuwamono gojikki bakari

Naka nimo Mionoya no Shirō to nanotte[26]

Massaki kakete mieshi tokoro ni

Heike no kata nimo Aku-Shichibyo-oe Kagekiyo to nanori[27]

Mionoya o megake tatakaishini                                130

Kano Mionoya wa sono toki ni
Tachi uchi-otte chikaranaku
Sukoshi migiwa ni hiki-shirizokishini

Kagekiyo okkake Mionoya ga

Kitaru kabuto no shikoro o tsukande                          135

Ushiro e hikeba Mionoya mo[28]

Mi o nogaren to mae e hiku.

Tagaini eiya to

---

[27]Aku-Shichibyōe Kagekiyo was a Taira (Heike) member of lower status, well-known for his bravery. *Aku* (bad) as a prefix to a name, means "strong." Yoshitsune's eldest brother, who is mentioned in *Tomonaga*, was called Aku-Genda (literally, strong, Genji's first son). Kagekiyo is the *Shite* of *Kagekiyo* and *Daibutsu Kuyō*.

[28]Lines 136--137. *Mionoya* alliterates with *mi o nogaren to* (body to save = to save oneself, to escape).

SHITE
Pulled with all their might, till

*Shura-nori*    JI
From the crown the neck plate torn asunder,
To left and right leaped off the two warriors.
Having seen all this, Ho-ogan[29]

*Shite rises and*    Came forward, advancing his horse to the water's edge,
*mimes the*    Then Sato-o Tsuginobu,[30]
*action.*    Hit by an arrow from Lord Noto's bow,[31]
Fell headlong from his horse, crashing to the ground.
Aboard the Heike vessels, Kikuo-o, too, was killed.[32]
Did their deaths so grieve the leaders on both sides?
Ships toward deeper waters, horsemen to camp[33]
Mutually withdrew, the tide receded,
After that war cries were heard no longer,[34]
Waves rolling to the beach, and pine wind alone
Sounded lonesome on the deserted coast.

*Shite sits*
*center stage.*
*Rongi au*    In wonder we have listened to the fisherman[35]
In such fullness to tell us the story.
Now reveal your name to us, we pray.

SHITE
My name . . . but what name?  Evening waves[36]
Ebbed with nocturnal tide, dawn still dark, Asakura's[37]
Kinomaru-dono . . . were this hut that palace,
One would give his name in passing.

JI
Indeed the very words that escape his lips
Make me yearn to know the name of the old man.[38]

SHITE
The stories of long-gone past he tells,

---

[29]Lines 142--150. from "The Battle of Yashima," ibid. *Hōgan*: A third-ranking officer of *Kenpiishi* (Police and Justice Department of Kyoto). Yoshitsune is often referred to by this title, and in Noh and Kabuki the word has come to mean him.
[30]Satō Tsuginobu: See footnote 2, introduction to *Yashima*.
[31]Noto-dono (Lord Noto): See footnote 1, Introduction to *Yashima*.
[32]Kikuō: Lord Noto's attendant boy. See the Introduction.
[33]*hiku* (to withdraw) in line 150 is the verb to *fune* (ships), *kuga* (land force) and *shio* (tide).
[34]*Ato* means: (a) "trace" in *shio no Ato* (tide's trace); (b) "afterward."
[35]*ama-bito* (fisherman) alliterates with *Amari* (exceedingly) in *Amari kuwashiki* (exceedingly detailed) in the next line.

Hiku chikara ni

Hachitsuke no ita yori hiki-chigitte    140
So-o e katto zo nokinikeru.
Kore o goranjite Ho-ogan[29]
Onma o migiwa ni uchi-yose-tamaeba
Sato-o Tsuginobu[30]
Noto-dono no yasaki ni kakatte[31]    145
Nma yori shimo ni do-o to otsureba
Fune niwa Kikuo-o mo utare kereba[32]
Tomoni aware to oboshikeru ka
Fune wa oki e kuga wa jin ni[33]
Aibiki ni hiku shio no    150
Ato wa toki no koe taete[34]
Iso no nami, matsu-kaze bakari no
Oto samishiku zo narinikeru.


Fushigi nari toyo ama-bito no[35]
Amari kuwashiki monogatari    155
Sono na o nanori-tamae ya.


Waga na o nanito iu-nami no[36]
Hiku ya yo-jio mo Asakura ya[37]
Kinomaru-dono ni araba koso
Nanori o shite mo yukamashi.    160


Geni ya kotoba o kikukarani
Sono na yukashiki oi-bito no[38]


Mukashi o kataru omi-goromo

---

[36]Lines 157--158. *nani to iu* (what to tell) --> *iu-nami no hiku* (evening waves recede) --> *hiku ya yo-jio* (receding night tide) --> *asa* (shallow) --> Asakura, the site of Empress Saimei's temporary palace in Kyushu. *Asa-kura* also means "morning dusk." *iu-nami ...yo-jio* is a *jo-shi* (introductory phrase) to Asakura.

[37]Lines 158--160. From a poem by Emperor Tenchi (624--671), composed when he was crown prince to Empress Saimei, in *Shin-Kokin-shū*: Asakura ya/ Kinomaru-dono ni/ Waga oreba/ Nanori o shi-tsutsu/ Yuku wa ta ga ko zo (At Asakura/ Palace of unbarked logwood/ Where I was staying,/ Announcing their names aloud,/ Who can be those that pass by?)

[38]Lines 162--164. *omi-goromo* (Shinto ceremonial robe. *goromo = koromo = robe*) is purely rhetorical here, a *jo-shi* to *koro* (the time), alliterates with it and *oi-bito* (old man).

|  | JI | SHITE |
|---|---|---|
|  | And now the season is | Vernal night. |

JI

Falling tide at break of day marks the hour

*Shite rises.*     When fighting in Asura's Hell starts again.[39]
When that time comes, I will reveal my name.
But whether or not it be made known to you,
'Tis as *well*, in *ever*-dreary life's[40]
Dream fast bound, do not awake from your sleep,
Dream fast bound, do not awake from your sleep,

NAKAIRI *Shite and Tsure exit.*[41]
AI-KYOGEN *Ai-kyogen, a villager, comes to the salt hut, tells the monks the episode of Kagekiyo and Mionoya,*[42] *thinks that the old man was Yoshitsune's ghost, and exits, having offered services to the monks who are going to stay all night expecting to witness further miracles.*

*Spoken*     WAKI
How strange!  The old man,
Being asked his name, answered,
"'Tis as *well*, the *ever*-dream-bound earthly soul,
Do not awake but wait," thus we heard

*Machi-utai au*     WAKI and WAKI-TSURE
The voice in the deepening night, the sea wind blows,[43]
The voice in the deepening night, the sea wind blows
The pines where, pillowed on the tree-root we listen,
Letting our thoughts unfold on the mat of moss,[44]
And awaiting for more dreams come piling on,
And awaiting for more dreams come piling on.

ISSEI *Nochi-shite enters and stands at jō-za.*

*Sashi awazu*     SHITE
A fallen flower returns not to the branch,[45]
A shattered mirror never again casts its light.

---

[39]*Shura no toki* (Asura's time):  The warrior ghosts who are condemned to Asura's realm in Hell haunt the earthly world at night, but have to return to their fighitng at the break of day.

[40]The line contains the name Yoshitsune, with *Yoshi* meaning "anyway" and *tsune* "ever, always."

[41]In some schools the *Tsure*, instead of exiting, takes part in the first part of the second act.

[42]Sometimes the *Ai-kyōgen* narrates different episodes, such as the death of Tsuginobu, or Nasu no Yoichi's shooting a fan the Heike hoisted on a pole in a boat, challenging their enemy to shoot it down.  The latter episode is told in the *kogaki* performance entitled *Yumi-nagashi* explained at the end of the Introduction.

Koro shimo ima wa      Haru no yo no

Ushio no otsuru akatsuki naraba                  165
Shura no toki ni naru-beshi.[39]
Sono toki wa waga na ya nanoran.
Tatoi nanorazutomo nanorutomo
Yoshi tsune no ukiyo no[40]
Yume bashi samashi tamo-o nayo,                   170
Yume bashi samashi tamo-o nayo.

Fushigi ya ima no rōjin no
Sono na o tazuneshi kotae nimo
Yoshi tsune no yo no yume-gokoro
Samasade mate to kikoetsuru                      175

Koe mo fuke-yuku ura-kaze no[43]
Koe mo fuke-yuku ura-kaze no
Matsu-ga-ne makura sobadatete
Omoi o noburu koke-mushiro[44]
Kasanete yume o machi-itari                     180
Kasanete yume o machi-itari.

Rakka eda ni kaerazu[45]
Hakyo-o futatabi terasazu

---

[43]*Koe mo fuke* (the voice aged, old) --> *fuke-yuku ura-kaze* (aging night's sea-wind), with *fuke* meaning "old" and "to grow late." *Fuke* also means "to blow" and is an *en-go* of *ura-kaze* (sea wind).

[44]Lines 179--180. In *Omoi o noburu* (thought to unfold, to meditate), *noburu* (to unfold, spread) is an *en-go* of *mushiro* (mat), and so is *kasanete* (again; to pile one on another).

[45]Lines 182--183. From *Keitoku Dentō-roku*, Chinese Buddhist anthology.

And yet, still to blind attachment bound, burning with anger,
My departed soul becomes a haunting spirit and
Inflicting torture upon itself,
Comes to Asura's shore, adrift on the waves of[46]
Deep-lying karma of former lives.

*kakaru*

*WAKI*
How strange! Already it must be dawn,
Thinking thus as I lie awake, to the pillow
An armor-clad figure appears.
Can it be Ho-ogan?

*Spoken*

*SHITE*
I am the ghost of Yoshitsune.
By anger's blind attachment driven,
Even now on the Western Sea's waves I drift,
To the Sea of Life and Death condemned.[47]

*kakaru*

*WAKI*
That was unwisely said. It is only in your mind that Life and Death's
Sea you behold. The Moon of Absolute Truth[48]

*SHITE*
Even though on a spring night, shines cloudless,[49]
the mind clear as tonight's sky,

*WAKI*
Calls back the past to the present,

*SHITE*
On land and sea battles fought

*WAKI*
At this very place[50]

*SHITE*
Never forgotten by

---

[46]*Shura no chimata* (Asura's place) here means a scene of carnage, a battlefield. *yori-kuru* (to approach, to drift to) refers to the ghost and *nami* (waves). *nami no asa* (waves shallow) --> *Asakarazarishi gōin* (not shallow karma).

[47]Sea of LIfe and Death: The scene of mutation men go through in the cycle of rebirths is compared to a rough, torturous sea.

[48]*Shinnyo no Tsuki* (the Moon of Absolute Truth): In Buddhism the moon is held as a symbol of truth, or *bhūtatathatà*.

[49]*kumorinaki* (cloudless) modifies *Shinnyo no Tsuki* (the Moon of Truth) in 198, and *kokoro* (the mind). *Sumeru* (clear) modifies *kokoro* and *koyoi no sora* (tonight's sky).

Shikaredomo nao mo-oshiu no shinni tote

Kishin konpaku no kyo-ogai ni kaeri      185
Ware to kono mi o kurushimete
Shura no chimata ni yori-kuru nami no[46]
Asakarazarishi go-oin kana.

Fushigi yana haya akatsuki nimo naru-yaran to
Omo-o nezame no makura yori      190
Katchiu o taishi mie-tamo-o wa
Moshi Ho-ogan nite mashimasu ka.

Ware Yoshitsune ga iurei naru ga
Shinni ni hikaruru mo-oshiu nite
Nao Saikai no nami ni tadayoi      195
Sho-oji no umi ni chinrin seri.[47]

Oroka yana kokoro kara koso ikishini no

Umi tomo miyure Shinnyo no Tsuki no[48]

Haru no yo naredo kumori naki kokoro mo sumeru
   koyoi no sora[49]

Mukashi o ima ni omoi-izuru      200

Fune to kuga tono kasen no michi

Tokoro kara tote[50]

Wasure-enu

---

[50]Lines 203--207. *Wasure-enu-mono* (unforgettable thing) --> *Mononofu* (warrior) --> Ya-shima (The name can mean "Arrow Isle.") --> *iru* (to let fly an arrow; to set, to sink) --> *tsuki* (the moon) --> *tsuki-yumi* (zelcova bow). There is an association between *yumi* (bow) and *tsuki* (the moon), from the expression, "to draw a bow to the shape of a full moon." *tsuki-yumi no moto* (zelkova bow's end, edge) --> *Moto no mi* (former self), with *tsuki-yumi* serving as a *jo-shi* (introductory phrase) to *moto no mi*.

Age-uta *au*      **JI**
The warrior at
Arrow Isle, shafts sailed high from his full-moon bow,
Arrow Isle, shafts sailed high from his full-moon bow,
My appearance as of yore, here again[51]
I come, the archer's way never losing, and yet[52]
A lost soul, wandering about Life and Death's
Sea and mountain, unable to free myself,
Flying back to Arrow Isle Bay, ah, bitterness![53]
In every way blind attachment
Remains, a sea unfathomable, deep at night[54]
A dream story I will relate to you.
A dream story I will relate to you.

Kuri *awazu*    Never forgotten, the earthly world, the home place
*Shite sits on a*   Left long ago, many years' waves[55]
*stool, center*    Have rolled, o'er the nocturnal dream's path drifted,
*stage.*         The sight of Asura's Hell I've come to reveal.

Sashi *awazu*     **SHITE**
Now revives in memory the bygone spring,[56]
The moon, too, on this night with her old brightness
   returns.

          **JI**
The beach of old, is this the same place?
Genji and Heike stood face to face, their arrow-heads in
   line,
Ships in formation, horsemen in thick array,
Plunged hoofs into water wave after wave, surges[57]
   washing horses' bits as they fought in hot attack.

Spoken        **SHITE**
Then it so happened, one knows not how,[58]
Hōgan let his bow drop into the sea,
Wave-drifted, it began to float away.

Kakaru        **JI**
The tide was then receding,
And the bow drifted further off.

---

[51]Lines 207--108. *koko ni ki* (here to come) --> *Kiusen* (bow and arrow).

[52]Lines 209--210. Sea of Life and Death: See 196.

[53]*Kaeru ya* (returning arrow) --> *Yashima no Ura* (Yashima Bay) --> *urameshi ya* (rueful).

[54]*fukaki* (deep) modifies *umi* (the sea) and *yo* (night).

[55]Lines 217--218. *toshi-nami* (year-waves, many successive years) --> *nami no yoru* (waves rolling to) --> *Yoru no yume-ji* (night's dream-path).

Mononofu no
Yashima ni iru ya tsuki-yumi no              205
Yashima ni iru ya tsuki-yumi no
Moto no mi nagara mata koko ni[51]
Kiusen no michi wa mayowanuni[52]
Mayoikeru zoya sho-oji no
Umi-yama o hanare-yarade              210
Kaeru Yashima no urameshi ya.[53]
Tonikaku ni shiushin no
Nokori no umi no fukaki yo ni[54]
Yume-monogatari mo-osu nari.
Yume-monogatari mo-osu nari.             215

Wasurenu mono o enbu no kokyo-o ni
Satte hisashiki toshinami no[55]
Yoru no yume-ji ni kayoi-kite
Shura-do-o no arisama arawasu nari.

Omoi zo izuru mukashi no haru[56]            220
Tsuki mo koyoi ni sae-kaeri

Moto no nagisa wa koko nare ya
Genpei tagai ni ya-saki o soroe
Fune o kumi koma o narabete
Uchi-ire uchi-ire ashinami ni kutsubami o hitashite[57]     225
  seme-tatako-o.

Sono toki nani toka shitariken[58]
Hōgan yumi o toriotoshi
Nami ni yurarete nagareshini

Sono orishimo wa hiku shio nite
Harukani to-oku nagare-yuku o            230

---

[56]Lines 221-222. In *sae-kaeri* (to shine bright), *kaeru* also means "to return," with the implication of the ghost and the moon returning to the past and to the old place. *kaeru* is an *en-go* of *moto* (former, of old) in *Moto no nagisa* (the old beach).

[57]*ashi-nami* (foot-pace, marching in line) --> *nami ni hitashi* (in the waves to dip).

[58]Lines 226--266. From "Dropping of the Bow" *ibid*.

| | |
|---|---|
| *Spoken* | **SHITE**<br>Lest the enemy should pick up the bow,<br>I swam my horse into the waves<br>Till I neared the enemy's ships. |
| *Kakaru* | **JI**<br>The foe, seeing this, lost no time,<br>They brought their boat up and with a rake hooked him.<br>"Now he falls into their hands," thought all. |
| *Spoken* | **SHITE**<br>However, with my sword cutting the rake off<br>And finally having retrieved the bow,<br>I regained the shore. |
| Sashi | **JI**<br>Then Kanefusa spoke thus to his lord,[59]<br>"Regrettable indeed was your conduct.<br>At Watanabe, Kagetoki had words with you,[60]<br>And it was the same story as this.[61]<br>Even if your bow were made of solid gold,<br>Should you forfeit your life for it?"<br>Tears running down his cheeks, thus he spoke.<br>Ho-ogan, listening, replied,<br>"No, I do not begrudge my bow. |
| Kuse *au* | "Yoshitsune against the Heike<br>Took up bow and arrows with no thought of self.<br>Yet it so happens<br>A fair name for myself I have not even half won.<br>As it is so, should this bow<br>Be taken by the foe and Yoshitsune<br>As a man of short stature known among them,[62]<br>Deeply humiliating it would be for me.<br>Were I to lose my life in the attempt,<br>'Twere beyond my power.  Yoshitusune's<br>Fortune had run out, thus I'd tell myself.<br>Not wanting to let fall in the enemy's hand<br>His wave-drawn bow, the warrior who retrieved it,[63]<br>Won't he leave his name to eternity?"<br>When Ho-ogan had spoken thus, Kanefusa<br>And other warriors in his presence |

---

[59]Kanefusa:  Mashio no Jūrō Kanefusa, Yoshitsune's wife's attendant since her birth.  He followed his master and mistress as they fled from Yoritomo, and finally died with them.  See *Futari Shizuka*, 79-83, and footnote, in *The Noh* Vol. 3, Book 3. He is a *tsure* in *Settai*.

[60]Watanabe:  A sea port, now a part of Osaka City.  Kagetoki: Yoritiomo's retainer.  See the Introduction.

Kataki ni yumi o torareji to
Koma o namima ni oyogasete
Tekisen chikaku narishi hodo ni

Kataki wa kore o mishi yori mo
Fune o yose kumade ni kakete                                          235
Sudeni ayo-oku mie-tamaishini

Saredomo kumade o kiri-harai
Tsuini yumi o torikaeshi
Moto no nagisa ni uchi-agareba

Sono toki Kanefusa mo-osu yo-o[59]                                    240
Kuchioshi no on-furumai yana,
Watanabe nite Kagetoki ga mo-oshishi mo[60]
Kore nite koso so-orae.[61]
Tatoi sen-kinno nobetaru onnyumi naritomo
Onninochi niwa kae-tamo-o beki kato                                   245
Namida o nagashi mo-oshikereba
Ho-ogan kore o kikoshimeshi
Iya toyo yumi o oshimu ni arazu

Yoshitsune Genpei ni
Yumiya o totte watakushi nashi.                                       250
Shikaredomo
Kamei wa imada nakaba narazu.
Sareba kono yumi o
Kataki ni torare Yoshitsune wa
Kohyo-o nari to iwarenna[62]                                          255
Munen no shidai naru-beshi.
Yoshi sore yue ni utarenna
Chikaranashi Yoshitsune ga
Un no kiwame to omo-o-beshi.
Sarazuwa kataki ni watasaji tote                                      260
Nami ni hikaruru yumitori no[63]
Na wa matsudai ni arazu ya to
Katari-tamaeba Kanefusa
Sate sono hoko no hito made mo

---

[61]The same story: Kanefusa means Yoshitsune's recklessness. See *ibid*.
[62]In *Heike Monogatari*, Yoshitsune is described as a small man.
[63]*Nami ni hikaruru yumi* (wave-driven bow) --> *yumi-tori* (bow man = archer, warrior). *Hikaruru* (driven) also means "stretched, pulled" and is an *en-go* of *yumi* (bow).

Were all moved to tears that ran down their cheeks.

**SHITE**
"A wise man is never at a loss;[64]

**JI**
"A man of courage has no fear,"

*Shite rises*
*and moves*
*making miming*
*gestures.*

A shaft high-bent his soul, a catalpa bow
In the enemy's hands he would not let fall,[65]
Begrudging it for his name's sake,
Never begrudged he his own life, ready
To throw it away, thus for the future records
His glorious name will remain forever,
In the bow-brush's bold strokes to be traced.[66]

*Sung awazu*

**SHITE**
Again from Asura's Hell rise war whoops.

**JI**
Archers' cries shake the air.

KAKERI *by Shite, at the end of which Shite stands at jō-za.*

*Spoken*

**SHITE**
In today's infernal battle who is my enemy?
What, Noto-no-kami Noritsune, do I hear?
How audacious! I have already measured out his skill.

*Kakaru*

Now I remember -- at Dan-no-Ura,[67]

*Shura-nori*
*Shite dances to*
*the end,*
*describing*
*the battle.*

**JI**
The sea-battle that was fought in the long gone past,
The sea-battle that was fought in the long gone past
In the earthly world where now I return, life and death's
Sea and mountain are quaking as one on all sides,
From the ships loud sound warriors' cries,

**SHITE**
Ashore, waves of shields,

**JI**　　　　　　　　　　　　　　**SHITE**
In the moonlight white flashes　　From gleaming swords,

---

[64]Lines 266--267. From the Analects of Confucius.

[65]*Yatake-gokoro* (brave, ardent heart), *ya-take* (ardent) also means "arrow bamboo" = "bamboo shaft" and is an *en-go* of *azusa-yumi* (catalpa bow).

[66]*Yumi-fude no ato* (bow-brush trace = what is written by a bow-brush = a record): *Yumi-fude* (bow brush) is a special brush for a warrior in battle attire. Here the word is in association with the bow in the story.

Mina kanrui o nagashikeri.                                    265

Chisha wa madowazu[64]

Yo-osha wa osorezu no
Yatake-gokoro no azusa-yumi
Kataki niwa tori-tsutaeji to[65]
Oshimu wa na no tame                                         270
Oshimanu wa ichimei nareba
Mi o sutete koso ko-oki nimo
Kamei o todomu-beki
Yumi-fude no ato naru-bekere.[66]

Mata Shura-do-o no toki no koe                               275

Ya-sakebi no oto shindo-o seri.

Kyō no Shura no kataki wa taso.
Nani Noto-no-kami Noritsune toya.
Ara monomonoshi ya tenami wa shirinu
Omoi zo izuru Dan-no-Ura no[67]                              280

Sono funa-ikusa ima wa haya
Sono funa-ikusa ima wa haya
Enbu ni kaeru iki-shini no
Umi yama ichido-o ni shindo-o shite
Fune yori wa toki no koe                                     285

Kuga niwa nami no tate

Tsuki ni shiramu wa          Tsurugi no hikari

---

[67]Dan-no-Ura: Coast along northern Kyushu, where the Heike fled from Yashima and was finally destroyed by Yoshitsune. Thus the finale describes the battle, not at Yashima, but at Dan-no-Ura.

      *JI*                          *SHITE*
Heaving waves reflect   Helmets' silvery stars sparkling
               bright,[68]

      *JI*
Water blends with the sky,
The sky rolling with clouds, a sea of billowing waves,[69]
Beating and thrusting at one another,
All the art of sea fight at command,
Floating up and sinking down, until
Spring night sees over the waves the first light of dawn.
The enemy seen all around were flocks of seagulls,[70]
Clamor of war so loud to the ear, was
Sea wind in the lofty pines of Takamatsu,[70]
Sea wind in the lofty pines of Takamatsu,
Morning wind the only sound in the air above.

---

[68]*hoshi* (stars): The rivets on a helmet.
[69]Lines 290--291. *Kumo no nami no* (cloud billows' = wave-like cloud's) -->
nami no Uchi (waves strike) --> *Uchi-ai* (strike at each other).

Ushio ni utsuru wa       Kabuto no hoshi no kage[68]


Mizu ya sora
Sora yuku mo mata kumo no nami no[69]            290
Uchiai sashichigo-oru
Funa-ikusa no kakehiki
Uki shizumu to seshi hodo ni
Haru no yo no nami yori akete
Kataki to mieshi wa mure-iru kamome[70]          295
Toki no koe to kikoeshi wa
Ura-kaze narikeri Takamatsu no[70]
Ura-kaze narikeri Takamatsu no
Asa-arashi tozo narinikeru.

---

[70]*mure-iru* (flocking) contains Mure, the name of a place near Yashima. *taka-matsu* (lofty pines) is also the name of the neighboring place. See 91 and 95.

# MICHIMORI

芦火の影と唔多、ろ、

--sea's wind
Blows the reed fire into flaring brightness

--urakaze mo
Ashibi no kage o fuki-tatete

-Lines 65-66

# INTRODUCTION

Taira no Michimori, the hero of the Noh *Michimori*, was a son of Norimori, a younger brother of Kiyomori. After he was killed in the battle at Ichinotani, his wife, Kozaishō no Tsubone, threw herself into the sea and died. Following is the story about them as told in *Heike Monogatari*. After Michimori was killed in the battle of Ichinotani and Heike survivors were drifting about in ships, Michimori's retainer, Tokikazu, came to his lord's wife and said, "When my lord lost his life at the hand of Kimura no Shigeakira, I ought to have followed him on his last journey. However, I remembered what he used to tell me: 'Even if the worst should happen to me,' he would say, 'you must not throw away your life. Instead, do your best to survive and seek out the whereabouts of my wife.' So I have saved this now useless life of mine and, steeling my heart, have fled and come to you." Hearing this, without a word the lady covered herself in her robe and wept bitterly. For two or three days she still hoped that the news of her husband's death might prove a mistake, and waited for his return, as if he had gone out just for a while. As days went by, however, she lost hope, and, together with her nurse, sank in tears of despair, keeping to her bed which she had not left since the sad news was first brought to her in the evening of the seventh day of the month. (February, 1184) Then on the fourteenth, when they were approaching Yashima, and all was quiet in her ship in the depth of night, the lady said to her nurse, "For some time after I heard about Michimori's death, I did not believe it, but now I think that is must be true. Everybody says that he was slain by a river named Minato, and not a single man has seen him alive. On the eve of the battle, when we met accidentally, he looked unusually sad and said to me, 'Surely I shall die in tomorrow's battle. When I am no more, what will become of you?' Being used to warfare, I did not heed his words specially. Now how I regret it! If I had known that it were our last meeting, I would have exchanged an eternal pledge with him that would last into our next life. The very thought grieves me deeply. I had kept my pregnancy in secret to him till then. However, lest he might think me too withdrawing, I told him about it. He looked very pleased and said, 'I have no child although I am already thirty. I wish it to be a boy. It shall be a keepsake that I leave in this sad life. I wonder how many months you are gone. How do you feel? Leading such a life as this, adrift in a ship over the waves, no one knows till when, what are you going to do when the time comes and you need peace and quietness?' Vain words were these! Nine out of ten women are sure to die of childbearing. For modesty's sake, I would not die in such a way. Sometimes I wish to bring up the baby as my dear husband's keepsake. However, every time I look at it, I shall miss my dead husband. The child will only add to my sorrow, instead of being my comfort. All that live must die in the end. Suppose you escape death and live in hiding, in this sad life where things never go as you wish, unexpected misfortune will visit you. The very thought breaks my heart. When I sleep I see him in dream, when awake, he appears to me like a vision. I have made up my mind to sink myself to the depths of water, rather than to live and pine for him. I am sorry for you who will be left behind to grieve for me, but I want you to get some priest to say prayers for my husband and myself, and give him my clothes for alms. Also take my letters to the people of Kyoto." The nurse replied in tears, "There are other ladies who grieve for their husbands killed in the battle at Ichinotani. You are not the only one. You should give birth to your child and bring it up. Finding a place to hide yourself, you may take the order and pray for the soul of the deceased. Even if you follow him now by taking your own life, there is no knowing which of the six ways in the rebirth's cycles you would go. There is small chance of your meeting him. So it is in vain that you drown yourself." Kozaishō tried to console the nurse, saying that she did not really mean to drown herself. Then late at night when her nurse fell asleep, she went out to the ship's side, and turning toward the mountain where the moon was sinking, she prayed quietly to Buddha, her chanting joined by the plaintive cries of beach plovers and the sound of ships' rudders. She called Buddha's name a hundred times, invoking him to lead her to Paradise, there to be united with her husband. Then she threw herself into the sea midway between Ichinotani and Yashima. As it was midnight, nobody saw her except a ruddersman on the watch, who called out, "Oh, look, from the ship over there, a most beautiful lady threw herself into the sea!" Awakened by the cry, the nurse looked about her, but her lady was nowhere to be seen. Many people dived into the water to save her. However, the sea was veiled in mist as was the wont of a spring night, and even buoyant clouds drifted out, covering the moonlight. When they at last picked her up after a long search, she was no longer of this life. --- From "Kozaishō," *Heike Monogatari*, Vol. 9.

The Noh, which is based largely on the above quoted episode in *Heike Monogatari* develops as follows: At Naruto (Thundering Straits) in Awa Province, while a monk and his attendant, the *Waki* and *Waki-tsure*, are chanting sutras in prayer for the Heike people who lost their lives in battle, an aged fisherman and his wife, the *Shite* and *Tsure*, appear in a fishing boat. After a description of their wearisome toil and the beautiful seascape that brings solace to their bleak life, they hear the voices chanting the sutra. They pole their boat to where the monks are chanting on a rocky bank. The monk unrolls the sutra scroll and reads from it in the light of the fishing fire, while the couple worshipfully listen. Then at the request of the monk, the fisherman and his wife narrate the tale of the death of Kozaishō no Tsubone. As the Chorus sings how she leapt into the sea, the woman, miming the action, steps out of the boat and withdraws to the *kōken-za*. The old man, miming the nurse trying to stop her lady, also steps out of the boat and makes the interim exit. The *Ai-kyōgen*, a local man who has come to listen to the sutra chanting, tells the monks about the romance and deaths of Michimori and his wife and exhorts them to pray for the couple, whose ghosts have just appeared in the guise of a fisherman and his wife. While the monks are offering prayers for the repose of their souls, the forms of an elegant lady and a warrior attired in splendid armor appear and reveal themselves as the ghosts of Michimori and Kozaishō. Then the *sashi* and *kuse* songs describe the parting of the couple, comparing their tragedy to that of the Chinese hero Hsiang Yü and his wife Yü-mêi-Jên. This is followed by a *kakeri* by the *Shite*, which expresses the excitement of battle. The final section in *shura-nori* presents Michimori's fighting and his fall, accompanied by a dance. The play ends with a brief *kiri* (epilogue)[1] to the effect that Michimori is delivered from the earthly attachment and attains Buddhahood thanks to the mercy of Buddha.

It has been pointed out that *shura*-Noh can be divided into two types: (1) those in which esthetic and poetic sensitivity of the hero is the key note of the play. In them a series of lyrical songs on an esthetic subject constitute the major feature of the first part, dance and music that of the second part; (2) those in which the narrative aspect is more prominent than dance and music. Some Noh in this group have no dance. Often they have a *katari* (narration, story telling), or a *katari*-like passge, in the first or second act, or in both.

*Michimori* belongs to the second group, and is characterized by certain features relative to a narrative play. Most *shura*-Noh, like a standard visional Noh, are two-character dramas, *shite* and *waki* (*waki-tsure* is not counted). In *Michimori*, not only is there a third character, a *tsure*, but as the hero Michimori's wife she plays an unusually important part for a *tsure* in the development of the drama of conjugal love. In this respect she is

---

[1]*Kiri* in its broader sense is "finale." In a more specific sense it means "epilogue." *Kiri* as "finale" can be all sorts of songs. An *age-uta* including *rongi* comes at the end of a majority of Noh. Example: *Takasago*. Many Noh end in an *ō-nori* song, especially when the *taiko* (stick drum) is playing. Examples: *Kakitsubata*, *Yōrō*. In some cases the *ō-nori* ends in *hira-nori*, this being the case with many visional *sanban-me-mono*, such as *Matsukaze*, *Hotoke-no-Hara* or *Futari Shizuka*. Typically the *shura*-Noh ends in a *shura-nori* song. *Kiri* in the more specific sense of "epilogue," as it is the case here with *Michimori*, is a short song in *hira-nori*, with a typical, rather matter-of-fact wording and melody pattern, usually beginning in the middle pitch and ending in the higher pitch. The song, as its name literally meaning "conclusion" indicates, serves to put an end to a play. In the Noh libretto, the section is marked as *kiri*. This occurs in comparatively few Noh. Usually by *kiri* we refer to the final section including the "epilogue" when there is one. *Michimori* and *Aoi-no-Ue* have the same *kiri*.

similar to the *Tsure* in *Kiyotsune*, the hero Kiyotsune's wife, with this difference: in *Kiyotsune*, the role of the *Tsure*, who meets the *Shite* after the exit of the *Waki*, is that of the antagonist to the *Shite*; in *Michimori*, the *Tsure*'s role is a companion to the *Shite*, and it is she who is presented as the chief narrator of the episode in the first act, herself the heroine of the story. It is the *Tsure* who speaks first after the entrance of the couple in a boat. In this unusual treatment of the *Tsure* in *Michimori*, originally written by Sei-ami and rewritten by Ze-ami, we see a trace of an older form of Noh before Ze-ami established the *Shite* as the single central figure.[2] The first act has other features of unusual appeal, such as the *tsukurimono* representing a fishing boat. The fishing torch made of a red wadding hung on a pole standing in the boat's prow effectively brings the atmosphere of the dark seascape into the audience's imagination. Very dramatic are the scenes of the encounter of the monks and the couple, who, attracted by the voices chanting the stura steer their boat to the shore; the monks reading sutra in the light of the fishing fire; *Tsure* stepping out of the boat in the gesture of leaping into the sea, which concludes her account of Kozaishō's self-drowning. The *Tsure* continues to take part in the second act in which the parting of the couple is compared to that of a defeated Chinese hero and his wife. The scene, a dramatic rendering of a brief passage in the original about the couple's last encounter, is also comparable to the parting of Hector and Andromache in its tragic appeal.

In *Heike Monogatari*, the account of Kozaishō's death is followed by a chapter devoted to Michimori's courtship of Kozaishō, who became his wife through the kindly intercession of a royal princess.[3] Thus Kozaishō

---

[2] In the second act, too, the *Tsure* is the first to answer the *Waki*'s question. A similar situation occurs in some other visional Noh of different genres. Examples: *Kayoi Komachi* and *Nishikigi*. In both the *Tsure* plays an important role.

[3] Michimori's courtship of Kozaishō no Tsubone is told in *Heike Monogatari* as follows: Kozaishō was a lady-in-waiting at the court of the royal princess Jōsaimon-in. When she was sixteen, Michimori saw her on the occasion of the Princess's flower-viewing excursion and fell in love. He sent her letters and poems for three years without receiving an answer. Then one day Michimori's messenger met her hurrying from her home to the royal residence in her father's coach, and threw his master's letter into the coach. Not wanting to leave the letter there, Kozaishō tucked it inside the belt of her long-trailing skirt and came into the royal presence. While she waited on her lady, she let fall the letter. The Princess picked it up, and hiding it in her sleeve, said, "I have come into possession of something very rare. I wonder to whom it belongs." All the ladies-in-waiting swore that they knew nothing about it. Only Kozaishō kept silence, her face flushing deep crimson. The Princess, who had known about Michimori's courtship, opened the letter which was permeated with exquisite smell of incense. The letter contained a card on which a poem was written in an elegant handwriting:

| | |
|---|---|
| Waga koi wa | My love for you is |
| Hosotani-gawa no | A narrow mountain river's |
| Maruki-bashi | Single-log foot bridge |
| Fumikaesarete | Being kicked o'er and turned down, |

is one of the heroines of the episodes that add romantic color to the epic. The introduction of this character as a *tsure* of no minor importance makes *Michimori* an unusually structured *shura*-Noh of deep romantic appeal.

Scene: The Straits of Naruto, Awa Province (present Tokushima Prefecture)

Season: Summer

Characters and costumes:

*Waki* A monk in the costume of an ordinary *waki* monk, such as the *Waki* in *Yashima*.

*Waki-tsure* An attendant monk, whose costume is similar to that of *Waki-tsure* in *Yashima*.

*Mai-shite* The ghost of Taira no Michimori in the guise of an old fisherman, in the costume of an old fisherman, such as the *Mae-shite* in *Yashima*, carries a rowing pole.

*Nochi-shite* The ghost of Michimori in the costume representing the military attire of a young nobleman, consisting of a *chujō* or *imawaka* mask, long black hair, a *nashiuchi-eboshi* hat, *chōken* or unlined *happi* robe over a *nuihakuu* or *atsuita karaori kitsuke* and white or colored *ōkuchi* divided skirt.

*Tsure* The ghost of Michimori's wife Kozaishō no Tsubone, in a *tsure* mask, and the costume of an ordinary young *tsure* woman, including a colorful *karaori* robe worn in the *kinagashi* style over a *surihaku kitsuke*. (The *Tsure* is an old woman in the first act and a young woman in the second. However, the actor always remains on the stage without making an interim exit. As it is, the *Tsure* appears from the beginning in a young woman's costume.)

---

| | |
|---|---|
| Nururu sode kana | My sleeves soaking with water. |

(Note: In the poem, *fumi-kaesarete* means (1) "being kicked over," (2) having a letter returned," with *fumi* meaning "to step on" and "letter," *kaesu* meaning "to turn or roll over," and "to return." "Wet sleeves" means "sleeves wet with tears.")

"This letter is a lament of an unreturned love," said the Princess. "Too much hard-heartedness sometimes brings unhappiness," she warned Kozaishō, quoting the example of Ono no Komachi, a lady of legendary beauty who turned down the courtship of many noblemen and died in misery. Then the gracious Princess wrote this poem in answer:

| | |
|---|---|
| Tada tanome | Do keep hoping on, |
| Hosotani-gawa no | A narrow mountain river's |
| Maruki-bashi | Single-log foot bridge, |
| Fumikaesarete wa | Being kicked o'er and turned down, |
| Ochizarameyawa | How will it not fall at last? |

(Note: *Ochi* (to fall) also means "to yield, to be conquered.")

In this way, through the royal mediation, Kozaishō became Michimori's wife and accompanied him to the Western provinces, to roam over the seawaves in boat, finally following him on the last voyage beyond this life.

    *Ai-kyōgen*  A local man.
*Kakeri* by the *Shite*.
The author: Sei-ami, revised by Ze-ami. (Sei-ami can be pronounced "I-ami.")

# MICHIMORI

NANORI-BUE *Waki enters accompanied by Waki-tsure.  Waki stands at nanori-za and Waki-tsure kneels by the first pine on the hashigakari.*

Nanori *spoken*　　　**WAKI**
I am a monk who is spending the summer at Thundering
　　　Straits of Awa.[1]
On this sea coast
The Heike people lost their lives, so in deep pity[2]
Nightly I go out to the beach and read a sutra.
Even now I am going out to pray for the repose of their
　　　souls.

*Waki goes to waki-za and sits down.  Waki-tsure sits on his right,*

Age-uta *au*　　　**WAKI** and **WAKI-TSURE**
On the beach dune,
As we sit by the pine-grown rocks and wait,[3]
As we sit by the pine-grown rocks and wait,
Whose night boat can it be?  Over the white waves[4]
The rudder's sound alone is heard, Thundering Straits[5]
Coast is calm and quiet this evening,
Coast is calm and quiet this evening.

ISSEI *A tsukurimono representing a fishing boat with a fishing fire hanging from a pole at the prow is placed stage left the prow foremost. Shite enters preceded by Tsure.  They step into the boat, Tsure standing in the middle of it, Shite behind her.  Shite takes a pole from a kōken and holds it in his left hand.*

Sashi *awazu*　　　**TSURE**
Ah, far away, a mountain temple bell is tolling,
To this beach so close reaches its sound.

　　　**SHITE**
It is the evening bell.  Let us make haste.

　　　**TSURE**
Soon passes away the light of this day.

---

[1]Awa-no-Naruto:  Literally "Awa's Sounding Straits," located between the Awaji Island and the coast of Awa Province in Shikoku is famous for the swirling tide waters. *Ichi-ge* (one summer):  Buddhist term referring to *ge-ango* (summer confinement), lasting from April 14 through July 15.  During this period, monks observe religious rites in seclusion.  See *Hajitomi*, line 3, *The Noh* Vol. 3, Book 1.

[2]Lines 2--3.  Actually no battle was fought on the coast, and nobody died there except Kozaishō.

Kore wa Awa-no-Naruto ni ichi-ge o okuru sō nite sōrō.[1]

Sate mo kono ura wa
Heike no ichimon hate-tamaitaru tokoro nareba itawashiku zonji[2]
Maiya kono isobe ni idete on-kyō o yomi-tatematsuri sōrō.
Tadaima mo idete tomurai-mōsabaya to omoi sōrō.                    5

Isoyama ni
Shibashi iwane no matsu hodo ni[3]
Shibashi iwane no matsu hodo ni
Ta ga yo-bune towa shira-nami ni[4]
Kaji-oto bakari Naruto no[5]                                       10
Ura shizuka naru koyoi kana
Ura shizuka naru koyoi kana.

Suwa to-o-yamadera no kane no koe
Kono iso chikaku kikoe so-oro-o.

Iriai gosamere isoga-tamae.                                       15

Hodonaku kururu hi no kazu kana.

---

[3]*Shibashi i* (for a while to stay) --> *iwa-ne no matsu* (rock-root pine tree, a pine growing on a rock) --> *matsu hodo ni* (waiting).

[4]*Ta ga yo-bune towa shirana* (whose night boat? Unknown . . .) --> *shira-nami* (white waves).

[5]*Kaji-oto bakari naru* (rudder sound only sounds) --> Naruto (Sounding Straits).

*SHITE*
Yesterday is gone,[6]

*TSURE*
Today comes to an end.

*SHITE*
Tomorrow, just another day like this.

*TSURE*
Yet old age does not count on

*SHITE*
The number of days left to it.

Issei *awazu*   *SHITE* and *TSURE*
How long thus, over the life's sea to cross,[7]
The fishers with little time to spare
In the wave-tossed boat.

*TSURE*
What hope have we
In our old age,

*SHITE*
In order to live

*SHITE* and *TSURE*
Toiling thus?

Age-uta *au*   *JI*
Adrift in sad life
Lonely souls find a little solace,
Lonely souls find a little solace,
Moonrise, the rising tide, fishers in their small boat,[8]
How enchanting
The bay's autumnal landscape!
A place famed for the evening waves,[9]
Thundering Straits, out o'er the sea clouds stretching to
Awaji Isle, inseparably attached,[10]

---

[6]Lines 17--19. From a poem by Harumichi no Tsuraki in *Kokin-shū*: Kinō to ii/
Kyō to kurashite/ Asuka-gawa/ Nagarete hayaki/ Tsukihi narikeri (Yesterday is gone,/
Today is already spent,/ The Morrow River/ Flows away with such swiftness,/ And so
do the days and months.) In the poem, Asuka-gawa (The Asuka River) contains *asu*
(tomorrow). *Nagarete* (to flow) is a verb to Asuka-gawa and *tsukihi* (days and months).

Kino-o sugi[6]

Kyo-o to kure

Asu mata kaku koso aru-bekere.

Saredomo oi ni tanomanu wa                                      20

Mi no yukusue no hikazu nari.

Itsu made yo oba watazumi no[7]
Amari ni hima mo
Nami-o-bune.

Nani o tanomi ni                                               25
Oi no mi no

Inochi no tame ni

Tsuko-o-beki.

Uki-nagara
Kokoro no sukoshi nagusamu wa                                  30
Kokoro no sukoshi nagusamu wa
Tsuki no de-jio no ama-obune[8]
Samo omoshiroki
Ura no aki no keshiki kana.
Tokoro wa iu-nami no[9]                                        35
Naruto no oki ni kumo tsuzuku
Awaji no Shima ya hanare-enu[10]

---

[7]Lines 22--23. *Yo oba wata* (life to cross, to live) --> *watazumi no ama* (crossing sea's fisherman = fisherman of the sea) --> *Amarini* (too), an adverb to the following phrase, *hima mo na* (time none, busy) --> *nami-o-bune* (wave-boat, a boat on the waves). *Nami-o-bune* alliterates with *Nani o* (what) in the next line.

[8]*Tsuki no de* (moon-rise) --> *de-jio* (rising tide).

[9]Lines 35--36. *iu-nami no Naru* (evening waves sound) --> Naruto (Sounding Straits).

[10]*hanare-enu* (inseparable) modifies Awaji no Shima (Awaji Isle), and *Ukiyo no waza* (the sad life's chore) in the next line.

The weary life's chore, ah, 'tis sad indeed,
The weary life's chore, ah, 'tis sad indeed!

Sashi *awazu*     **SHITE**
The dark seas engulf the moon, her clear light gone;

    **TSURE**
On the boat burns the fisherman's torch, the night wearing on.

    **SHITE** and **TSURE**
Through the rush-woven covering drips night rain,[11]
In the reeds, rustling of the wind, besides them,
No sound comes knocking on the wave-tossed pillows, and yet[12]
Dreaming or awakening, voices reading a sutra,
With the sound of wind mingling, are heard.

*Shite puts right* Let the rudder's sound be stilled, rest the hand on the
*hand on the* oar,
*pole and listens.* Listen to the sutra being chanted.

*Kakaru*     **WAKI**
Who is there? Over Thundering Straits away from the coast I hear a sound.

    **SHITE**
For no haven bound, a fisherman's boat this is.

    **WAKI**
If so, I have a word to say.
Close to this beach row your boat.

*Shite puts right*     **SHITE**
*hand on the* Obeying the word, I steer the boat to the shore and
*pole, a kata of* see . . .
*poling.*

    **WAKI**
Two monks seated on a rock,

    **SHITE**
A fishing boat by the bank.

*Waki takes out*     **WAKI**
*sutra and* Reed-fire light I borrow for a while and[13]
*unrolls it.* The holy scroll I unfold and recite.

---

[11]Lines 42--43. *ame no ashi* ("rain's feet" = rain falling in lines; rain's speed or density) --> *Ashi-ma* (reed's gap, meaning the wind blowing through the reed growth).

Ukiyo no waza zo kanashiki
Ukiyo no waza zo kanashiki.

Anto-o tsuki o uzunde seiko-o nashi                              40

Fune ni taku ama no kagaribi fuke-sugite

Toma yori kuguru yoru no ame no[11]
Ashi-ma ni kayo-o kaze naradewa
Oto suru mono mo nami-makura ni[12]

Yume ka utsutsuka o-kyo-o no koe no                             45
Arashi ni tsurete kikoyuru zoya.
Kaji-oto o shizume kara-ro o osaete

Cho-omon sebaya to omoi soro-o.

Ta-so ya kono Naruto no oki ni oto suru wa

Tomari sadamenu ama no tsuri-bune zo-oro-o yo.                  50

Samo araba omo-o shisai ari
Kono iso chikaku yose-tamae.

O-ose ni shitagai sashi-yose mireba

Ni-nin no so-o wa iwao no ue

Isari no fune wa kishi no kage                                  55

Ashi-bi no kage o karisome ni[13]
On-kyo-o o hiraki dokuju suru.

---

[12]*Oto suru mono mo nami* (sound-maker none = There is no sound/visitor) with *oto suru* meaning "to make sound" and "to visit." --> *nami-makura* (wave-pillow = sleeping in a boat).
[13]*kage o kari* (light to borrow) --> *karisome ni* (temporarily, for a while).

> *SHITE*
> Ah, what bliss!  Since 'tis to catch fish,
> Reed fire as an evil fire thought I, but[14]

*Shite drops*
*the pole,*

> *WAKI*
> Into a blissful light[15]

> *SHITE*
> Turned at Thundering Straits.

*Shite makes kata*
*of prayer.*

> *SHITE* and *WAKI*
> "All embracing pledge sea-deep, lasting to eternity[16]
> a miracle . . ." this encounter,
> "To the fiftieth are passed on" the blessings told in[17]
> the *Ecstatic Devotion Book.*

Sage-uta *au*

*Shite fans the*
*fire, Shite and*
*Tsure kneel.*

> *JI*
> Oh, blissful sutra!  The sacred scroll's[18]
> Face obscure and dark, sea's wind
> Blows the reed fire into flaring brightness
> As we listen to the holy words, oh what bliss!

Age-uta *au*

> Dragon Maiden was reborn as man, hearing this,[19]
> Dragon Maiden was reborn as man, hearing this,
> The old woman, too, is hopeful.
> Not to mention the venerable man,
> Prayer is led to fulfillment by the Three Carts.[20]
> Let the reed fire burn pure and bright all night.
> Continue with your sutra reading, we pray,
> Continue with your sutra reading, we pray.

*Spoken*

> *WAKI*
> Oh, what joy!
> In the light of the fire, my heart in peace and quiet,
>   I have read the sutra.
> Now by this bay[21]
> Heike people lost their lives.  As it is so,

---

[14]*Waza wa ashi* (practice bad) --> *ashi-bi* (a. reedfire. b. bad fire).  In Buddhism killing even fish is considered as a grave sin.

[15]Lines 60--61.  *Yoki tomoshibi ni naru* (good light to become) --> *Naruto no umi* (Naruto Sea), an introductory phrase to the next passage.

[16]The quotation is from the twenty-fifth book of *Saddharmapundarīka-sūtra.*

[17]In the eighteenth book of *Saddharmapundarīka-sūtra,* entitled "Ecstatic devotion," it is said that the blessing of the sutra is passed on from person to person down to the fiftieth as each hears it recited and passes it on to another.  Cf. *Yorimasa* 141--142.

[18]Lines 64--65.  *kuraki* (dark) modifies *omote* (face, surface) and *ura* (sea).  *Ura* also means "back," the antonym of *omote.*

Arigata ya isari suru
Waza wa ashi-bi to omoishi ni[14]

Yoki tomoshibi ni[15]                                              60

Naruto no umi no

"Guzei jinnyokai ryakko-o fushigi" no kien ni yorite[16]

Go-jiu tenden no Zuiki Kudoku-bon[17]

Geni arigata ya kono kyo-o no[18]
Omote zo kuraki ura-kaze mo                                       65
Ashi-bi no kage o fuki-tatete
Cho-omon suru zo arigataki.

Riunyo henjo-o to kiku toki wa[19]
Riunyo henjo-o to kiku toki wa
Nba mo tanomoshi ya                                               70
O-oji wa iu ni oyobazu
Negai mo mitsu no kuruma no[20]
Ashi-bi wa kiyoku akasu-beshi
Nao nao o-kyo-o asobase
Nao nao o-kyo-o asobase.                                          75

Ara ureshi ya zōrō.
Hi no hikari nite kokoro shizuka ni on-kyō o
    yomi-tatematsurite sōrō.
Mazu mazu kono ura wa[21]
Heike no ichimon hate-tamaitaru tokoro nareba

---

[19]Buddhahood is denied to women. However, according to the twelfth book of *Saddharmapundarīka-sūtra*, entitled *Devadatta*, the dragon king's daughter became a Buddha through transformation into a man.
[20]Lines 72--73. *Negai mo mitsu* (wish fulfilled) --> *mitsu no kuruma* (three carts). In the third book of *Saddharmapundarīka-sūtra*, entitled "Parables," Buddha who leads illusion-bound men to enlightenment is compared to a father who coaxes his children out of their burning house, a symbol of the earthy life, luring them with a promise to give them three carts, each drawn by either an ox, sheep or deer. *Kuruma no Ashi* (wheel's feet, wheel's speed) --> *Ashi-bi* (reed fire). In *akasu* (to spend the night), *aka* (bright) is related to *"ashi-bi."*
[21]Lines 78--79. See footnote 2.

Every night I come out to this beach and read the sutra
for them.
Among them was there any one of special note?  Please
tell me in detail about such a person.

*SHITE*
As you say, some were slain in battle,
Some threw themselves into the sea.
Among them Kozaishō no Tsubone . . .

*To Tsure*     I say, tell the story together with me.

*Sings in free*     *TSURE*
*rhythm*     Before long people of Heike
Having forsaken their horses,
Boarded small fishing boats,
At times they would pole in the moonlight.[22]

Sashi *awazu*     *SHITE*
There already from the Capital remote enough they lived
on Suma Coast,

*SHITE* and *TSURE*
All of a sudden by the enemy even from there driven
out[23]
Those who should honor their names, the men at arms,[24]
Past Onokoro Island and Awaji Bay,
To Awa's Thundering Straits they came.

*TSURE*
Then Kozaisho-o no Tsubone called her nurse to
her side.

*SHITE* and *TSURE*
"What would you say?" said she,
"Those who would help me remain in the Capital.
Michimori was killed in battle.
Whom am I to turn to and live on?
Into this sea I want to throw myself."

*Shite and Tsure*     Mistress and servant in tears held each other's hand
*rise.*     and went to the ship's side.

---

[22]Lines 89--90.  In 89 there is a hint at moonlight excursion, an elegant pastime of
noblemen who played music and wrote poems on the boats.  Suma near Heike's
headquarters, Ichinotani, was celebrated for its landscape, especially on moonlight
autumn nights.  The line alludes to the romantic spirit and esthetics of the Heike
noblemen even in tragic situations.  In *Miyako ni to-oki Suma* (From the Capital remote
Suma), Suma implies *sumai* (dwelling place).
[23]The Heike lost their battle when a troop of Genji warriors led by Minamoto no
Yoshitsune drove down the sheer cliff, Hiyodori-goe (Bulbul Pass) and attacked the
Heike from behind.  See line 149.

Maiya kono isobe ni idete on-kyō o yomi-tatematsuri sōrō.                    80

Toriwaki ikanaru hito kono ura nite hate-tamaite
sōrō zo kuwashiku on-monogatari sōarae.

Ōse no gotoku aruiwa utare
Mata wa umi nimo shizumi-tamaite sōrō.
Nakanimo Kozaishō no Tsubone koso . . .
Ya, morotomo ni on-monogatari sōrae.                    85

Saruhodoni Heike no ichimon
Basho-o o aratame
Ama no o-bune ni nori-utsuri
Tsuki ni sao sasu toki mo ari.[22]

Koko dani mo Miyako no to-oki Suma-no-Ura                    90

Omowanu kataki ni otosarete[23]

Geni na o oshimu mononofu no[24]
Onokoro-jima ya Awaji-gata
Awa-no-Naruto ni tsukinikeri.

Saruhodoni Kozaisho-o no Tsubone menoto o chikazuke                    95

Ikani nani toka omo-o.
Ware tanomoshiki hitobito wa Miyako ni todomari
Michimori wa utarenu.
Tare o tanomite nagaro-o-beki.
Kono umi ni shizuman tote                    100
Shiujiu nakunaku te o tori-kumi funabata ni nozomi

---

[24]Lines 92--93. *mononofu no* (warrior's) serves as a pillow word to Onokoro
Island, in which *onoko* can mean "a (manly) man." Onokoro Island is a legendary
island which was popularly identified with Awaji Island. "Onokoro" means "of itself to
congeal." According to the *Kojiki*, when god Izanigi and goddess Izanami let a halberd
down into the sea to create land, drippings from the halberd hardened and became an
island, which was named Onokoro Island.

                     *TSURE*
                     "So into this sea I would sink.

Sage-uta *au*         JI
                     "To sink down was my fate," the thought seemed
                        to prompt[25]

*Tsure makes kata* Tears that already were floating up to the eyes.
*of weeping.*

Age-uta *au*       Which way is the west?  Where the moon is sinking,[26]
                     Which way is the wets?  Where the moon is sinking,
                     The sky is all blurred, maybe it is just because
                     Spring night, as its wont, is closed in mist,
                     Tears, too, cast clouds, obscuring the sight.
                     The nurse in tears held fast to her lady's robe,
                     "Now your heart is heavy with deep sorrow, but
                     You are not the only one to suffer.
                     Think it over, change your mind," she pleaded,
*Shite holds*       Clinging to the sleeve of her lady,
*Tsure's sleeve.*    Who seemed to shake her off and plunge into the deep,
*Tsure steps out* The old man in the same way, under the rising tide,[27]
*of the boat,*      To the bottom sank down, to rot with the sea dusts,
*kneels, goes to* To the bottom sank down, to rot with the sea dusts.
*kōken-za. Shite*
*looks down, steps*
*out of the boat,*
*kneels, exits.*

    NAKAIRI *Shite exits.*
    AI-KYŌGEN *Ai-kyōgen, a local man, who has come to listen to the*
    *monks chanting the sutra, tells them about the romance and deaths of*
    *Michimori and Kozaishō no Tsubone, and exhorts them to pray for the*
    *souls of the departed.*

Machi-utai *au*    *WAKI* and *WAKI-TSURE*
                     These eight sacred scrolls, scripture of divine pledge,[28]
                     These eight sacred scrolls, scripture of divine pledge
                     Will not leave a single man unabsolved.
                     The words from the Book of *Upāya* now we chant.[29]

*Awazu*              WAKI
                     "What I wished in the past . . ."[30]

---

[25]Lines 103--104.  *Shizumu* (to sink) and *ukami* (to float, to well out) are antonyms.
[26]*Nishi* (west) where Buddha's Paradise is.
[27]*onaji michi* (the same way) --> *michi-jio* (rising tide).
[28]eight scrolls: Refers to the *Saddharmapundarīka-sūtra*, which consists of eight volumes.

Sarunitemo ano umi ni koso shizumo-ozurame.

Shizumu-beki mi no kokoro niya[25]

Namida no kanete ukamuran.

Nishi wa to toeba tsuki no iru[26]                            105
Nishi wa to toeba tsuki no iru
Sonata mo miezu o-okata no
Haru no yo ya kasumuran
Namida mo tomo ni kumoruran.
Menoto nakunaku toritsukite                                   110
Kono toki no mono-omoi
Kimi ichi-nin ni kagirazu.
Oboshimeshi-tomari-tamae to
On-kinu no sode ni toritsuku o
Furikiri umi ni iru to mite                                   115
Ro-ojin mo onaji michi-jio no[27]
Soko no mikuzu to narinikeri
Soko no mikuzu to narinikeri.

Kono hachi-jiku no chikai nite[28]
Kono hachi-jiku no chikai nite                                120
Ichi-nin mo morasaji no
Ho-oben-bonno dokuju suru.[29]

"Nyoga-shaku-shogan. . ."[30]

---

[29]*Hōben-bon* (Book of *Upāya*): the second book of the sūtra, *upāya* means wisdom
of Buddha to lead people to enlightenment.
[30]Lines 123--127. From the second book of the *Saddharmapundarīka-sūtra*. Line
124 is not in the texts of *shite* schools.

DEHA *Nochi-shite enters. Tsure rises and stands in front of daishō. Shite enters the main stage, stands at jō-za and makes the kata of prayer, facing Waki.*

*Awazu*
*Waki makes kata of prayer.*

WAKI
"What I wished in the past . . ."

SHITE
"Has now been fulfilled;

*Noru*

WAKI
"Enlightenment for all on earth,

SHITE
"Every soul led to Buddha's Way."[31]

JI
Michimori and his wife
To the sutra attracted,
Rise and return o'er the surging waves,[32]

*Awazu*

*Shite prays.*

SHITE
Ah, highly blissful
Law of Buddha!

*Kakaru*

WAKI
How strange! A beautiful lady's form
Over the waves is seen afloat.
Who can you be?

TSURE
Her name alone still not vanishing, in the foamy
waves of[33]
Awa's thundering Straits sank low
Kozaisho-o no Tsubone, and this her ghost.

*Tsure sits to the left of Waki.*

WAKI
The other is in helmet and armor attired,
His arms a glittering splendor.
Tell me who you are.

SHITE
I am he who in the battle of Ikuta Wood[34]
His name to the world made known,

---

[31]Lines 127--128. In *niubutsudo-o* (enter the Buddha's way), the Chinese character *dō* (the way) is pronounced *michi* in the *kun* reading and leads to Michimori.

[32]*Tachi-kaeru* (to return; to rise and roll), verb to *Michimori fu-ufu* (Michimori and his wife) and *nami* (waves) --> *Ara* (violent; ah!).

"Nyoga-shaku-shogan. . .

"Konja-i-manzoku;                                                          125

"Ke-issai shuju-o

"Kairyo-o-niubutsudo-o" no[31]

Michimori fu-ufu
O-kyo-o ni hikarete
Tachi-kaeru nami no[32]                                                   130

Ara arigata no
Minori yana.

Fushigi yana samo namamekeru on-sugata no
Nami ni ukamite mie-tamo-o wa
Ikanaru hito nite mashimasu zo.                                           135

Na bakari wa mada kie-hatenu ada-nami no[33]

Awa-no-Naruto ni shizumi-hateshi
Kozaisho-o no Tsubone no iurei nari.

Ima ichi-ninna katchiu o taishi
Hyo-ogu imijiku mie-tamo-o wa                                             140
Ikanaru hito nite mashimasu zo.

Kore wa Ikuta no Mori no kasen ni oite[34]
Na o tenga ni age

---

[33]Lines 136--137. *Na...kie-hatenu* (name...not vanishing) --> *ada nami* (vain waves) --> *awa* (foam) --> Awa-no-Naruto (Awa's Thundering Straits).
[34]Ikuta: The site of the front gate of the Heike fort at Ichinotani.

As great general of high renown[35]
Won Echizen's Lord of the Third Court Rank, Michimori.
Remote past's story to recount
As far as this place I have appeared.

| | |
|---|---|
| Sashi *awazu* | **JI** |
| *Shite sits on a* | Now this place, Ichinotani, faces the sea.[36] |
| *stool, center* | Behind rises steep Hiyodori Pass, |
| *stage.* | True to its name none but birds on their wings can |
| | cross it, for the beasts |
| | To set their feet no ground. |

**SHITE**

As it is, again and again Ikuta's front gate stood first in[37]
our concern.

**JI**

Clan leaders were sent to guard the place,
Michimori foremost among them. However,

*Shite kneels* Stealthily returning to his camp,
*on the floor,* To Kozaisho-o no Tsubone he spoke thus;
*facing Tsure.*

Kuse *au* "Now the battle will
Tomorrow come to a decisive end.
How my heart aches with pity for you!
Except Michimori among all these people
A person to turn to you have none.
Should I meet my fate, as most likely I shall,
Return home, and if you don't forget me,
For my departed soul please say prayers."
In grief of parting they took up a farewell cup.

*Shite makes* Michimori filled it with sake,
*kata of serving* Serving it to his wife. As evening hours mellowed,[38]
*sake.* In slumbrous embrace words of love they exchanged.
There is a Chinese story,
Ko-ou, by Ko-oso being attacked,[39]
In lines trickled down Lady Gu's tears. Their grief,
Compared with this, could have never been greater.
A taper was flickering dimly,

---

[35]Lines 144--145. *homare o E* (renown to win) --> Echizen, the northeastern part of present Fukui Prefecture.

[36]Ichinotani: In the present Suma Ward, Kobe City. Hiyodori = Bulbul, a song bird.

[37]*ikutabimo*: Literally "many times, again and again," an emphatic word, contains "Ikuta."

[38]*yoi*: Means "intoxication" and "evening."

Busho-o tasshi homare o[35]
Echizen no Sanmi Michimori 145
Mukashi o kataran sono tame ni
Kore made araware-idetaru nari.


Somosomo kono Ichinotani to mo-osuni mae wa umi[36]
Ue wa kewashiki Hiyodoroi-goe
Makotoni tori naradewa kakeri-gataku kedamono mo 150

Ashi o tatsu-beki chi ni arazu.


Tada ikutabi mo o-ote no jinno kokoromotonaki zo tote[37]


Muneto no ichimon sashi-tsukawasaru.
Michimori mo sono zuiichi tarishiga
Shinonde waga jin ni kaeri 155
Kozaisho-o no Tsubone ni mukai


Sudeni ikusa
Myo-onichi ni kiwamarinu.
Itawashi ya onmi wa
Michimori narade kono uchi ni 160
Tanomu-beki hito nashi.
Ware tomokaku mo naru naraba
Miyako ni kaeri wasurezuwa
Naki ato toite tabi-tamae.
Nagori oshimi no o-sakazuki 165
Michimori shaku o tori
Sasu sakazuki no yoi no ma mo[38]
Utatane narishi mutsugoto wa
Tatoeba Morokoshi no
Ko-ou Ko-oso no seme o uke[39] 170
Suko-o Gu-shi ga nanda mo
Kore niwa ikade masaru-beki.
Tomoshibi kuro-oshite

---

[39]Lines 170--173. Kōu (Hsiang Yü, 232--202 B.C.), Ch'u's ruler, was defeated by his former assistant Kōso (Kao Tsu, 247--195 B.C.), and killed himself. Kao Tsu became the first Emperor of the former Han dynasty. Gu-shi (Yü-mêi-Jên), Hsiang Yü's mistress, died with him. 171 is from a poem by Tachibana no Hiromi (837--890) in *Wakan Rōei-shū*: "The taper was burning dimly; In lines tears ran down Lady Gu's cheeks."

In the moonlight, their eyes fastened on each other,
As they thus talked, comforting each other,

*SHITE*

My younger brother, Lord of Noto,[40]

*JI*

Already in armor and helmet attired,
"Michimori, where are you?
Why is it that you are so late?"
He was calling, the sound of his voice
So loud. "Ah, I'm ashamed. That is Lord of Noto.[41]
My own younger brother, and yet
More than others he makes me ashamed.

*Shite rises.*  Now I must part with you. Farewell," he said.
But he finds it hard to leave her, at Ichinotani
Where Suma's mountains rise high, feeling as if[42]
From behind he is pulled back by his hair.

KAKERI *by Shite. After kakeri Shite stands at jō-za.*

*Spoken*  *SHITE*
Then in the midst of hard fighting,
Lord of Tajima, Tsunemasa, I heard, had already
been killed.[43]

*Kakaru*  *WAKI*
Now, Lord of Satsuma, Tadanori, how did he meet
his end?[44]

*Spoken*  *SHITE*
*To the end Shite*  With Okabe no Rokuyata Tadazumi he came to a grapple
*describes the*  and was slain.[45]
*fight in dance.*

Ah, Michimori, too, wants an enemy of name,
I would die fighting with him, as I waited thinking thus,
*Kakaru*  Oh, look there, a worthy enemy,[46]

---

[40]Noto-no-kami: Taira no Noritsune. Cf. lines 144 and 278, *Yashima*.
[41]*Ara* (ah!) also means "violent" and modifies *koe* (voice) in the preceding line. Cf.
131.
[42]Lines 186--187. *Suma no yama no ushiro* (Suma's mountain behind) --> *ushiro-gami* (back hair, hair at the back of the head). *Ushiro-gami o hikaruru* (the back hair being pulled) means "to take leave with reluctance." Suma's mountain behind: From the following passage in the Suma Chapter, *Genji Monogatari*: "the smoke rising from what they call brushwood they were burning on the mountain behind." Cf. *Atsumori* 178, and *Tadanori*, 72, Vol. 2, Book 1, *Matsukaze* 286, Vol. 3, Book 2.

Tsuki no hikari ni sashi-mukai
Katari nagusamu tokoro ni                                    175

Shatei no Noto-no-kami[40]

Haya katchiu o yoroi-tsutsu
Michimori wa izuku nizo
Nado osonawari-tamo-o zo to
Yobawarishi sono koe no                                      180
Ara hazukashi ya Noto-no-kami[41]
Waga oto-oto to ii nagara
Tanin yori nao hazukashi ya.
Itoma mo-oshite saraba tote
Yuku mo yukarenu Ichinotani no                               185
Tokorokara Suma no yama no[42]
Ushiro-gami zo hikaruru.

Saruhodoni kasen mo nakaba narishikaba
Tajima-no-kami Tsunemasa mo haya utarenu to kikoyu.[43]

Sate Satsuma-no-kami Tadanori no hate wa ikani.[44]          190

Okabe no Rokuyata Tadazumi to kunde utareshikaba[45]

Appare Michimori mo na aru samurai mogana,
Uchijini sen to matsu tokoro ni
Suwa are o miyo yoki kataki ni[46]

---

[43]Tajima-no kami Tsunemasa: Kiyomori's brother Tsunemori's son and Atsumori's elder brother, the *Shite* of *Tsunemasa*.
[44]Satsuma-no-kami Tadanori: Kiyomori's brother and the *Shite* of *Tadanori*.
[45]See *Tadanori*.
[46]Lines 194--195. *yoki kataki ni O-o* (with a worthy enemy to encounter) --> O-omi (a province which is present Shiga Prefecture.

*Shura-nori*

**JI**

O-omi Province was where he came from,
O-omi Province was where he came from,
Kimura no Gengo Shigeakira,
Whipping hard his horse, he came galloping.
Michimori, who, not in the least disturbed,
With his sword already drawn, stood waiting,
On the enemy's helmet dealt a crashing blow,
Then he and the enemy stabbing each other,
Both to Asura Hell's torture were doomed,
Take pity on me, I beseech you,
And pray well for the repose of my soul.

Kiri *au*

To the sutra-reciting voice listening,[47]
To the sutra-reciting voice listening,
Even an evil fiend is placated.
Patient sufferance and mercy's embodiment,
Bodhi-sattva comes to receive and
To Buddhahood and enlightenment
To deliver the lost soul, oh, how blissful,
To deliver the lost soul, oh, how blissful!

---

[47]Lines 206--213. In the libretto this section is specifically designated as *kiri* (epilogue). See the Introduction note 1. The same *kiri* is used in *Aoi-no-ue*.

O-omi no Kuni no jiunin ni                                    195
O-omi no Kuni no jiunin ni
Kimura no Gengo Shigeakira ga
Muchi o agete kake-kitaru.
Michimori sukoshimo sawagazu
Nuki-mo-oketaru tachi nareba                                  200
Kabuto no makko-o cho-o to uchi
Kaesu tachi nite sashichigae
Tomoni Shura-do-o no ku o ukuru
Awaremi o tare-tamai
Yoku tomuraite tabi-tamae.                                    205

Dokuju no koe o kiku toki wa[47]
Dokuju no koe o kiku toki wa
Akki kokoro o yawarage
Ninniku jihi no sugata nite
Bosatsu mo koko ni raiko-o su.                                210
Jo-obutsu tokudatsu no
Mi to nari-yuku zo arigataki
Mi to nari-yuku zo arigataki.

知

章

TOMOAKIRA

取つて押さへて首掻き切つて。
ナア

--Pressed the enemy down and cut off his head.

Totte osaete kubi kaki-kitte

-Line 248

# INTRODUCTION

The death of Taira no Tomoakira, the hero of Noh *Tomoakira*, is told in its source chapter, *"Death of Tomoakira"* from *Heike Monogatari* Vol. 9, as follows:

Shin-junagon Tomomori,[1] Taira no Kiyomori's son and the leader of the force posted at Ikuta Wood to the east of the Heike headquarters at Fukuhara, lost all followers but his son Musashi-no-kami (Lord of Musashi Province) Tomoakira and a retainer Kenmotsu Tarō Yorikata. The three men fled toward the beach to make their escape to the ships lying at anchor off the coast. About ten enemy horsemen came running after them with loud cries, hoisting a flag with the pattern of a fan, the crest of the Kodama clan. Kenmotsu Tarō, a mighty archer, let fly an arrow at the enemy's ensign who was running foremost. The arrow pierced his neck bone and he fell from his horse. One of the warriors who seemed to be the leader ran up to Shin-jūnagon and was about to grapple with him, but his son, Musashi-no-kami Tomoakira, wedged himself between them and in a grapple falling from his horse with the enemy, pressed him down and cut off his head. As he was rising to his feet, the enemy's page boy came up and cut his head off. Kenmotsu Tarō threw himself over the boy and slew him. . . . He killed many enemy men but finally an arrow hit his knee. Unable to rise to his feet, he died. During the skirmish, Shin-jūnagon, who was mounted on a stalwart horse, plunged into the sea and reached the Inner Minister's[2] ship lying at a distance. The ship was full of people with no place for the horse, so Shin-jūagon urged it to return to the beach. "Let me kill him," said Awa no Minbu Shigeyoshi, a Heike retainer, notching an arrow to his bow, "Otherwise the enemy will take him." "Any one can have him," said Shin-jūnagon. "He has saved my life. How can I let him

---

[1]Shin(new)-jūnagon Tomomori: A brave general who threw himself into the sea and died when the battle of Dan-no-Ura ended in the total defeat of the Heike. He is the *Nochi-shite* of *Ikari-kazuki* and *Funa-Benkei*. *Jū* (= chū = middle)-*nagon*: the title of the second of the three-ranked officials, who stand immediately under the grand minister, left and right ministers and inner ministers in the Imperial Ministry. Jiunagon in the text is an archaic pronunciation.

[2]Taira no Munemori, Kiyomori's second son and Tomomori's elder brother, the leader of the Heike after his elder brother Shigemori's death.

die?" Shigeyoshi dared not contradict him. The horse, loath to part with its master, would not go back, but swam about in the offing for a while. However, as the ship sailed far away, it swam back to the beach. Coming near the shore where it could stand, the horse looked back toward the ship and neighed two or three times. As it finally came ashore and stood still, it was taken by Kawagoe no Kotarō Shigefusa, who later presented it to the Ex-Emperor Goshirakawa. The horse came from Inoue in Shinano Province, so it was called Inoue-guro (Inoue the Black).

Shin-jūnagon came into the presence of the Inner Minister and said, "Musashi-no-kami passed away, leaving me behind, and I saw Kenmotsu Tarō being slain. My heart is heavy with grief. What a brave child he who grapples with an enemy to save his parent! What a parent I am who, instead of defending his child, made his escape like this! If it had been somebody else, and not myself, I would have been furious! Now I realize that life was so dear to me. Oh, I am ashamed to think how people will look at me." Covering his face with his sleeve, he wept bitterly. The Inner Minister said, "It is most extraordinary that Musashi-no-kami died for his father. He was skilled in military arts and was brave of heart, a fine captain. He must have been of the same age as Kiyomune, who is sixteen." As he looked at his son Kiyomune, tears stood in his eyes. All the Heike warriors present, those with sensitive hearts, or who were not easily moved, alike wet their sleeves with tears.

The Noh *Tomoakira* is structured as follows:

1. *Shidai, nanori, michiyuki* and *tsuki-zerifu* by the *Waki*, a traveling monk from a western province, who arrives at Suma Coast. Finding a newly erected stupa on which the name of Taira no Tomoakira is inscribed, he is moved to pity.

2. *Yobikate, mondō, kakeai, sage-uta* and *age-uta*: The *Shite*, the ghost of Taira no Tomoakira, in the guise of a local person, enters calling to the *Waki*, who asks him to tell him about Taira no Tomoakira. The *Shite* answers that Tomoakira was Shin-jūnagon Tomomori's son, who was slain in the battle of Ichinotani on this coast on February seventh. It is his anniversary day so a person related to him has erected the stupa. The *Shite* asks the *Waki* to pray for the deceased. Then the *Shite* and *Waki* pray together, while the Chorus sings in praise of Buddha's Law by whose power even a prayer a stranger offers by the wayside will save a soul.

3. *Katari* by the *Shite* followed by an *age-uta*: At the request of the *Waki*, the *Shite* narrates how Shin-junagon Tomomori escaped to the ship off shore, swimming the sea on horseback, how the horse, abandoned by its master, swam back to the beach, where it looked at the ships and neighed as if grieving the separation from its master. Then the *age-uta* describes the sorrow of the animal who would have followed its master even if it had to be tethered to the ship's rope.

4. *Rongi* and *nakairi*: It gets dark, and the *Waki* intends to pass the night on the beach, praying for Tomoakira's soul. The *Shite* thanks the *Waki*, revealing himself as one of the members of the Heike. Then he departs toward the shore, where his figure seems to sink and float over the waves till it disappears.

5. *Ai-kyōgen* and *machi-utai*: At the request of the *Waki*, the *Ai-kyōgen*, a villager, tells him the episode about Tomomori and Tomoakira as told in *Heike Monogatari*, then he exhorts the *Waki* to pray for Tomoakira's soul. The *Waki* sings *machi-utai*, describing himself reading the sutra all night on the wind-swept coast of Suma.

6. Entrance of *Nochi-shite*, Tomoakira's ghost in full military attire: *Sashi* by *Shite* and *kakeai* between *Shite* and Chorus followed by *age-uta*. The lines express the joy of Tomoakira who, attracted by the blessed sutra, has floated up to the shore. He reveals himself as Tomoakira's ghost who, thanks to the prayer offered for him, has returned to the Suma Coast, where the winging geese, the moon's face and ships receding behind Awaji Island are dimmed in spring mist. He begs the monk to pray on.

7. *Kuri-sashi-kuse*: *Kuri* and *sashi* about the defeated Heike people making their escape by ships; deaths of Tomoakira and Kenmotsu Tarō; Tomomori's escape to the Inner Minister's ship; *kuse* about his lament; the Inner Minister, who has a young son of Tomoakira's age, is deeply touched.

8. *Rongi* and finale in *shura-nori*: describe Tomoakira's fighting with the enemy and his death. The song ends with Tomoakira asking the monk to pray for the repose of his soul.

The above outline indicates that the Noh *Tomoakira* is a faithful adaptation of its original source. As it is, throughout the Noh, the hero's father Tomomori is in the limelight as much as, if not more than, the hero himself. The Noh begins according to the structural pattern of a visional Noh: the traveling monk on his arrival at the scene notices Tomoakira's name on a newly erected stupa. In pity he wonders who he can be. A local man, actually Tomoakira's ghost, tells the monk that Tomoakira was Tomomori's son. According to the standard pattern, this is to be followed by questions and answers about Tomoakira, the *Shite*. Instead, the *Waki* monk rather abruptly asks the villager about the fate of Tomoakira's father Tomomori. Upon this the villager narrates in a *katari* (not designated as *katari* in the Kanze text) how Tomomori escaped to the ship on his faithful horse. After this, the first act ends with a *rongi* in which the Chorus sings for the *Waki*, who is going to pass the night on the coast, praying, he does not specify for whom. It may be either Tomoakira or Tomomori, or both. The *Shite* makes his interim exit with a hint that he is one of the Heike members, but his name is not revealed. In the second act, the *Nochi-shite* appears as the ghost of the noble young warrior Tomoakira. In the ensuing questions and answers he reveals his name. There again is a reference to his father in *age-uta* that follows, describing sailing boats disappearing behind an island, which sadly remind Tomoakira of the separation from his father. The *kuri-sashi* is a description of the battle, with Tomoakira, Tomomori and their retainer Kenmotsu Tarō making their escape to the beach, the deaths of Tomoakira and Kenmotsu Tarō, and Tomomori's escape to the Inner Minister's ship. The major part of the *kuse* section is devoted to the description of Tomomori in the presence of the Inner Minister, to whom he pours out his lament over his son's death. Only in the finale does Tomoakira play his full part as *Shite*. During the song in *shura-nori* he describes in dance his mortal fight and then begs the monk to say prayers for his soul sunk to Asura's Hell.

The presentation of the father and son episode in the manner described above makes *Tomoakira* a sort of two-character Noh. In this respect it deviates from the standard *shura*-Noh, which is typically a Noh of one character. There are a few *shura*-Noh, such as *Kiyotsune* and *Michimori*, in which a second character, the *Tsure*, plays an important role. In *Tomonaga* the *Shite* in acts one and two are different characters. The difference between these multi-character *shura*-Noh and *Tomoakira* is that, in the former the second character makes her appearance on the stage in person, whereas in *Tomoakira*, Tomomori is a shadow character who never appears in person. He is only talked about, often the *Shite* as Tomoakira assuming the role of a narrator impersonating Tomomori. Examples: the *katari* in the first act and the *kuse* in the second act. The impersonation of a shadow character by the *shite* occurs in other *shura*-Noh, too, as in *Sanemori, Tadanori* and *Yorimasa*. However, in these this occurs only in a limited section. Also in the first two, during the impersonation of a shadow character, the *Shite* character is always the subject talked about. For example, in *Sanemori*, a shadow character tells about Sanemori, and in *Tadanori*, Okabe no Rokuyata impersonated by the *Shite* player describes the *Shite* Tadanori's death. In *Tomoakira*, on the contrary, references to Tomomori are made throughout the play, and in the *kuse*, the *Shite* character, instead of telling his own story, describes the father's plight.

*Tomoakira*, as a double-fucussed Noh, distinguishes itself from standard *shura*-Noh, which is characterized by a clear-cut imagery, where unity is achieved through concentration on the single important character, and in which the original narrative is refined and sublimated to pure poesy presented through graceful dancing. In contrast to such a "pure *shura*-Noh," *Tomoakira* adapts the original source as it is. Reflecting the characteristic of the original as a narrative literature, a greater emphasis is placed on the story development than on pure lyrical appeal.[3] As a narrative, play, it has a *katari* in the first act. In a two-act Noh with a *kuse*

---

[3]In this connection, there is the episode of Tomomori's faithful horse. It adds, at the same time, to the deviation of the Noh from the pure unity of imagery and to its human interest appeal.

in the second act, it is the general rule that the lyricism of the drama attains climax in that section with the accompaniment of a graceful dance. But the *kuse* in *Tomoakira*, although it occurs in the second act, exceptionally has no dance. Instead it is predominated by a narrative feature. While the Chorus sings about Tomomori pouring out his grief on board the Inner Minister's ship, the *Shite* remains seated on a stool, playing in a way the role of a *heike* (reciter of *Heike Monogatari*), who chants his lines to the accompaniment of his *biwa* (lute).

*Tomoakira* is classed by some scholars among half a dozen *shura*-Noh (including three that are no longer performed) that, with some probability, can be considered as Ze-ami's works. Whether this be the case or not, the dramatic structure of *Tomoakira* is of a different order from that of *Atsumori, Kiyotsune* and *Tadanori*, the young-warrior *shura*-Noh whose authorship is definitely attributed to Ze-ami by the same authorities.[4] In these Noh we find the structure based on a clearly established thematic unity which distinguishes Ze-ami's works, especially his visional Noh. *Tomoakira*, with its dual focus on two characters, lacks a clear-cut dramatic unity. A less refined product from the point of view of thematic sublimation, none the less, *Tomoakira*, based on one of the touching stories about a father and son, has a deep human appeal, which finds a highly poetic expression in such lines as:

| | |
|---|---|
| All blurred in spring mist | Oboro naru |
| Geese in flight, a passing shadow, the moon's face, | Kari no sugata ya tsuki no kage |
| Geese in flight, a passing shadow, the moon's face, | Kari no sugata ya tsuki no kage |
| Penciled faint o'er Picture Isle. Hiding behind it | Utsusu E-jima no shima-gakure |
| Sailed away the boat. | Yuku fune o |
| With wistfulness watched I, from my father | Oshi tozo omo-o waga chichi ni |

---

[4]Professor Akira Omote: *"Ze-ami Sakunō-kō"*, a consideration on Ze-ami's authorship, *Kanze* magazine, August 1960; Professor Haruo Nishino: *"Ze-ami no Noh Gaikan,"* a comment on Professor Omote's article, *Kaishaku to Kansho*, February, 1977. According to these articles, the Noh plays which can be considered as Ze-ami's works in the light of his writings or words, or of contemporary documents, can be classed into the following four groups:

A. Eighteen Noh, unquestionably written by Ze-ami, being mentioned by him in *Sarugaku Dangi* as his works.

B. Thirteen, with high probability of Ze-ami's authorship, based on *Goin* and *Sarugaku Dangi*.

C. Twenty-six, whose authorship is attributed to Ze-ami on the basis of documents, but with less probability because supporting sources are lacking. *Tomoakira* belongs to this group.

D. Thirteen Noh which are known to have been revised by Ze-ami.

Professor Nishino thinks that two of the *shura*-Noh in C, *Koremori* and *Norimori*, both no longer performed, were probably written by Ze-ami's son, Jūrō Motomasa, who wrote only a few Noh in his short life, all masterpieces. Of these, three are tragedies of parent and child. Of these, two, *Yoroboshi* and *Utaura*, are about father and son. This suggests, together with the structural characteristics pointed out above, that *Tomoakira* may have been written by Motomasa. On the other hand, quite a few Noh in the two professor's lists treat the parent-son theme. Of these, three, namely *Tomoakira, Tokusa* and *Tōsen*, are about father and son, a theme of universal appeal.

| | |
|---|---|
| Parted, his ship diminishing to a shadow,<br>Leaving no trace but white waves and deep longing<br>in me. | Wakareshi funa-kage no<br>Ato shira-nami mo natsukashi<br>150 -- 157 |

Season: Seventh day of February, early spring by the lunar calendar.
Scene: Suma Coast in Settsu Province (present Kobe City)
Characters and costumes

*Waki* A traveling monk attired like the *Waki* in *Yashima*.

*Mae-shite* The ghost of Taira no Tomoakira in the guise of a villager, maskless, in *dan-noshime* or plain dark *atsuita kitsuke*, and white *ōkuchi* divided skirt under a *suō* or *mizugoromo* robe.

*Nochi-shite* Tomoakira's ghost in the costume representing the military attire of a young nobleman, similar to that of Michimori, wearing an *atsumori* (mask for a noble boy warrior) or *dōji* (a boy mask).

*Ai-kyōgen* A villager.
The author: See footnote 4 above.

TOMOAKIRA

SHIDAI    *Waki enters and stands at nanori-za, facing the pine tree painted on the back panel.*

Shidai *au*        **WAKI**
Spring will be my roving soul's guide,[1]
Spring will be my roving soul's guide,
On a carefree journey let me start.

Jidori *awazu*    **JI**
*Waki turns around*  Spring will be my roving soul's guide,
*and faces the*      On a carefree journey let me start.
*audience.*

Nanori *spoken*    **WAKI**
I am a monk from a western province.
As I have never seen the Capital,
I have decided to make a visit there.

Michiyuki *au*     In a travel robe,[2]
Eight-layered briny way far I traverse,
Eight-layered briny way far I traverse,
Crossing wave beyond endlessly rolling wave.
Through clouds sails the boat away from the coast.
I, too, the earthly world's way have left behind,
And drifting, to an unknown edge of sea,
At a coastal terminus the boat has arrived,[3]
At a coastal terminus the boat has arrived.

Tsuki-zerifu *spoken*   From a remote province, traveling a long way,
*At center stage.*  I have arrived at this sea coast, where I see
A new stupa erected,
For a deceased one's repose, it seems.
Blissful sutra words diverse are written on it.
"The late Taira no Tomoakira," the name is inscribed.
*Kakaru*          Tomoakira . . . among the members of the Heike,
Which one could he have been?
Ah, my heart fills with pity.

YOBIKAKE   *Waki takes a few steps toward waki-za.  Shite enters calling to Waki, who stops near waki-za.*

Yobikake *spoken*     **SHITE**
You, you holy man, what was that you were saying?

---

[1]Lines 1--3.  The same *shidai* as is sung by the *Waki* in *Ebira*.
[2]Lines 9--10.  *Ya-e* (eight-fold/layers) modifies *Tabi-goromo* (travel robe) and *shio-ji* (briny ways).  This, and *haru* (wash and full) in *harubaru* (far) are *en-go* (associate word) of *tabi-goromo*.

Haru o kokoro no shirube nite[1]
Haru o kokoro no shirube nite
Ukaranu tabi ni ijo-o yo.

Haru o kokoro no shirube nite
Ukaranu tabi ni ijo-o yo.                                              5


Kore wa Saikoku-gata yori idetaru sō nite sōrō.
Ware imada Miyako o mizu sōrō hodoni
Tadaima omoitachi Miyako ikken to kokorozashi sōrō.

Tabi-goromo[2]
Yae no shioji o harubaru to                                          10
Yae no shioji o harubaru to
Nao sue ari to yuku nami no
Kumo omo wakuru oki-tsu-bune
Ware mo ukiyo no michi idete
Izuku tomo naki umi-giwa ya                                          15
Ura naru seki ni tsukinikeri[3]
Ura naru seki ni tsukinikeri.

Sate mo ware hina no kuni yori harubaru to
Kore naru isobe ni kite mireba
Atarashiki sotoba o tate-okitari.                                    20
Naki hito no tsuizen to oboshikute
Yōmon samazama kaki-shirushi
Mokku Taira no Tomoakira to kakaretari.
Tomoakira towa Heike no go-ichimon no on-naka nite wa
Tare nite ka mashimasu ran                                           25
Ara itawashi ya zo-oro-o.


Nō, nō, on-sō wa nani goto o ōse sōrō zo.

---

[3]*Ura naru seki* (coastal terminus) = Suma. There was a *seki* (barrier, checking station) there.

| | |
|---|---|
| Mondō *spoken* | **WAKI** |
| *Waki at waki-za* | I am a monk from a remote land. |
| | On this stupa I see |
| | An inscription which reads, "The Late Taira no Tomoakira." |

| | |
|---|---|
| *Shite enters* | A member of Heike he must be, thinking thus, in |
| *main stage and* | deep pity |
| *and stands at* | I have said a prayer for him. |
| *jō-za.* | |

**SHITE**
Indeed, since you are from a remote land,
It is no wonder that you do not know about him.
Tomoakira was the son of the late grand minister's third son,
Shin-jiuagon Tomomori.[4]
In the battle on the seventh day of February,[5]
Here at Ichinotani he was killed.[6]
Since today is that day,
A person related to him has erected the stupa.
Of all days, holy man,
On this very day you have come here
And have said a prayer for him. Oh, what a blessing!

*Kakaru*    A tree casting a shady shadow, a river stream...[7]
Our former lives' karma must have drawn us together.
Pray well for the repose of the departed soul, I beseech you.

**WAKI**
Indeed, as you say,
It is all because of our former lives' karma,
As a mere passer-by my coming to this place.

**SHITE**
And on a stranger you bestow a benefit.

**WAKI**
Believing thus, the votive beads I count off[8]

**SHITE**
And pray. Even if it were not for this,

---

[4]See the first three paragraphs of the Introduction.
[5]The seventh day of February: 1184 A.D.
[6]Ichinotani: On Suma Coast, to the east of Fukuhara, Heike's headquarters.
Defeated by Minamoto no Yoshitsune, they fled from there to Yashima.

Kore wa ongoku yori noboritaru sō nite sōrō ga
Kore naru sotoba o mireba
Mokko Taira no Tomoakira to kakarete sōrō. 30


Go-ichimon no on-naka nite sōrō yaran to itawashiku zonji

Ippen no nenbutto ekō moshite sōrō


Geni geni ongoku no hito nite mashimaseba
Shiroshimesanu wa on-kotowari
Tomoakira towa Shōkoku no sannan 35

Shin-jiunagon Tomomori no go-shisoku nite sōrō.[4]
Kisaragi nanuka no kasen ni[5]
Kono Ichinotani nite utaresase-tamaite sōrō.[6]
Sareba sono hi mo kyō ni ataritareba
Yukari no hito no tatetaru sotoba nite sōrō. 40
Toki mo koso are on-sō no
Kyō shimo koko ni kitari-tamai
Ekō shi-tamō arigata-sa yo.
Ichi-ju no kage ichi-ga no nagare[7]
Kore mata tasho-o no en naru-beshi. 45
Yoku yoku tomurai-tamai so-orae.


Geni geni o-ose no gotoku
Tasho-o no en no areba koso
Karisome nagara koko ni kite

Muen no riyaku o nasu koto yo to 50

Omoi no tama no kazu kurite[8]

Tomuro-o koto yo sanakidani

---

[7]Lines 44--45. A Buddhist expression found in a number of Noh, meaning: Strangers come together to take shelter under a tree or draw water from a stream, all through their former lives' karma. See *Tomoe* 66--67.
[8]*Omoi* (to think; to pray) --> *Omoi no tama* (prayer's beads = rosary).

*Waki sits center stage,*    *SHITE* and *WAKI*
*Shite also sitting,*    "One look at a stupa, and one is forever free
*they make kata of*    from Three Evil Ways.[9]
*prayer, facing*    Not to speak of those who erect one.
*each other.*    Assured of rebirth in the Blessed Land."
   May the deceased, Taira no Tomoakira, attain
   enlightenment.

*Sage-uta au*    *JI*
   Yesterday it was others' plight,
   Today if the same may befall us we never know.
   Moreo'er, of an archer and cavalier's house you are,[10]
   Ride straight, by the holy Law drawn,
*Waki sits at waki-za.* The fruit of Buddhahood to attain.

Age-uta *au*    Just one calling of Buddha's name evokes power,
   Just one calling of Buddha's name evokes power
   That absolves a sinner condemned to Three Evil Ways.
   More so the exquisite preaching of the Law's[11]
   Way by the roadside where the man ceased to be,
   Though by a stranger, how can it be fruitless?
   Though by a stranger, how can it be fruitless?

*Shite sits center stage.*
Spoken    *WAKI*
   Now tell me what happened to Tomomori.

   *SHITE*
   Oh, you ask about Tomomori.
   Away there you see a fishing boat.    At about that
   distance,
   Far out on the sea was the Imperial ship.
   He reached it and was saved.

   *WAKI*
   Did he get there by boat?

   *SHITE*
   No, he was on horseback.
   The horse named Inoue-guro was one of the finest.
   More than two thousand meters over the seawaves
   Easily he swam
   And saved the master's life.
   However, on board there was no room left, so
   Nobody would take the horse up onto the ship.

---

   [9]Lines 53--55. A Buddhist verse in couplet. Three Evil Ways: Inferno, Beastly
Hell and Hunger Hell.
   [10]Lines 59--60. *Nori* (the holy Law; to ride) and *hikare* (drawn; driven) are *engo* of
*kiu-ba* (bow and horse) in *kiu-ba no ie* (bow and horse family).

"Ikken sotoba yo-ori san-akudo-o[9]

Gakyo-o zo-oriusha
Hisshō-o Anrakkoku."                                          55
Mokko Taira no Tomoakira jo-oto-osho-ogaku.


Kino-o wa hito no ue
Kyo-o wa ware omo shiranu mi no
Shikamo kiuba no iebito naraba[10]
Nori ni hikare-tsutsu                                        60
Bukka ni itari-tamae ya.

Tada ichinen no kuriki dani
Tada ichinen no kuriki dani
Sannaku no tsumi wa kienu-beshi.
Mashite tae nimo toku nori no[11]                            65
Michi no hotori no naki ato o
Gyakuen nado ka nakaru-beki
Gyakuen nado ka nakaru-beki.


Sate Tomomori no go-saigo wa nani toka narase-tamaite sōrōzo.

Sanzōrō Tomomori wa                                          70
Are ni mietaru tsuribune no hodo narishi
Haruka no oki no gozabune ni
Oitsuki tasukari-tamaite sōrō.


Sate are made wa shōsen ni mesarete sōrō ka.

Iya bashō nite sōraishi.                                     75
Sono koro Inoue-guro tote kukkyō no meiba tarishiga
Nijiu-yo-chō no umi no omote o
Yasuyasu to oyogi-watari
Nushi o tasukeshi nma nari.
Saredomo senchiu ni tokoro nakarishi aida                    80
Nosuru hito mo nakushite

---

[11]Lines 65--66. *tae* (exquisite) and *nori* (the holy Law) are the *kun* (Japanese)
reading of *myō* and *hō* from *Myōhōrenge-kyō* (Saddharmapundarīka-sūtra). *nori no*
*Michi* (Law's way) --> *Michi no hotori* (wayside).

So again to the coast swam back
The horse, and as if in grief over the separation from the
  master,
Turning to the sea, gave a loud neigh,
Pawed the air with his feet and stood still.

*Kakaru*     "Even the beast has a feeling heart," thinking thus,
Those looking on were moved to pity.

*Au*

### JI

A Yüeh bird builds its nest on a southern branch,[12]
A horse from Hu neighs when the wind blows from the
  north,
Their home lands with so deep longing they recall.
A Hu horse pines after the north wind,
As for this horse, to the westward sailing ship's
Hawser even if they must tether him,
He would follow the bark that bears the master.

Rongi *au*     In the meantime
Dusk has already fallen over Suma Coast.
In the fisherman's hut passing the night,
Although a stranger, let me pray for the deceased.

### SHITE

Oh, how gracious! As for myself, truth to tell,
I am no outsider, a man within the clan,[13]
In and out passes the moon, leaving
Night's darkness after. Enlighten me, I pray.

### JI

Among the clansmen you say you are.
Which of those people can you be?

### SHITE

What should I hide now? A grass-shaded well-[14]
Water clear, hidden from the eye . . . this foam of a life

| JI | SHITE |
|---|---|
| You have left, your name | Untraced, an arrow off the bow, |

---

[12]Lines 88--89. From *Monzen*. *Etteu* = Etsu bird. Etsu (Yüeh) was one of the twelve states of ancient China, located in the south. Ko (Hu), a barbaric state in the north.

[13]Lines 100--101. *Ichimon no uchi* (the clan's within = among the clan members) --> *uchi-to ni kayo-o* (in and out to go, that is, in and out of the land of the dead), with *kayo-o* (to go, to sail) as the verb to *ware* (myself) in 99 and *iu-zuki* (evening moon), --> *nochi no yo no yami* (after(-moon)-night's/afterlife's darkness), implying the after-life's darkness when the moon embodying enlightenment has sunk, *yo* meaning "night" and "life."

Mata moto no migiwa ni oyogi agari
Kono nma nushi no wakare o shitō kato oboshikute

Oki no kata ni mukai taka-inanaki shi
Ashigaki shite zo tattarikeru.                                    85
Chikurui mo kokoro arikeru yo to
Miru hito aware o moyo-oshikeri.

Etteu nanshi ni su o kake[12]
Koba hokufu-u ni ibaeshi mo

Kiuko-o o shinobu yue nari toka.                                  90
Koba wa hokufu-u o shitai
Kono nma wa nishi ni yuku fune no
Tomozuna ni tsunagaretemo
Yukabaya to omo-o kokoro nari.

Saruhodo ni                                                      95
Hi mo haya kurete Suma no Ura
Ama no isoya ni yadorishite
Gyakuen nagara tomurawan.

Geni arigata ya ware totemo
Yosobito narazu ichimon no[13]                                   100
Uchito ni kayo-o iu-zuki no
Nochi no yo no yami o toi-tamae.

Somo ichimon no uchi zo towa
Onmi ikanaru hito yaran.

Ima wa nani oka tsutsumi-i no[14]                                105
Migakurete sumu aware yo ni

Naki ato no na wa  Shira-mayumi no

---

[14]Lines 105--108. *nani oka tsutsumi* (what to hide?) --> *tsutsumi-i* (hidden well)
--> *mi-gakurete sumu* (water hidden clear; body hidden to live = living in hiding),
with *mi* meaning "water" and "body," and *sumu* meaning "to be clear" and "to live"
--> *awa* (foam), an *en-go* (associate word) of the water image --> *aware yo* (sad life)
--> *yo ni naki* (in life no more). *na wa Shira* (name unknown) --> *Shira-mayumi*
(white zelkova bow) --> *kaeru* (to return, to be bent), an *en-go* of *yumi* (bow).

*JI*
Departing, the eye following sees
Him not to Suma's hamlet, field or mountain
Go, but to the coast where, of the dry beach bereft.[15]
Heading for the reedy marshes cranes are moving,
Now afloat, now seeming to sink into the water,[16]
The diminishing form faded out of sight,
The diminishing form faded out of sight.

NAKAIRI   *Shite makes interim exit.*
AI-KYOGEN   *Ai-kyogen, a villager, enters. At the monk's request, he tells him how Tomoakira fell, fighting in defence of his father Tomomori, who escaped to the ship, crossing the sea on his horse. Then the villager exhorts the monk to pray for the repose of Tomoakira whose ghost has just appeared in the guise of a villager.*

Machi-utai *au*   *WAKI*
On the evening waves plovers now sleep in flocks,[17]
On the evening waves plovers now sleep in flocks,
Here at Suma, along the long stretch of coast,
O'er field and hill blows wind of piercing chill,
My heart keen and clear, wrapped in the ink-black
   cloak[18]
The sacred script I chant for the departed soul,
The sacred script I chant for the departed soul.

ISSEI   *Nochi-shite enters and stands at jō-za.*

Sashi *awazu*   *SHITE*
Oh, blissful prayers for the repose of my soul!
From the Asura Hell where I suffer tortures
Without respite, now, as you see,
By my illusory attachment drawn I come,

Issei *awazu*   To be freed, floating[18]

---

[15]Lines 110--111. *migiwa no kata* (beach toward, toward the beach) --> *kata o nami* (the beach being none, gone): From a poem by Yamabe no Akahito (ca. 8th cent.) in *Mannyō-shū*: Waka-no-Ura ni/ Shio michikureba/Kata o nami/Ashibe o sashite/ Tazu naki-wataru (At Waka-no-Ura/ When the tide comes flowing in,/ Of dry beach bereft,/ Heading for the reedy marsh/ Cranes go whooping away). See *Matsukaze* lines 75--77, *The Noh* Vol. 3, Book 3.

[16]*mieshi* (visible) refers to *tazu* (cranes) and *Ushiro-kage* (literally, "a form seen from behind"). The mention of the cranes enhances the poetic associations of this passage.

Kaeru kata o mireba
Suma no sato nimo noyama nimo
Yukade migiwa no kata o nami[15]       110
Ashibe o sashite yuku tazu no
Ukinu shizumu to mieshi mama ni[16]
Ushiro-kage mo usenikeri ya
Ushiro-kage mo usenikeri.


Iunami-chidori tomone shite[17]       115
Iunami-chidori tomone shite
Tokoro mo Suma no ura-zutai
Noyama no kaze mo saekaeri
Kokoro mo sumi no koromode ni[18]
Kono on-kyo-o o dokuju suru       120
Kono on-kyo-o o dokuju suru.


Ara arigata no on-tomurai yana.
Ware shura-do-o no kurushimi no
Hima naki uchi ni kaku bakari
Hakurei ni hikarete kitaritari.       125

Ukamu-beki[19]

---

[17]*Iunami-chidori* (on-eve's-waves-flying plovers): From a poem by Kakinomoto no Hitomaru (ca. 7th cent.) in *Mannyō-shū*: Ōmi no mi/ Yūnami-chidori/ Na ga nakaba/ Kokoro mo shinu ni/ Inishie omohoyu (At Ōmi Lake/ On-eve's-waves-flying plovers,/ Hearing you twitter/ My heart pains with heavy grief/ Thinking of the days gone by.) In 119, there is an echo of the fourth phrase.

[18]*Kokoro mo sumi* (the mind clears) --> *sumi no koromode* (ink-black sleeve = a monk's cloak).

[19]Lines 126--127. *Ukamu-beki* (to float), meaning "freed from illusory attachment" --> *Nami* (waves).

On the waves rolling so close to Suma coast[20]

*JI*
The sea lies at a little distance from the path,

    *SHITE*
Behind, mountain gale,[21]
On the plateau, stormy wind,[22]

    *JI*
Grasses, trees, beings of this earth,[23]
Sentient and non-sentient,
One and all attain Buddhahood
On yonder shore.  Close to the sea coast

*Shite makes kata*    Floating up I have come, oh, what bliss![24]
*of prayer to Waki.*

*Kakaru*       *WAKI*
How strange!  An elegant and noble young warrior
Over the waves is seen afloat.
Tell me who you are.

*Spoken*      *SHITE*
You ask who I am, but wherefor?
At your blissful prayer, in joy worshipful
Tomoakira has come here.

*Kakaru*      *WAKI*
Then a young Heike nobleman
Before my very eyes I see now.
To the past roll back the sea waves,[25]

    *SHITE*
Floating patterns embossed on the robe,
To the fringe exquisitely shading off the color of armor,

    *WAKI*
A flower-bright figure,

    *SHITE*
The place none other than

---

[20]Lines 127--128. From the *Suma* chapter, *Genji Monogatari*:  "At Suma the heart-breaking autumn wind blows.  Although the sea lies at some distance. . . . the beach waves at night are heard quite close by."  See *Matsukaze* lines 26, 29, *ibid*.

[21]*Ushiro no yama* (back mountain, mountain behind):  "'Some fishermen are burning saltwood,' he thought, looking at the smoke rising from what they call brushwood that they were burning on the mountain behind."  *Ibid*.  See *Atsumori* line 179 and *Tadanori* lines 72--74, *The Noh*, Vol. 2, Book 1.

Nami kokomoto ya Suma no Ura[20]

Umi sukoshi aru kayoi-ji no

Ushiro no yama-kaze[21]
Ueno no arashi[22]                                               130

So-omoku kokudo[23]
Ujo-o hijo-o mo
Shikkai jo-obutsu no
Kano kishi no umi-giwa ni
Ukami-idetaru arigata-sa yo.[24]                                 135


Fushigi yana samo namamekitaru waka-musha no
Nami ni ukamite mie-tamo-o wa
Ikanaru hito nite mashimasu zo.

Tare towa nado ya oroka nari
On-tomurai no arigata-sa ni                                       140
Tomoakira koremade mairitari.

Satewa Heike no kindachi o
Ma no atari ni mi-tatematsuru koto yo to
Mukashi ni kaeru ura-nami no[25]

Uki-orimono no hitatare ni                                        145
Tsuma-nioi no yoroi kite

Samo hanayaka naru on-sugata

Tokoro mo sazo na

---

[22]*Ueno* ("plateau"): Like *Ushiro no Yama*, Ueno at Suma is a poetic place. *arashi* (stormy wind) leads to *So-omoku* (grasses and trees).

[23]Lines 131--133. From *Nirvana-sūtra* and other Buddhist writings. The couplet is found in a number of Noh. See *Kakitsubata* 221--222, *The Noh*, Vol. 3, Book 2.

[24]*Ukami-idetaru* (floated up): Cf. 126.

[25]Lines 144--145. *Mukashi ni kaeru* (to the past to return) --> *kaeru ura-nami* (returning sea waves) *Uki* (to float) --> *Uki-orimono* (floating-patterned textile = textile with embossed patterns).

WAKI
Suma Coast,

Age-uta *au*         JI
All blurred in spring mist,[26]
Geese in flight, a passing shadow, the moon's face,[27]
Geese in flight, a passing shadow, the moon's face,
Penciled faint o'er Picture Isle.  Hiding behind it[28]
Sailed away the boat.
With wistfulness watched I, from my father
Parted, his ship diminishing to a shadow,
Leaving no trace but white waves and deep longing in
me.[29]
Fate had it that finally my own[30]
Miserable self I should throw into the Western Sea,
The seaweed dust adrift in the bay waves,[31]
Roll out again the holy scroll and pray for me,
Roll out again the holy scroll and pray for me.

*Spoken*              WAKI
*Shite sits on a*     Yes, but tell me in detail all that happened at that time.[32]
*stool, center stage*

Kuri *awazu*          JI
Ah, what happened at that time - a story of disgrace, a
taint to our name,
Tatsuta Mountain's maple leaves . . .
Our crimson streaming banners, fast[33]
Scattering away in the hostile wind.[34]

Sashi *awazu*         SHITE
The Emperor and Ni-i-dono, as well as[35]
The Inner Minister and his son,[36]

---

[26]Lines 150--151.  "Thinking of these people who would be looking at the moon, he kept gazing at the moon's face. . . .  As he looked at geese flying in a line, . . . tears flowed down his cheeks."  From the *Suma* chapter, *Genji Monogatari*.  In *Kari no sugata* (geese's figure), *kari* (geese) also means "assumed, not actual," alluding to the ghostly figure described above.

[27]Lines 151--153.  *tsuki no kage* (moon's light) --> *kage Utsusu* (light reflects), with *utsusu* also meaning "to reflect; to sketch" --> E-jima (Picture Island).

[28]Lines 153--154.  From an anonymous poem, attributed to Kakinomoto no Hitomaro, in *Kokin-shū*: Honobono to/ Akashi no Ura no/ Asagiri ni/ Shima-gakure yuku/ Fune o shizo omo (Slowly the day dawns/ Pale crimson, Akashi Bay/ Draped in morning mist/ Where behind the isles vanish/ Boats I think of in longing.)  In the poem, *honobono to Akashi* (pale red, slowly dawning) --> Akashi-no-Ura (Akashi Bay).  *Aka* means "red; to dawn."

Suma no Ura ni

Oboro naru[26]                                                    150
Kari no sugata ya tsuki no kage[27]
Kari no sugata ya tsuki no kage
Utsusu E-jima no shima-gakure[28]
Yuku fune o
Oshi tozo omo-o waga chichi ni                                   155
Wakareshi funa-kage no
Ato shira-nami mo natsukashi ya.[29]

Yoshi totemo tsuini waga[30]
Ukimi o sutete Saikai no
Mokuzu to narishi ura no nami[31]                                160
Kasanete toite tabi-tamae
Kasanete toite tabi-tamae.

Saraba sono toki no arisama kuwashiku on-monogatari sōrae.[32]

Sate mo sono toki no arisama kataruni tsukete uki na nomi

Tatsuta no Yama no momiji-ba no                                   165
Kurenai nabiku hata no ashi[33]
Chirijiri ni naru keshiki kana.[34]

Shusho-o Ni-i-dono o hajime-tatematsuri[35]
Sonohoka O-oi-tono fushi[36]

---

[29]*Ato shirana* (the trace/whereabouts unknown) --> *Ato shira-nami* (after-white waves, waves in the ship's wake), with *ato* meaning "trace, whereabouts, after."

[30]Lines 158--160. There is an illusion to Tomomori who later threw himself into the sea and was drowned. In lines 157 and 222 are the same imagery of sea-death.

[31]Lines 160--161. *Kasanete* (again, one over another) modifies *toi* (to pray) and is an *en-go* of *nami* (waves).

[32]Lines 164--165. *uki na nomi Tatsu* (sad name only rises) --> Tatsuta no Yama (Tatsuta Mountain), famous for autumn leaves.

[33]Refers to the Heike's crimson banners.

[34]*Chirijiri ni* (scattered in all directions): autumn-leaf imagery.

[35]The Emperor: The boy Emperor Antoku. Ni-i = the second court rank; dono = an honorific suffix; mother of the Emperor's mother Kenreimon-in.

[36]*O-oi-tono* (Lord Minister) = the Inner Minister Munemori, Kiyomori's son and Tomoakira's elder brother.

*JI*
And other clan members all boarded the ships,
Floating on the sea, seeming
Like water fowls on green waves' crests rising
　　and sinking.

*SHITE*
Among them, my father, Shin-jiunagon,
Myself, Tomoakira, and Kenmottaro-o
Our retainer, only three, all the rest of our men slain,

*JI*
Marking the Imperial ship, rode as far as this beach.
The enemy relentlessly came to our attack,
So again we turned back and fought with them, till
Tomoakira and Kenmottaro-o
Master and servant, were killed at this place.

*SHITE*
While we were thus engaged, Tomomori,

*JI*
Far out on the sea perceiving
The Inner Minister's ship,
Swam his horse till he reached
The ship and went on board,
His futile life thus saved.

Kuse *au*　　Tomomori, who then came
Into the presence of the Inner Minister,
Tears streaming down his cheeks spoke thus to him,
"Musashi-no-kami has been slain.[37]
Kenmottaro-o Yorikata, too,
On the beach fell by the enemy's hand.
Seeing all this, I left them to their fate and came here.
Oh, deeply ashamed I am of myself!
Why is it indeed
That a child for his parent
His life with readiness gives up?
What parent am I, I ask myself,
A parent who abandoned his child to his death?
Life . . . ah, that I should have been so loath to lose it!"
Having thus spoken, he wept bitterly,
Other people's sleeves, too, were moistened with tears.
The Inner Minister then spoke,
"Musashi-no-kami beyond all doubt

---

[37]Musashi-no-kami (Lord of Musashi Province): Tomoakira.

Ichimon minamina fune ni tori-nori                    170
Kaisho-o ni ukamu yoso-oi
Tada so-oha no une ni uki-shizumu mizutori no gotoshi.


Sono naka nimo oya nite so-oro-o Shin-jiunagon
Ware Tomoakira, Kenmottaro-o
Shiujiu san-gi ni uchinasare                          175


Gozabune o ukagai kono migiwa ni uchi-idetarishini
Kataki teshigeku kakarishi aida
Mata hikkaeshi uchio-o hodoni
Tomoakira Kenmottaro-o

Shiujiu koko nite uchijini suru.                      180


Sono hima ni Tomomori wa


Nijiu-yo-cho-o no oki ni mietaru
O-oi-tono no on-fune made
Nma o oyogase oitsuite
On-fune ni nori-utsuri                                185
Kainaki onninochi tasukari-tamo-o.

Tomomori sono toki ni
O-oi-tono no on-mac nitc
Namida o nagashi notamawaku
Musashi-no-kami mo utarenu[37]                         190
Kenmottaro-o Yorikata mo
Ano migiwa nite utaruru o
Misutete kore made mairu koto
Menboku mo naki shidai nari.
Ikanareba                                             195
Ko wa oya no tame
Inochi o oshimanu kokoro zoya
Ikanaru oya nareba
Ko no utaruru o misuteken
Inochi wa oshiki mono nari tote                        200
Samezame to naki-tamaeba
Yoso no sode mo nurenikeri.
O-oi-tono mo notamawaku
Musashi-no-kami wa moto yori mo

Was a youth of valiant spirit,
A worthy captain, that is how I thought of him,"
And toward his son Kiyomune
He cast a glance, while tears
Ran streaming down his cheeks.  At this, those on board
Who sat around the minister,
Wept, till their armor sleeves were wet with tears.

*SHITE*
Musashi-no-kami Tomoakira was

*Shite rises, goes*        *JI*
*forward, turns*        Aged sixteen in the blooming spring of life,
*round and*        Kiyomune the same age as he,
*stands at jō-za,*        Two fresh green beach pines growing together,[38]
*facing Waki.*        Many thousand years of prosperity promised,
        Thick-leafed boughs piling one over another,[39]
        Clansmen's stately gates stood side by side,
        Till this year, this day it has come to this, but why?
        At this very place, Suma's mountain cherry blossom,[40]
        Still a sapling, has fallen, while the rotten wood[41]
        Floats about on the water, the sea-farer adrift,
        Such is the fated end of the clan, oh, how sad!

Rongi *au*        Indeed a deeply touching story it is.
        Now further about your own end
        For the sake of redemption I pray you to tell.

*SHITE*
'Tis rightly said.  About my own end
In penitence I will confess to you,
From Asura Hell's torment to deliver myself.

*JI*
Indeed in Asura's Hell suffering tortures,
My soul as vindicative as when I fell fighting,

*SHITE*
I hear my foe's name, the same old enemy,

*JI*
Now coming in attack, rolling[42]

---

[38]Lines 215--216.  *so* (beach) *-nare* (intimate) *-matsu* (pine tree), a beach pine
hanging branches as if kissing the beach; implies the intimacy of the two youths.  A
pine was thought to live for a thousand years.
   [39]Lines 217--218.  Cf. *Atsumori* lines 153--154, Vol. 2, Book 1.
   [40]Lines 220--221, "The young cherry tree" in the *Suma* chapter, *Genji Monogatari.*
Cf. *Tadanori* line 83, Vol. 2, Book 1.

Kokoro mo ko-o nishite                                       205
Yoki taisho-o to mishi zo tote
On-ko Kiyomune no kata o
Miyarite on-namida o
Nagashi-tamaeba fune no uchi ni
Tsuranareru hitobito mo                                       210
Yoroi no sode o nurashikeri.


Musashi-no-kami Tomoakira wa


Sho-onen ni-hachi no haru nareba
Kiyomune mo do-onen nite
Tomoni wakaba no sonare-matsu[38]                             215
Chiyo o kasanete sakayuku ya
Ruiyo-o eda o tsurane-tsutsu[39]
Ichimon kado o narabeshi mo
Kotoshi no kyo-o no ikanareba
Tokoro mo Suma no yama-zakura[40]                             220
Wakaki wa chirinu nmoregi no[41]
Ukite tadayo-o funabito to
Nariyuku hate zo kanashiki.

Geni itawashiki monogatari
Onajikuwa go-saigo o                                          225
Sange ni katari-tamae ya.


Geni ya saigo no arisama o
Zangi sange ni arawashi
Shura-do-o no kugen manukaren.


Geni Shura-do-o no kurushimi no                               230
Sono ichinen mo saigo yori


Kikitsuru mama no kataki nite


Suwa ya yose-kuru[42]

---

[41]Lines 221--222. *Ukite* (floating) is an *en-go* of *gi* = *ki* (tree) in *nmore-gi* (rotten tree).

[42]Lines 233--235. *yose-kuru* (come in attack; come rolling) --> *ura no nami uchi* (sea waves beat) --> Uchiwa (fan). Kodama clan: One of the Seven well-known clans in Musashi Province. Kodama is their district.

*Shite*
Sea waves,

*Shura-nori*
*Shite dances,*
*describing*
*fighting.*

"A fan pattern on their flag, is that Kodama clan?
Oh, how presumptious!" with these words
Kenmottaro-o let fly an arrow.
It hit the enemy's ensign,
Piercing his neck bone inches deep.
Head foremost he fell from his horse with a crash.

*SHITE*
A warrior whom I took for their master,

*JI*
A warrior whom I took for their master,
On Shin-jiunagon fixing his eyes,
Ran his horse up and was about to strike him.
Not to let him kill my father,
I, Tomoakira, cut in between them,
And in grappling fell from my horse,
Pressed the enemy down and cut off his head.
I was about to rise again, when
One of the enemy's retainers dashed at me
And cut off Tomoakira's head.
Thus here at this place, slain by the enemy,
Straight to Asura Hell's retribution I fell.
But unexpectedly the holy man
Now prays for my soul, oh, what bliss!
This is a true friend bound by the sacred Law,
A true friend you are for Tomoakira,[43]
For my soul's repose say prayers,
For the repose of my departed soul say prayers.

---

[43]*makoto no tomo* (true friend) --> Tomoakira.

Ura no nami,

Uchiwa no hata wa Kodama-to-o ka                    235
Monomonoshi to iu mama ni
Kenmottaro-o ga hanatsu ya ni
Kataki no hatasashi no
Kubi no hone nobuka ni isasete
Massakasama ni do-o to otsureba                     240


Shujin to oboshiki musha


Shujin to oboshiki musha
Shin-jiunagon o me ni kakete
Kakeyosete utsu tokoro o
Oya o utasejito                                     245
Tomoakira kake-fusagatte
Muzu to kunde do-o to ochi
Totte osaete kubi kaki-kitte
Okiagaru tokoro o mata
Kataki no ro-odo-o ochiaite                         250
Tomoakira ga kubi o toreba
Tsuini koko nite utare-tsutsu
Sonomama shura no go-o ni shizumu o
Omowazaruni on-so-o no
Tomurai wa arigata ya                               255
Kore zo makoto no nori no tomo yo
Kore zo makoto no Tomoakira ga[43]
Ato toite tabi-tamae
Naki ato o toite tabi-tamae.

賴

改

YORIMASA

ざつざつと。うち入れた。や

Splashing water they plunged--

Zazzatto uchi-irete

-Line 207

# INTRODUCTION

The hero in the title role of *Yorimasa* was a Seiwa Genji, that is, a descendant of one of Emperor Seiwa's grandsons, Prince Tsunemoto (917--961), who assumed the status of a subject with the family name of Minamoto. (Gen-ji means "Minamoto family." Most royal princes who became subjects were given this family name. For example, the hero of *Genji Monogatari* is called Genji no Kimi, that is, Lord Genji. The Taira, also Hei-ke, or Hei-shi, descended from Emperor Kanmu, assumed the family name of Taira and was called the Kanmu Heishi.) While Yorimasa descended from one of Tsunemoto's grandsons, a younger grandson is the progenitor of Yoshitomo and his sons, Tomonaga and Yoshitsune, the *Shite* of *Tomonaga* and *Yashima* respectively, as well as their brother Yoritomo. (See the Pedigree at the end of the book.)

Yorimasa and Yoshitomo were respectively the leaders of two main branches of the Genji. In the Hōgen and Heiji rebellions in 1156 and 1159, Yorimasa joined the Heike and defeated the rebels. Yoshitomo, a leader of the Heiji warfare, and his father Tameyoshi, a general of the rebels in the Hōgen uprising, perished with their sons. Thus in the two riots, Yorimasa fought for the Emperor against his own kinsmen. In spite of his services, he was not rewarded to his satisfaction. Yorimasa, already an old man, saw with mounting rancor his rival Taira no Kiyomori and his clansmen rapidly promoted to highest ranks and occupying the key government posts. When his eldest son, Nakatsuna, was humiliated by Kiyomori's son Munemori,[1] he could no longer contain his anger: Munemori forced Nakatsuna to give him his celebrated horse, and having branded it Nakatsuna, would call it by this name in public. Yorimasa decided to overthrow the Heike, effect a coup d'état and enthrone a new emperor of his choice. Most of the fourth volume of *Heike Monogatri* devotes itself to the rebellion of Yorimasa and some episodes about him, which are outlined briefly below:

Mochihito, a son of retired Emperor Goshirakawa, with every qualification

---

[1] For Munemori, see the footnote 2, in the Introduction to *Tomoakira*, and 183--211, *ibid.*

for an able ruler, had been looked upon as the first successor to the throne after his elder brother, the late Emperor Nijō, and his infant son, Emperor Rokujō.  However, Goshirakawa dethroned the boy emperor in favor of Mochihito's younger brother, whose mother was Goshirakawa's favorite consort.  Mochihito suffered humiliation at his father's unfair treatment not only in the issue of the Imperial succession:  Goshirakawa did not even bestow him the status of *shinnō* (royal prince), in consequence of which Mochihito remained a plain ō (prince).

In May, 1180, Yorimasa went to this prince and persuaded him to effect a coup d'état, telling him that, at the prince's summons, the Genji warriors all over Japan, including Yoritomo who was exiled in Izu, and his younger brother Yoshitsune in the northernmost province of Mutsu, would rise against the Heike.  Messengers bearing the prince's message were at once sent to Genji clansmen in various provinces.  However, in no time the conspiracy became known to Kiyomori.  On May 15, hearing that Heike soldiers were on their way to his palace, the prince, disguised as a court lady and followed only by a couple of attendants, fled to Mii Temple by Lake Biwa in Ōmi Province, where he was warmly received by the monks.  On the next day, having set fire to his residence, Yorimasa hastened to Mii Temple with his two sons and about three hundred horsemen.  The monks of the temple sent a letter to Kōfuku Temple in Nara, asking its monks to come to the Prince's assistance.  The latter decided to take the Prince's side and seven thousand armed monks made themselves ready to join Mochihito.  When the day was dawning on May 23, the Prince thought that he should escape to Nara before it was too late.  So he left Mii Temple, followed by Yorimasa and his men, as well as by those of the monks who were young and strong enough to fight.  They were one thousand in number.  While the Prince and his men were resting at Byōdō Temple on the further bank of the River Uji, half way between Kyoto and Nara, the Heike force who came in pursuit arrived at the opposite bank and they fought on the river bank there.  The Prince was defeated, Yorimasa's two sons died and Yorimasa committed suicide.  The Prince died, wounded by an arrow as he was fleeing toward Nara.  The story of the battle is told as follows in *Heike Monogatari*:

On the way from Mii Temple to Uji, the Prince fell from his horse no less than six times.  They thought that it was because he had not slept the night before, so, having removed the boards in the central part of the bridge for the length of four posts, they let the Prince rest for a while in Byōdō Temple.  Meanwhile the large army of the Heike who came in pursuit arrived at the opposite bank of the river.  Seeing the Prince's force assembled around Byōdō Temple, they rushed to the bridge with loud war cries.  Those in the van guard shouted aloud to those behind, warning in vain to be beware of the removed bridge boards.  Pushed from behind, about two hundred men fell into the river and were drowned.  (Then follows a description of the hot fighting on the bridge and the bravery of Yorimasa's men and the monks of Mii Temple, among them Ichirai Hosshi and Tsutsui no Jōmyō mentioned in the Noh *Yorimasa*.) The Heike captain, realizing the difficulty of crossing the river in high flood after the long rain of early summer, with the enemy fighting desperately in defence, suggested to his generals to make a detour and cross the river at some other place. Hearing this, Tawara no Matatarō Tadatsuna, a seventeen-year old warrior of the Ashikaga clan, came forward and said how his clansmen had once crossed the mighty Tone River in the Kantō district on horseback to attack their enemy on the opposite bank. "It is the way with the warriors of the Eastern Provinces," he said, "not to consider the depth of a river when confronting an enemy on the yonder bank. What difference is there in the depth of the Tone River and this one?" Then calling to his men to follow him, he plunged his horse into the river. Following his example, more than three hundred horsemen rushed into the river.

To them Tadatsuna shouted in a loud voice, "Let strong horses go upstream, with weak ones in their lee. As long as the horses' feet reach the bottom, slack the reins and make them walk. When they start prancing, pull in the reins and let them swim. Let those struggling behind hold to your bows. Cross the river, hand in hand, shoulder to shoulder. Sit squarely on your saddle, pressing the stirrups hard with your feet. If the horse's head sinks, pull it up, but not too hard, lest you are thrown back. Where the water is high, move back and sit on the horse's hips. Be gentle with your horse, but firm with the water. Don't shoot an arrow while crossing, even if the enemy does. Keep your head down, but not too much, or you may be hit on the top of your helmet. Don't go straight against the current, but follow the flow of the water. Now, to the yonder bank, everybody!" Under the command of one warrior, the three hundred horsemen reached the opposite bank without a single loss.

Seeing this, Taira no Tomomori,[2] the commander of the Heike forces, ordered his men to cross the river, and an army of twenty-eight thousand horsemen plunged into the river. Stopped by so many men and horses, the river water rose high upper stream, while the water that leaked through rushed down, sweeping men and horses down with the current. It is hard to say how it happened, but the warriors from the Ise and Iyo Provinces had their horse-made dam broken by the rushing water and about six hundred horsemen were carried away. In their colorful armor threaded in red, crimson or yellow, they drifted in the water like so many autumn leaves on Mt. Kannabi scattered by the wind from the mountain top and caught in the weirs of the Tatsuta River of an autumn evening. Yorimasa's son Nakatsuna, Lord of Izu Province, saw three warriors in scarlet armor caught in the wickerwork fishing net, and composed this witty poem:

| | |
|---|---|
| Ise-musha wa | The Ise warriors |
| Mina hi-odoshi no | All in the scarlet-threaded |

---

[2]For Tomomori, see the Introduction to *Tomoakira*, in which Noh he plays an important part as a shadow character.

| Yoroi kite | Armor attired, |
| Uji no ajiro ni | In Uji's wickerwork nets |
| Kakarinuru kana | Were trapped like the river's fish. |

Note:    In the poem, *hi-odoshi* (scarlet-threaded) contains *hi-o*, fish which the Uji fishermen caught with *ajiro* (wickerwork net) stretched in the river.

Having crossed the river, the mighty Heike army rushed to the temple. Yorimasa made the Prince flee to Nara, while he remained with this men to cover the Prince's escape.    The over-seventy-year-old warrior was severely wounded in the left knee, and withdrew inside the temple gate to commit suicide.    His second son, Gendayū Kanetsuna, fought with the enemy, keeping them away from his father, and fell in the combat. Yorimasa's eldest son, Nakatsuna, was heavily wounded and killed himself in the fishing pavilion of the temple.    Yorimasa, about to kill himself, turned to the west, called Buddha's name aloud, and then composed his last poem, a deeply touching one:

| Umoregi no | I, a fossil wood, |
| Hana saku koto mo | From coming into blossom |
| Nakarishini | Forever estranged, |
| Mi no naru hate zo | And this is the final fruit, |
| Kanashikarikeru | Ah, the bitter taste of it! |

Note:    *Mi no naru hate*: (a) one's coming to a (sad) end; (b) fruit coming to fruition, with *mi* meaning "one's being"; "fruit," *naru* meaning "to come to"; "to bear fruit." The character *hate* (end) also means "fruit."    The fruit image is in association with *umoregi* (fossil wood).

Then he fell on his sword and died.    An ordinary man would not think of composing a poem at such a time.    However, Yorimasa had loved poetry ever since he was a young man, and did not forget it at his last moment. (From "The Battle over the Bridge," Vol. 4, *Heike Monogatari*.)

Hida-no-kami Kageie, a veteran warrior, thought that the Prince must have escaped for Nara in the general confusion, so, instead of fighting, he went in hot pursuit with a hundred horsemen under his command.    As he had expected, he caught up with the Prince in flight.    He and his men rained down arrows at him, one of which hit the Prince.    He fell from his horse and was decapitated.    By that time the seven thousand monks of Kōfuku Temple who were on their way to join the Prince's forces were only at a distance of about four miles from where the Prince was attacked. Hearing about his death, in sorrow they returned to Nara. (From "The Death of the Prince," *Ibid.*)

The last chapter of the fourth volume of *Heike Monogatari*, entitled *Nue (Nue* is a legendary monster bird), tells some episodes which present Yorimasa as a talented poet and archer.    By virtue of his poems, twice he successfully appealed to the Imperial court for promotion. Lamenting that, after the Hōgen and Heiji rebellions, his status remained low in spite of his services, he made a petition with his poem, comparing himself to an obscure garden keeper of the Imperial palace, and was promoted to the rank which entitled him to enter the Imperial hall. This is the poem he presented:

| | |
|---|---|
| Hito shirenu | Unknown and alone |
| Ōuchiyama no | The Imperial Palace |
| Yama-mori wa | Garden keeper |
| Kogakurete nomi | Only through the shade of trees |
| Tsuki o miru kana | Gazes at the moon on high |

Later he presented another metaphorical poem which hinted at his desire to be promoted to the third court rank, and obtained that rank as he had wished.

Yorimasa's fame as a poet and great archer rose for the first time when he shot a monstrous bird which had nightly afflicted the Emperor. The Minister of the Right, about to bestow him an Imperial gift in award for his meritorious deeds, extemporized the first three lines of a *tanka* (Tanka, literally "short poem," is a thirty-one syllable poem in five lines. The poems quoted in this introduction are *tanka*.).

| | |
|---|---|
| Hototogisu | The cuckoo bird |
| Na omo kuomi ni | His name to cloud-bound heaven |
| Aguru kana | Raised, calling aloud. |

Yorimasa, kneeling before the Minister, extemporized the finishing lines:

| | |
|---|---|
| Yumihari-zuki no | What time the crescent moon from |
| Iru ni makasete | On high shot itself and sank. |

Note: Cuckoos' cries were poetically described as "a cuckoo giving its name." *Na o aguru* means: (a) to give one's name; (b) to achieve fame. *kumoi* (cloud-bound place) means "heaven" and "Imperial court." *Yumi-hari zuki* = literally, "bow-stretched moon." *iru*: (a) "to set" refers to -*zuki* (moon); (b) "to shoot" refers to *yumi* (bow).

After this Yorimasa shot down another monster which tormented another emperor and again composed a couplet in answer to a court lord who extemporized the first lines as he gave him the Imperial award.

Six hundred and ninety-one poems by Yorimasa are collected in *Ju-sanmi Yorimasa-kyō-shū* (Collected Poems of Lord Yorimasa of the Junior Third Court Rank). Fifty-five of his poems with duplications are found in various Imperial anthologies.[3]

In the Noh *Yorimisa*, the scene is Uji, a place celebrated for its scenic beauty as well as for literary and historical associations. In the first act Yorimasa's ghost appears in the form of an old villager to a traveling monk, and at the monk's request tells about the famous places they see before them. Then he takes the monk to Byōdō Temple by the river. In the temple garden a patch of turf is cut in the shape of a fan. The old man explains in a *katari* that Yorimasa laid an open fan on the turf and killed himself seated on it. In commemoration of this, says the old man, to this day the turf is cut in that way and is called *Ōgi no Shiba* (fan-shaped turf). Then with a hint that he is the ghost of Yorimasa, the old man disappears in the falling dusk.

In the second act, Yorimasa's ghost appears as the aged warrior. Description of the battle is the major feature of the second act, which attains a climax with the crossing of the river, described first by the *Shite's katari*, then by a song. The guttural *tsuyo-gin* (strong singing) in lively *shura*-rhythm heightens the effect of the sound of the flooded river water with hundreds of horsemen struggling with the rushing currents. The chorus song in narrative style is unaccompanied by any sort of dancing. The *Shite*, who all the while remains seated on a stool stage center, accompanies the song with occasional gestures of his hands and an open fan, suggestive of the horsemen plunging into the water, a bow held out to a man about to be submerged, and other actions, and he punctuates the singing with the stamping of his feet. The lines sung are based largely on the passage in *Heike Monogatari* quoted above. After the crossing of the river, the song telling about Yorimasa's death resumes the *hira-nori* (ordinary rhythm) and the play ends quietly as Yorimasa's ghost recites his last poem, asks the monk to pray for his soul and disappears.

*Yorimasa*, like most shura-Noh, is a two-act Noh with *kuri-sashi-kuse* in the second act. According to the standard structure, there should be a dance with chorus during the *kuse* and the finale, with a *kakeri* between them. *Yorimasa* lacks all these. Instead, there is miming by the *Shite* which describes the river-crossing and Yorimasa's suicide. In the river-crossing scene, the *Shite* who has been playing the role of Yorimasa's ghost, acts as a narrator and role-player of the enemy warrior Tadatsuna commanding his men crossing the river. Although we see all the while the figure attired as the ghost warrior Yorimasa miming, it is a picture from which Yorimasa is left out. In this Yorimasa differs from the similar examples in two other shura-Noh, *Tadanori* and *Sanemori*. In these,

---

[3]These Imperial anthologies and the number of Yorimasa's poems in them, given in the parentheses, are: *Shika* (1), *Senzai* (14), *Shin-Kokin* (3), *Shin-Chokusen* (3), *Shoku-Gosen* (2), *Shoku-Kokin* (4), *Shoku-Shūi* (1), *Shin-Gosen* (2), *Gyokuyō* (5), *Shoku-Senzai* (2), *Shoku-Goshūi* (12), *Shin-Senzai* (1), *Shin-Shūi* (2), *Shin-Goshūi* (2), *Shin-Shoku-kokin* (4).

although the *Shite*-hero's death is told by the *Shite* actor acting as a third party, it is a story about the hero. Similar examples of such role-playing of a shadow character by a *shite*-actor where the hero is absent occur in *Kanehira* and *Tomoakira*, as well as in *Tomoe* to a lesser extent. (See the Introduction to *Tomoakira*.) This absence of dance, the *Shite*'s two *katari*, with his role-playing of a shadow character in the second *katari*, reflect the characteristic of its source *Heike Monogatari* as narrative literature.

Yorimasa was a man of frustrated ambition. On more than one occasion he composed poems which alluded to his tardy promotion. In one of them he compared himself to a guard of the Imperial Palace who gazed at the moon only through the shade of trees, away from the eyes of the celebrities at His Majesty's moon-viewing party. In his last poem he compared himself to a fossil wood that would never blossom. Yorimasa, a talented poet and tragic hero of thwarted ambition constitutes the dual motif of the Noh *Yorimasa*. This reminds us of another *shura*-Noh hero, Tadanori, poet-warrior with thwarted poetic aspiration. (See *Tadanori*, Vol. 2, Book 1.) What is vitally different from *Tadanori* is the age of *Yorimasa*'s hero. While Tadanori is a *kindachi* (young nobleman) like most *shura*-Noh heroes, Yorimasa is an aged warrior, over seventy. There is another *shura*-Noh with an old hero, *Sanemori*. These two Noh, referred to as *rō-musha-mono* (old-warrior pieces), constitutes a group which distinguishes itself from the rest in various ways. They are pervaded with the pathos peculiar to the old age, which reflects itself in the severe, subdued style. Yet there is beauty in these old-warrior pieces, which reminds us of Ze-ami's words, "an old tree in bloom," found in *Fūshi Kaden* and some other writings of his. As it is, *Yorimasa* is rich in lyrical appeal imbued with an undertone suggestive of the deep-rooted rancor of the aged warrior. Uji, the scene of the Noh, is a place famous for the beauty of its landscape and literary associations. All through the first act, songs and speeches are interwoven with fragments of well-known poems and phrases of literary interests, including allusions to some passages in the *Uji* Chapters of *Genji Monogatari*. The beautiful poetic imagery attains a climax with the *shodō* (the first *age-uta* style chorus song), which describes the mist-bound country faintly lit by the rising moon:

| | |
|---|---|
| Na nimo nizu | Unlike the name, |
| Tsuki koso izure Asahi-yama | The moon is rising above the Morning-sun Mountain. |
| Yamabuki no Se ni kage miete | In the Yellow-rose Waters casting shadows, |
| Yuki sashi-kudasu shiba-obune | Down the snow-white stream go boats brushwood laden. |
| Yama mo kawa mo oboro oboro toshite | Mountain and river are all blurred, enshrouded in the veil of mist, |
| Zehi o wakanu keshiki kana. | Indistinct and dim spreads the landscape. |
| | 55--61, with refrain |

Uji, a place of exquisite beauty was a hiding place for people who had renounced life, and is referred to in poetic expressions as *yo o Uji* (life-weary Uji). The phrase occurs more than once in the Noh, creating an atmosphere of pathos and sense of defeat, together with other pathetic expressions in Yorimasa's last poem or in such lines as "It was during the Jisho-o Era, time summer,/ Into a fruitless rebellion I drew/ High-renowned Prince Takakura." (158--160).

*Yorimasa* with the subtlety of its dual motif, its background rich in poetic imagery, and its effectively structured climax scene, is a masterpiece of its genre worthy of its claimed author, Ze-ami.

Season   Early summer.*
Scene   Uji Village in present Kyoto Prefecture.
Characters and costumes:
  *Waki*   A traveling monk in ordinary monk's costume in *kinagashi* style, the same as that of the *Waki* in *Yashima*.
  *Mae-shite*   The ghost of Minamoto no Yorimasa appearing as an aged villager, in the costume of a humble old man such as the *Mae-shite* in *Yashima*.
  *Nochi-shite*   The ghost Yorimasa in a *yorimasa* mask, in a costume representing the military attire of a lay priest, including a special head covering named *yorimasa zukin*, an *atsuita kitsuke* in subdued colors under a *happi* robe and *hangire* divided skirt, wearing a sword.
  *Ai-kyōgen*   A villager.
The author:  Ze-ami Motokiyo according to his words in *Sarugaku Dangi*.
*   According to line 90, the date is same as that of the battle, May 26, summer by the lunar calendar. However, the landscape described is that of spring.

# YORIMASA

NANORI-BUE *Waki enters and stands at nanori-za.*

Nanori *spoken*

**WAKI**
I am a monk on pilgrimages through various provinces.
This time I have been in the Capital,[1]
Visiting all the shrines and temples in the city.[2]
Now I intend to go to the Southern City.[3]

Michiyuki *au*

Clouds sit high above[4]
Inari Shrine. Bowing on my knees in passing,
Inari Shrine. Bowing on my knees in passing,
Further I go on my way. Fukakusa and[5]
Kowata Barrier are left behind, and
Fushimi's Marshy Paddies now come into view.
The water's headspring trying to trace,[6]
At Uji Village I have arrived,[7]
At Uji Village I have arrived.

Tsuki-zerifu
*spoken*

Having hastened,
Already I have arrived at the Village of Uji.
At my leisure, in tranquility, I will take a look at the place.

*Kakaru*

Ah, in the remote countryside I have heard about this Uji Village.

*Spoken*

The mountain ranges, the river stream,[8]

*Sung, awazu*

Distant hamlets, the view of the bridge,[9]
So rich in scenic beauty is this celebrated place.

*Spoken*

Oh, I hope to meet a villager.

YOBIKAKE  *Shite enters calling to Waki, and walking along the hashigakari, speaks with Waki who stands near waki-za.*

Yobikake and mondō
*spoken*

*SHITE*
You, you holy man, what was that you were saying?

---

[1]Miyako (the Capital) = Kyoto.

[2]Rakuyō: Loyan = Kyoto, from the ancient Chinese capital of this name.

[3]Nantọ (Southern City) = Nara.

[4]Lines 5--6. *Ama-gumo no i* (heavenly cloud sits) --> Inari, the deity of harvest. The Inari Shrine at Fushimi, mentioned here, is the head of all the Inari Shrines. *Ama-gumo no* (heavenly cloud) is used as a *makura-kotoba* (pillow word) to Inari.

[5]Lines 8--10. Fukakusa, Kowata, Fushimi and Sawada are located on the way from Kyoto to Uji, and are among the places of the district celebrated for their associations with classic poems. Fukakusa literally means "thick grass," and Sawada means "swampy paddy." *mie-wataru* (seen far and wide) modifies Sawada and *Mizu* (water) in the next line.

[6]Line 11. Cf. Yamagawa no/ Mizu no minakami/ Tazunekite/ Hoshi ka tozo miru/ Shiragiku no hana. (Up a mountain stream,/ Whereabouts of its headspring/ As

Kore wa shokoku ikken no sō nite sōrō.
Ware kono hodo wa Miyako ni sōraite[1]
Rakuyō no jisha nokorinaku ogami-megurite sōrō.[2]
Mata kore yori Nanto ni mairabaya to omoi sōrō.[3]

Ama-gumo no[4]                                                    5
Inari no Yashiro fushi-ogami
Inari no Yashiro fushi-ogami
Nao yukusue wa Fukakusa ya[5]
Kowata no Seki o ima koete
Fushimi no Sawada mie-wataru                                     10
Mizu no minakami tazune-kite[6]
Uji no Sato nimo tsukinikeri,[7]
Uji no Sato nimo tsukinikeri.

Isogi sōrō hodoni
Kore wa haya Uji no Sato ni tsukite sōrō.                        15
Kokoroshizukani ikken sebaya to omoi sōrō.

Geni ya ongoku nite kiki-oyobinishi Uji no Sato

Yama no sugata kawa no nagare[8]
Ochi no sato, hashi no keshiki[9]
Midokoro o-oki meisho kana.                                      20
Aware satobito no kitari sōraekashi.

Nō, nō, on-sō wa nanigoto o ōse sōrō zo.

---

I went in quest,/ Like so many stars I saw/ White chrysanthemums in bloom.) by
Fujiwara no Toshinari in *Chôshû Eisô*.

[7]*Uji no Sato* (Uji village) was located where present Uji City is, in the southern part
of Kyoto Prefecture, celebrated for its scenic beauty and historical and literary
associations. See also note to 97-99.

[8]*Kawa* (the river) = the Uji River. With its bridge and the wickerwork fishing
nets, the river was a popular poetic theme. Also its name is associated with famous
battles fought there.

[9]*Ochi no sato* (distant hamlets): Cf. the following poem, sent to the heroine
Ukifune (Drifting Boat) living in Uji, from Chapter *Ukifune, Genji Monogatari*: Mizu
masaru/ Ochi no sato-bito/ Ikanaran/ Harenu nagame ni/ Kaki-kurasu koro (With the
rising water,/ You in the remote hamlet,/ How are you faring/ When one gazes at
ceaseless rain/ On these dark and dreary days?) In the poem, *nagame* means "long
rain" (*naga-ame*) and "to contemplate pensively." *hashi* (the bridge) = Uji Bridge.

*WAKI*

I am one who has come to see this place for the first
time.
About this Uji Village,
The celebrated places and historic sites there, please tell
me all about them.

*SHITE*

Though I live at this place,
Being a humble villager of Uji,[10]
About celebrated places and historic sites

*Kakaru*      My knowledge uncertain as white waves of Uji River,[11]
Boats and the bridge are there to cross it, but[12]
Hard to cross is the tide of this earthly life.
He who barely makes his living in the celebrated place,
What can he tell you in reply?

*Spoken*      *WAKI*

Although you speak like that,
"Kangaku-in's sparrows twitter phrases from *Mōgiu*,"[13]
they say,
You, an inhabitant of the place, have spoken with
modesty.
First of all, the hermitage where Monk Kisen lived,
where is it?[14]

*Shite enters the*      *SHITE*
*main stage and*      Ah, just as I thought! You ask a difficult question.
*stands at jō-za.*      Monk Kisen's hermitage . . .
*Sings, awazu*      "My hermitage is southeast of the City. There I live as
I like.[15]

*Spoken*      'Life-weary Mountain,' this is how people speak of the
place."

*Kakaru*      "This is how people speak,"
He himself said thus in the poem.
This old man knows even less.

---

[10]*Iyashiki uji* (humble family) --> *Uji no sato-bito* (Uji villager).

[11]*Isa shirana-* (Well, I don't know) --> shira-nami (white waves), a *jo-shi*
(introductory word) to Uji no Kawa (the Uji River).

[12]Lines 30-31. *Fune* (boats): Uji was famous for the boats sailing down the river
carrying brushwood. Cf. Yononaka ni/ Fune to hashi towa/ arinagara/ Watari-kanetaru/
Mi o ikani sen. (In this floating life,/ Neither boats nor bridges/ Do we lack, and yet,/
Hardly able to steer across, I'm driven to helpless despair.), quoted in *Yōkyoku
Shūyōshô*, its source unknown.

Kore wa kono tokoro hajimete ikken no mono nite sōrō.

Kono Uji no Sato ni oite
Meisho kiuseki nokorinaku onnoshie sōrae.                    25

Tokoro niwa sumi sōraedomo
Iyashiki Uji no satobito nareba[10]
Meisho tomo kiuseki tomo
Isa shira-nami no Uji no Kawa ni[11]
Fune to hashi towa ari-nagara[12]                             30
Watari-kanetaru yononaka ni
Sumu bakari naru meisho kiuseki
Nani toka kotae-mo-osu-beki.

Iya sayō niwa uketamawari sōraedomo
Kangaku-in no suzume wa Mōgiu o saezuru to ieri.[13]          35

Tokoro no hito nite mashimaseba on-kokoro nikū koso sōrae.

Mazu Kisen Hosshi ga sumikeru io wa izuku no hodo nite sōrō zo.[14]

Sareba koso daiji no koto o o-tazune are.
Kisen Hosshi ga io wa
"Waga io wa Miyako no tatsumi shika zo sumu[15]              40

Yo o Uji-yama to hito wa iunari."

Hito wa iunari to koso
Nushi danimo mo-oshi so-orae.
Jo-o wa shirazu so-oro-o.

---

[13]The quotation is a proverb. Kangaku-in was a private school built by Prime Minister Fujiwara no Fuyutsugu (775--826) for the children of the Fujiwara family. *Mōgiu/Mōgyū*: *Men-ch'iu*, a collection of sayings and anecdotes of eminent Chinese people, compiled during the Tang Dynasty by Li Kan. The book was used in Japan as a text book for young noblemen.

[14]Kisen Hosshi (Monk Kisen) was one of the Six Great Poets of the early Heian era. He lived in a hermitage on Mt. Uji, now called Mt. Kisen.

[15]Lines 40--41. A poem by Kisen in *Kokin-shū*. *Yo o u* (life-weary) --> Uji. *Yo o Uji* is a poetic phrase.

| | |
|---|---|
| Spoken | **WAKI**<br>And yonder I see a hamlet with a cluster of houses.[16]<br>Is that Black Pine Island? |
| | **SHITE**<br>That is right, that is Black Pine Island.<br>It is also called the River Island of Uji. |
| Kakaru | **WAKI**<br>And down there, I see a small headland. |
| Spoken | **SHITE**<br>Its fragrant name reaches far, the Small Headland of Orange.[17] |
| Kakaru | **WAKI**<br>And over there I see a temple.<br>I guess that Bishop Eshin[18]<br>Preached the Holy Law in that temple. |
| | **SHITE**<br>Ah, traveler,<br>Look up there. |
| Age-uta *au* | Unlike the name,<br>The moon is rising above Morning-sun Mountain,[19] |
| | **JI**<br>The moon is rising above Morning-sun Mountain. |
| Shite circles<br>the stage,<br>gazing about. | In the Yellow-rose Waters casting shadows,[20]<br>Down the snow-white stream go boats brushwood laden.<br>Mountain and river are all blurred, enshrouded in a<br>    veil of mist,<br>Indistinct and dim lies the landscape.<br>Indeed this celebrated place[21] |

---

[16]Lines 45--46. Maki no Shima (Black Pine Island), now a part of the main land, is an *utamakura* (place of poetic association).

[17]*Na ni tachi* (the name rises) --> tachibana (orange). Tachibana no Kojima-ga-saki (Small Headland of Orange) was well known in association with classic poems including those in *Genji Monogatari*.

[18]Eshin no Sōzu (Bishop of Eshin Temple) = Genshin (942--1017), the author of *Ōjō Yōshū* and other Buddhist writings.

[19]Asahi-yama (Rising-sun Mountain) is located on the eastern side of the Uji River. Eshin Temple was on that mountain.

[20]Lines 58--59. Yamabuki-no-Se (Yellow-rose Shallows) is a part of the Uji River. The name is found in classic poems, but the site is no longer known. *Yuki sashi-kudasu* (through the snow to steer boats down): The landscape is wrapped in the white moonlight as if in snow. *shiba-obune* (brushwood boat): The Uji River was famous for the boats poling down the river carrying brushwood. For these two lines,

Mata are ni hito-mura no sato no miete sōrō wa[16]  45
Maki-no-Shima zōro ka.


Sanzōrō Maki-no-Shima tomo mōshi,
Mata Uji no Kawashima tomo mōsu nari.


Kore ni mietaru kojima-ga-saki wa


Na ni Tachibana no Kojima-ga-saki.[17]


Mukai ni mietaru tera wa  50
Ikasama Eshin no So-ozu no[18]
Mi-nori o tokishi tera zo-oro-o na.


No-o, no-o tabibito
Are goranzeyo.


Na nimo nizu  55
Tsuki koso izure Asahi-yama[19]


Tsuki koso izure Asahi-yama,
Yamabuki-no-Se ni kage miete[20]
Yuki sashi-kudasu shiba-obune
Yama mo kawa mo oboro oboro toshite  60


Zehi o wakanu keshiki kana.
Geni ya nanishio-o[21]

---

cf. Chiri-hatsuru/ Yamabuki-no-Se ni/ Yuku haru no/ Hana ni sao sasu/ Uji no kawa-osa. (Where fall and scatter/ Yellow-roses on the stream,/ Spring is now passing,/ Through flower petals steers his pole/ The Uji River boatman.) by Saionji no Kintsune (1171--1244) in *Shin-shūi-shū*. *Hana* in the fourth verse of the original poem is here changed to *yuki* (snow).

[21]Lines 62--63. *nanishio-o Miyako* (celebrated Capital): Cf. Na nishi owaba/ Iza koto towan/ Miyako-dori/ Waga omō hito wa/ Ari ya nashi ya to (Since you have the name,/ I have a question for you,/ The Capital bird./ The one I am pining for,/ Is she well or is she not?), by Ariwara no Narihira in *Ise Monogatari*. When Narihira left Kyoto in self-exile and after a long and weary journey came to the Sumida River in Musashi Province, he saw white birds swimming in the river. They told him that the birds' name is *miyako-dori* (Capital bird). At this Narihira composed the above poem. Etymologically in *nanishiō* (celebrated), *na* means "name" and *ō* means "to have, to carry," *shi* is an emphatic particle, *ni* a preposition. "Celebrated," a sort of pillow word to "Miyako", here modifies "Uji".

Near the Capital, the Village of Uji ---
Its lovely landscape surpasses all its renown,
Its lovely landscape surpasses all its renown.

*Spoken*

**SHITE**
I have something to say.
There is a temple named Byōdō-in.  Have you
    been there?[22]

**WAKI**
No, as I know nothing about this place,
I have not yet visited it.  Please tell me where it is.

**SHITE**
Come this way.

*Shite goes to*
*front left, Waki*
*near Chorus*

This is Byōdō-in.
And this is the fishing pavilion,[23]
An interesting place.  Look at it well.

**WAKI**
Indeed, it is an interesting place.
And here I see a patch of turf
Which is cut in the shape of a fan.
What does it mean?

**SHITE**
There is a story about this turf.  I will tell you about it.

*Katari spoken*
*Shite sits*
*center stage,*
*Waki at*
*waki-za.*

Long ago, at this place a battle was fought for a royal
    prince.
Gen-zanmi Yorimasa, being defeated,
Here, spreading out a fan and seated on it, killed himself.
In memory of the renowned general,
The turf, cut in the shape of a fan, is left there,
And to this day it is called the Turf of Fan.[24]

*Kakaru*

**WAKI**
How pathetic!  Although he was famous as warrior
    and poet,[25]

---

[22]Byōdō-in (Byōdō Temple), located on the western bank of Uji River, originally a detached palace of Minamoto no Tōru (822--895), a son of Emperor Saga, was converted into a temple in 1052.  It is famous for a beautiful building facing a pond, the central part of which is joined by the left and right wings in the form of a phoenix spreading its wings and is named Hō-ō-dō (Phoenix Building).

[23]*tsuri-dono* (fishing pavilion) is a part of the typical aristocrat's mansion of the Heian era, located in the southwestern part of the garden, connected with the main building by a covered passage, and overlooking the pond.  Yorimasa's eldest son, Izu-no-kami Nakatsuna, committed suicide in the fishing pavilion of the Byōdō Temple.  See the Introduction.

Miyako ni chikaki Uji no Sato
Kikishi ni masaru meisho kana,
Kikishi ni masaru meisho kana.  65


Ikani mōshi sōrō.
Kono tokoro ni Byōdō-in to mōsu mi-tera no sōrō o
    goranzerarete sōrō ka.[22]


Fuchi annai no koto nite sōrō hodo ni
Imada mizu sōrō.  Onnoshie sōrae.


Konata e onnide sōrae.  70
Kore koso Byōdō-in nite sōrae.
Mata kore naru wa tsuri-dono to mōshite[23]
Omoshiroki tokoro nite sōrō, yoku yoku goran sōrae.


Geni geni omoshiroki tokoro nite sōrō.
Mata kore naru shiba o mireba  75
Ōgi no gotoku tori-nokosarete sōrō wa
Nani to mōshitaru koto nite sōrō zo.


Sanzōrō kono shiba ni tsuite monogatari no sōrō
    katatte kikase-mōshi sōrō-beshi.

Mukashi kono tokoro ni-miya-ikusa no arishini


Gen-zanmi Yorimasa kasen ni uchi-make-tamai  80
Kono tokoro ni ōgi o shiki jigai shi hate-tamainu.
Sareba meishō no koseki nareba tote
Ōgi no nari ni tori-nokoshite
Ima ni Ōgi no Shiba to mōshi sōrō.[24]


Itawashi ya sashimo bunbu ni na o eshi hito naredomo[25]  85

---

[24]*Ōgi no Shiba* (Fan Turf) still exists today.  However, no mention is made of the
turf in *Heike Monogatari* and other history books.
[25]See the Introduction.

No trace of him is left where dew-laden grass grows
   by the road.
Like a traveler on his horse is he gone,
Oh, how pathetic!

Spoken

> **SHITE**
> Indeed you have prayed well for him.
> Moreover it so happens that the royal battle was fought
>    on the same day of the same month as today.[26]

> **WAKI**
> What!  Do you say that the royal battle was fought on
>    the same day of the same month as today?

Kakaru

> **SHITE**
> The tale I have just related
> Is not about a stranger.  To the traveler
> Pillowed on the grass in the dew-transient earthly
>    world,[27]
> To reveal myself I have come.
> What you see must not be thought as real.[28]

Age-uta *au*

Shite rises.

> **JI**
> Dreamlike floating world's midway lodging place,
> Dreamlike floating world's midway lodging place,[29]
> The woeful Uji, whose bridge keeper of many years
> On the rolling waves of age has so far gone,[30]
> To you who are far away, I have a word to say,
> I am the ghost of Yorimasa,
> But hardly had he told his name before he vanished,
> But hardly had he told his name before he vanished.

---

[26]The battle was fought on May 26, 1180, summer by the lunar calendar, but the songs describe spring scenes. Cf. Line 158.

[27]*Kusa no makura no tsuyu* (grass pillow's dew) --> *tsuyu no yo* (dew-like life). *Kusa no makura* (grass pillow) is a metonym for "passing a night on a trip."

[28]Lines 96--97. *Utsutsu* (real, actual) --> *Yume* (dream).

[29]Lines 97--99. *naka-yado no Uji* (midway lodging place Uji) --> *Uji no hashimori* (Uji Bridge keeper). This life is considered in Buddhism as a brief midway lodging place between the former and future lives, and Uji used to be a midway lodging place between Kyoto and Nara, mentioned in the chapter *Shi-i-ga-moto, Genji Monogatari*. "Aged keeper of Uji Bridge" is a poetic phrase found in classic poems. Example:  Toshi hetaru/ Uji no hashimori/ Koto towan/ Iku-yo ni narinu/ Mizu no minakami (For many years you've been/ the Keeper of Uji Bridge./ I'd like to ask you,/ How many generations/ Old is the water's source?) by Fujiwara no Kiyosuke (1108--1177) in *Shin-Kokin-shū*.

Ato wa so-oro no michinobe to natte

Ko-ojin seiba no yukue no gotoshi.
Ara itawashi ya zo-oro.

Geni yoku on-tomurai sōrō mono kana.
Shikamo sono miya-ikusa no tsuki mo hi mo kyō ni atarite
sōrō wa ikani.[26]                                                   90

Nani to sono miya-ikusa no tsuki mo hi mo kyō ni
ataritaruto zorō ya.

Kayo-o ni mo-oseba warc-nagara
Yoso niwa arazu tabibito no
Kusa no makura no tsuyu no yo ni[27]

Sugata micn to kitaritari                                              95
Utsutsu to na omoi-tamaiso toyo.[28]

Yume no ukiyo no naka-yado no
Yume no ukiyo no naka-yado no[29]
Uji no hashimori toshi o hete
Oi no nami mo uchi-watasu[30]                                          100
Ochikata-bito ni mono mo-osu
Ware Yorimasa ga iurei to
Nanori mo aezu usenikeri
Nanori mo aezu usenikeri.

---

[30]Lines 100--102. *Oi no nami mo uchi* ("old age's waves roll", implying wrinkles)
--> *uchi-watasu* (seen far away), a *makura-kotoba* (pillow word) to *ochikata-bito* (far-
away person). These phrases lead to the quotation of another interrogative poem by an
anonymous poet in *Shin-Kokin-shū*: Uchiwatasu/ Ochikata-bito ni/ Mono mōsu ware/
Sono soko ni/ Shiroku sakeru wa/ Nani no hana zomo (My eyes reach out/ To you who
are far away./ I have a word to say. Right there where you are,/ A white flower is in
bloom./ Tell me, what flower is that?) *Mono mōsu ware* (A word to say have I) -->
*Ware Yorimasa ga iurei* (I Yorimasa's ghost). The song is associated with the famous
passage in the Chapter *Yūgao* (Moon-flower) of *Genji Monogatari*, where, quoting the
second verse of the poem, Lord Genji asks his attendant the name of a white flower
blooming in the hedge. The word *naka-yado* (midway lodging) is also used in the
opening sentence of the same chapter, meaning Genji's nurse's home he visits on his
way from the Imperial Palace to Princess Rokujō's.

NAKAIRI  *Shite makes the interim exit.*
AI-KYŌGEN  *Ai-kyōgen, a villager, enters and tells Waki the story of the Battle of Uji. Waki tells the villager about an old man who, having told him the story about the Turf of Fan and the Battle of Uji, revealed himself as Yorimasa's ghost and disappeared. The villager, thinking that the old man was Yorimasa's ghost, suggests to Waki to pray for his soul, offers his services and exits.*

| | |
|---|---|
| Spoken | **WAKI** |
| | So Yorimasa's ghost appeared in an assumed form |
| | And exchanged words with me. |
| *Kakaru* | Now let me pray for his soul's repose. |
| Machi-utai *au* | My thoughts drift on the waves rolling to my pillow.[31] |
| | My thoughts drift on the waves rolling to my pillow |
| | By the river bank in the temple garden, |
| | On the Turf of Fan laying me down, |
| | In a dream let me wait for the promised meeting, |
| | In a dream let me wait for the promised meeting. |

ISSEI  *Nochi-shite enters and stands by the first pine.*

| | |
|---|---|
| Sashi *awazu* | **SHITE** |
| | Blood, as at Takuroku, flows, forming a river,[32] |
| | Crimson waves run with floating shields.[33] |
| | White-flashing swords smash bones. |
| | Life-weary Uji River's wickerwork nets white with waves . . .[34] |
| | Violently my heart yearns for the earthly world. |
| *Awazu* | "The Ise warriors, |
| | All in the crimson-threaded |
| | Armor attired, |
| | In Uji's wickerwork nets |
| | Were trapped like the river's fish."[35] |
| Issei *awazu* | Fast-vanishing, frothy[36] |
| *Shite enters the* | Foam is this sad, vain world. |
| *main stage and* | |
| *stands at jō-za.* | |

---

[31]*Omoi-yoru* (to think of) --> *yorube no nami* rolling to shore waves --> *nami-makura* (wave-pillow), a metonym for sleeping near water or in a ship.

[32]Takuroku (Chulu): Huang-ti, legendary emperor of ancient China, defeated a traitor at this place, which came to be used as a synomym of a hard-fought battles.

[33]Lines 115--116. Cf. *Kanehira* 117--119.

Satewa Yorimasa no iurei karini araware　　　　　　105
Ware ni kotoba o kawashikeru zoya.

Izaya onnato tomurawan to

Omoi yorube no nami-makura[31]
Omoi yorube no nami-makura
Migiwa mo chikashi kono niwa no　　　　　　　　110
O-ogi no Shiba o kata-shikite
Yume no chigiri o mato-o yo
Yume no chigiri o mato-o yo.

Chi wa Takuroku no Kawa to natte[32]
Ko-oha tate o nagashi[33]　　　　　　　　　　　　115
Hakujin hone o kudaku
Yo o Uji-gawa no ajiro no nami[34]

Ara enbu koishi ya.

"Ise-musha wa
Mina hi-odoshi no
Yoroi kite　　　　　　　　　　　　　　　　　120
Uji no ajiro ni
Kakarikeru kana."[35]

Utakata no[36]
Aware hakanaki yononaka ni　　　　　　　　　125

---

[34]Lines 117--118. *Yo o u* (life-weary) --> Uji-gawa (Uji Rover). Cf. 40--41. *ajiro* is a fishing net laid in the river. It is made of small bamboo and tree twigs. Uji was famous for *ajiro*. See the Introduction and footnote (1). *ajiro no nami* (wickerwork net's waves) --> *Ara* (a) "violent"; (b) "ah!" The phrase has an image of white waves with *jiro (shiro)* meaning "white."

[35]*Kakarikeru kana* (were trapped): Only in the Kanze and Hōshō schools. The other three schools have *kakarinuru kana* as in the original poem in *Heike Monogatari*. See the Introduction.

[36]*Utakata no* (foam-like), an water image --> *Aware (sad)*, in which *awa* means "foam."

*JI*
On a snail's horns[37]
To wage a battle,

*SHITE*
Oh, how vain indeed
The thought of man.

Spoken

Oh, holy sutra!
Continue your chanting, I pray.

Kakaru

*WAKI*
How strange!  In appearance a monk, and yet in armor
  attired,[38]
You tell me to chant the sutra.
Surely you are the one I have heard about, Gen-zanmi.
Who now reveals himself as a ghost.

Spoken

*SHITE*
Indeed the scarlet herb planted in the garden is
  never hidden from the eye.[39]

Kakaru

Even before I had revealed my name,

Spoken

As Yorimasa you knew me.  That puts me to shame.
Do keep chanting the sutra, I pray.

Kakaru

*WAKI*
Do set your heart at rest.
Down to the fiftieth is passed on the sutra's virtue,[40]
Leading men to Buddhahood beyond all doubt.
Even more so when, in this way, directly

*SHITE*
A prayer is offered.  With the Holy Law's power

*WAKI*
You meet at the place with a name that means[41]

*SHITE*
"All equal."  In the temple garden

*WAKI*
Now I remember,

---

[37]From a fable in *Chuang-tzu* about two war lords who fought with each other, one from the right, the other from the left horn of a snail, an allusion to petty quarrels and struggles.

[38]*hottai* (monk's form):  In his old age, Yorimasa became a lay monk like many people of his time.

[39]A saying found also in the Noh *Ataka*.

Kagiu no tsuno no[37]
Arasoi mo

Hakanakarikeru
Kokoro kana.

Ara tatto no on-koto ya.     130
Nao nao on-kyō yomi-tamae.

Fushigi yana hottai no mi nite katchiu o taishi[38]

On-kyo-o yome to uketamawaru wa
Ikasama kikitsuru Genzanmi no
Sono iurei nite mashimasu ka.     135

Geni ya kurenai wa sono-o ni uetemo kakurenashi.[39]

Nanoranu saki ni

Yorimasa to goranzuru koso hazukashikere.
Tada tada on-kyō yomi-tamae.

On-kokoroyasuku oboshimese     140
Gojiu tenden no kuriki dani[40]
Jo-obutsu masani utagai nashi.
Mashite ya kore wa jikido-o ni

Tomurai-naseru nori no chikara

Ai ni aitari tokoro no na mo[41]     145

Byo-odo-in no niwa no omo

Omoi-idetari

---

[40]Lines 141--142. From *Saddharmapundarīka-sūtra*: "If a man, having heard of the blessing of the sutra, and passes it on to a second man, and he and others after him do the same, the blessings the fiftieth man receives is clearly foreseen." Cf. *Michimori* 63.

    [41]Lines 145--146. *Ai ni aitari*: (a) "met and met, miraculously encountered," (b) "very suitable, propitious," modifying *tokoro no na* (the place's name) = Byōdo-in (Equal Temple). This leads to *byōdō daie* (all equally embracing great wisdom of Buddha) in 152.

*SHITE*
The time when Buddha was in life.

Age-uta *au*

*JI*
Buddha preached of Law in the sacred temple,
Buddha preached of Law in the sacred temple,[42]
At this place named after his all equal great wisdom,
Through holy power Yorimasa[43]
Will obtain the fruit of Buddhahood, on what bliss!

Kuri *Awazu*
*Shite sits on a*
*stool center*
*stage.*

*SHITE*
Now what should I conceal?
I am Gen-zanmi Yorimasa,
In the waves of illustory attachment floating
    and sinking,
This is my former lives' karma I reveal to you.

Sashi *awazu*

*JI*
It was during the Jisho-o Era, time summer,[44]
Into a fruitless rebellion I drew
High-renowned Prince Takakura.  From his noble
    palace[45]
Cloud-bound he fled when the day was dawning, leaving
    the moon-lit Capital in stealth.

*SHITE*
Sad fortunes waited him[46]
O-omi Road as he took,

*JI*
Mii Temple the destination of his escape.

Kuse *au*

In the meantime,
By the Heike, who wasted no time,

*Shite sitting on*
*the stool makes*
*gestures*
*describing*
*battle, 165--221.*

A huge army of mighty soldiers
Was sent to the east of the Barrier.[47]
Hearing this, past the echoing Otowa Mountain range,[48]
Yamashina Village, and close to it,
The Kowata Barrier viewed in passing,

---

[42]Lines 150--151. *nori no niwa* (holy Law's temple): (a) Ryōju-sen, or Grdhrakūta, where Buddha preached; (b) *Koko zo Byo-odo-o* (Here Byōdō Temple). The temple name Byōdō then leads to *byōdō daie* (all equally embracing great wisdom of Buddha). *Niwa* (temple) is used here also in the sense of "garden."

[43]*Kuriki ni yori* (power by = by the power of) --> Yorimasa.

[44]From line 158--the end: Refer to the Introduction.

[45]Lines 160--161. *Na mo takaku* (name high, renowned) --> Takakura = the name of the house of Prince Mochihito). *yoso ni ari* (outside be, to be outside of) --> *ariake no tsuki* (dawn's moon) --> *tsuki no Miyako* (moon Capital = beautiful Capital, an epithet). The lines can be paraphrased: The renowned Prince Takakura from

Butsu zaise ni

Hotoke no tokishi nori no niwa
Hotoke no tokishi nori no niwa[42]                                    150
Koko zo byo-odo-o daie no
Kuriki ni Yorimasa ga[43]
Bukka o en zo arigataki.

Ima wa nani oka tsutsumu-beki
Kore wa Gen-zanmi Yorimasa                                           155
Shiushin no nami ni uki shizumu

Inga no arisama arawasu nari.

Somo somo Jisho-o no natsu no koro[44]
Yoshinaki go-muhonno susume-mo-oshi
Na mo Takakura no Miya no uchi[45]                                   160

Kumoi no yoso ni ariake no tsuki no Miyako o
    shinobi-idete

Uki toki shimo ni[46]
O-omi-ji ya

Mii-dera sashite ochi-tamo-o.

Saruhodoni                                                           165
Heike wa toki o megurasazu
Su-man-gi no tsuwamono o
Seki no higashi ni tsukawasu to[47]
Kiku ya Otowa no yama-tsuzuku[48]
Yamashina no Sato chikaki                                            170
Kowata no Seki o yoso ni mite

---

within his palace went beyond the cloundbound (Imperial) site, the crescent moon
emerging out of cloud, the moon-beautiful Capital he left in stealth.
    [46]Lines 162--163. *Uki toki shimo ni ô* (sad time to encounter. *shimo* is an emphatic
particle.) --> *O-omi-ji* (Ōmi Road).
    [47]*Seki* (barrier) = Osaka Barrier to the south of Mii Temple.
    [48]*Kiku* (to hear) --> Otowa no Yama (Otowa Mountain), in which *oto* means
"sound." Otowa Mountain lies to the south of Ōsaka Barrier.

To this place came we, weary life's travelers[49]
Way-worn, Uji River's bridge we crossed,
And toward Yamato hastened on.

### SHITE
On the way between the temple and Uji,

### JI
Highway horses trudging on incessantly,[50]
The Prince as often as six times fell from his horse,
Overcome as he was with fatigue,
All because the night before
He had scarcely had any sleep. So
At Byo-odo-o-in
A place to rest him awhile was arranged.
The boards of the Uji Bridge were removed in the center.
Under it, the river waves, and men above
Alike let flow white streamers,[51]
Waiting for the advancing enemy.

Katari *spoken*

### SHITE
Before long the Genji and Heike warriors
Had advanced to the southern and northern banks of the
    Uji River,
The clamor of the battle, the archers' cries
With the roaring waves mingling in loud sound,
The bridge stripped to beams between them. So they
    fought.

*Kakaru*
*Spoken*

Among our men, Tsutsui no Jo-omyo-o[52]
Ichirai, the monk,
Surprised the men of both sides with their bravery.
The numerous Heike warriors,
With the bridge stripped of its boards, the water in flood,

*Sings, awazu*
*Spoken*
*Sings, awazu*

The dangerous great river before them,
Were faced with difficulty crossing it. At that moment,
Tawara no Matataro-o Tadatsuna gave his name in a loud
    voice,

*Spoken*

"The Uji River will be crossed first by none other but
    myself."

*Sings awazu*

Hardly had he called out thus before three hundred
    horsemen,

---

[49]Lines 172--173. *tabi-gokoro U* (traveler's feeling sad) --> Uji. *Ukiyo* (sad
world), Uji and *uchi-watari* (to cross): Alliterations of *u* sound.
    [50]*Seki-ji no koma* (highway horses) is a *makura-kotoba* (pillow word) to *hima mo
naku* (incessant). *"Hima"* (interval; narrow opening in a wall etc.) and *"koma"* (horse)
are related to a proverb, *"Hima yuku koma"* (narrow opening passing horse = a horse
passing seen through a narrow opening), alluding to the swiftness of time.

Koko zo ukiyo no tabi-gokoro[49]
Uji no kawa-hashi uchi-watari
Yamato-ji sashite isogishi ni

Tera to Uji tono aida nite                                        175

Seki-ji no koma no hima mo naku[50]
Miya wa roku-do made go-rakuba nite
Wazurawase-tamaikeri.
Kore wa saki no yo
Gyoshin narazaru yue nari tote                                    180
Byo-odo-o-in nishite
Shibaraku go-za o kamae-tsutsu
Uji-bashi no naka no ma hiki-hanashi
Shita wa kawa-nami ue ni tatsu mo
Tomo ni shira-hata o nabikashite[51]                             185
Yosuru kataki o machi-itari.

Saruhodoni Gen-pei no tsuwamono
Uji-gawa no nanboku no kishi ni uchi-nozomi

Toki no koe yasakebi no oto
Nami ni taguete obitatashi                                        190
Hashi no yukigeta o hedatete tatakō.

Mikata niwa Tsutsui no Jo-omyo-o[52]
Ichirai Hosshi
Kataki mikata no me o odorokasu.
Kakute Heike no ōzei                                              195
Hashi wa hi-itari mizu wa takashi
Sasuga nanjo no daiga nareha
Sō nō watasu-beki yō mo nakasshi tokoro ni
Tawara no Matataro-oTadatsuna to nanotte

Uji-gawa no senjin ware nari to                                   200

Nanori mo aezu sanbyaku-yo-ki

---

[51]*shira-hata* (white flag): Genji flags were white and Heike flags were red.
[52]Lines 192--193. Tsutsui no Jōmyō, Ichirai Hosshi: They were among the monks of Mii Temple who joined the Prince's warriors. See the Introduction.

*Shura-nori*

**JI**

Their horses' bits all in a line, into the water,
Showing no hesitation,
Like a flock of numerous birds,
Their wings side by side in lines,
Making loud whirring sound, into the white waves[53]
Splashing water, they plunged and
Now floating, now sinking, began to cross the river.

**SHITE**

Tadatsuna to the warriors
Called out his instructions,

**JI**

"At the spots where the water is rolling back,
Beware of hidden shoals beneath.
Let the weaker horses go in the current's lee,
Make the stronger ones break the coursing water.
If a man is being swept away, let him seize your bow.
Unite yourselves as one to help each other,"
Thus he commanded, and led by but one man,
Though it was a mighty river,
Not a horseman lost, on this side of the stream
With loud outcries they landed.  At this, our men,

*Shite stands up and makes fighting gestures.*

Woe to them, unable to hold their ground,
In spite of themselves fell back some hundred paces, then
Their swords thrust in one line,
Determined there to give up their lives, they fought.

*Hira-nori*

Now men of both sides in a melée,
Vied one another, fighting desperately.

**SHITE**

Yorimasa's hope and strength,

**JI**

His elder and younger sons, were slain with the rest.[54]

**SHITE**

Now what is left for me to look forward to?

**JI**

No other thought but this had the aged warrior.

**SHITE**

This is the end, thinking thus,

---

[53]*kaku ya to shira-* ("So," thus we knew) = "It was like a flock of birds flying up all at once," thus we felt. --> *shira-nami* (white waves).

Kutsubami o soroe kawa-mizu ni
Sukoshi mo tamerawazu
Mure-iru mura-tori no
Tsubasa o naraburu                                                    205
Ha-oto mo kaku ya to shira-nami ni[53]
Zazzatto uchi-irete
Ukinu shizuminu watashikeri.


Tadatsuna tsuwamono o
Geji shite iwaku                                                      210


Mizu no sakamaku tokoro oba
Iwa ari to shiru-beshi.
Yowaki nma oba shitade ni tatete
Tsuyoki ni mizu o fusegase yo.
Nagaren musha niwa yuhazu o torase                                    215
Tagai ni chikara o awasu-beshi to
Tada ichi-nin no geji ni yotte
Sabakari no daiga naredomo
Ikki mo nagarezu konata no kishi ni
Omeite agareba mikata no sei wa                                       220
Warenagara fumi mo tamezu
Hancho-o bakari oboezu shisatte
Kissaki o soroete
Koko o saigo to tatako-otari.

Saruhodoni irimidare                                                  225
Ware mo ware mo to tatakaeba


Yorimasa ga tanomitsuru


Kyo-odai no mono mo utarekereba[54]


Ima wa nani oka gosu-beki to


Tada hitosuji ni ro-o-musha no                                       230


Kore made to omoite

---

[54]Minamoto Nakatsuna and Kanetsuna. See the Introduction.

*JI*

This is the end, thinking thus,
In the garden of Byo-odo-o-in,
Here on this patch of turf,

*Shite kneels at* Having spread out his fan,
*center left and* He cast off his armor. Then seated on the fan,
*makes gesture* And drawing out his dagger,
*of suicide.* A man worthy of his fame, he recited thus:

*Awazu* **SHITE**

I, a fossil wood,
From coming into blossom forever estranged,
And this is the final fruit,[55]
*Au* Ah, the bitter taste of it!

*JI*

Please say prayers for my soul, you holy man.
A casual encounter though this be,[56]
*Shite, rising,* A seed from former lives' karma has drawn us[57]
*throws his fan* To the Turf of Fan. Into the shadowy grass
*down, kneels,* I return. With these words the form faded,
*then exits* With these words the form faded out of sight.

---

[55]Lines 241--242. The words are slightly different from the original poem in *Heike Monogatari*, but the meaning is practically the same. See the Introduction.
[56]In *Karisome* (casual), *kari* (to cut, reap) is an *en-go* (associate word) of *kusa* (grass) and *Shiba* (turf) in 246.

Kore made to omoite
Byo-odo-o-in no niwa no omo
Kore naru shiba no ue ni
O-ogi o uchi-shiki                                          235
Yoroi nugisute za o kumite
Katana o nuki-nagara
Sasuga na o eshi sono mi tote


Nmoregi no
Hana saku koto no nakarishini                              240
Mi no naru hate wa[55]
Aware narikeri.


Ato toi-tamae on-so-o yo
Karisomenagara kore tote mo[56]
Tasho-o no tane no en ni ima[57]                           245
O-ogi no Shiba no kusa no kage ni
Kaeru tote usenikeri
Tachi-kaeru tote usenikeri.

---

[57]Lines 245--246. *tane* (seed) is *en-go* of *hana* (flower) and *mi* (fruit) in the above poem. *en ni ima o-o* (through the karma now encountered --> *O-ogi* (fan). *Shiba no kusa* (turf grass) --> *kusa no kage* (grass's shade), the realm of the dead.

兼平

KANEHIRA

Lose no time but come aboard, I pray you

Toku toku mesare so-orae

-Line 46

# INTRODUCTION

Two *shura*-Noh, *Kanehira* and *Tomoe*, can be considered as companion pieces. *Tomoe* is unique among *shura*-Noh because the *Shite* in the title role is a female warrior, sister of Imai no Shirô Kanehira, the *Shite* of *Kanehira*. Their mother was a nurse of Minamoto no Yoshinaka, a cousin of Yoritomo and his brother Yoshitsune. When Yoshinaka was two years old, his father was killed by a kinsman, and he was brought up by his nurse's husband, Nakahara no Kanetô, in the Province of Kiso (present Nagano Prefecture), and came to be known as Kiso Yoshinaka. Kanehira, like his elder brother, Higuchi no Jirô Kanemitsu (mentioned in the *shura*-Noh *Sanemori*), was Yoshinaka's most trusted retainer and a brave warrior. When his cousin Yoritomo raised forces in Kamakura against the Heike, Yoshinaka also rose in arms and attacked the warring lords in the neighboring districts who sided with the Heike. In 1183 the Heike fled from Kyoto before the advancing army of Yoshinaka and the latter occupied the Capital. His cousin Yoritomo, who had been estranged from him, now sent an army led by his younger brothers Noriyori and Yoshitsune, to attack Yoshinaka, who, defeated, fled as far as the coast of Lake Biwa in Ōmi Province (present Shiga Prefecture), where he was killed by the enemy. Tomoe, the only woman among a handful of warriors who fled with Yoshinaka as far as Awazu (literally "Foamy Ford") on the coast of Lake Biwa, was not allowed to follow her lord to the end because she was a woman, so, much against her will, she left her lord after fighting bravely for the last time to cover his retreat. Kanehira was with Yoshinaka until there were only the two of them left. When Yoshinaka was finally slain, Kanehira fell on his sword. In the Noh *Tomoe*, the ghost of Tomoe, whose grief at being left behind her lord on his last journey binds her to the earthly world, appears to the monk to be delivered from her worldly attachment. In *Kanehira*, the ghost of Kanehira comes to the monk to ask him to pray for the afterlife of his lord and himself. The two Noh are based on the chapter entitled "Death of Kiso" in the ninth volume of *Heike Monogatari*, outlined below:

Yoshinaka and his warriors fled eastward, followed by the Genji forces who came in hot pursuit after them. When Yoshinaka left Shinano Province the year before, he had fifty thousand horsemen with him. Now he was leaving the Capital with only six of his retainers. Sadly he thought of the solitary journey beyond this life he would soon be making. From Shinano he was accompanied by two lovely women, one named Tomoe and the other Yamabuki. As he fled from Kyoto, the latter remained there because of illness. Tomoe, a woman of great beauty with fair complexion and long streaming hair, was a matchless warrior, a mighty archer who would wield her weapon against any god or devil, on horseback or on foot; she went down steep cliffs on a wild horse. In battles, Yoshinaka would have her wear handsome armor, give her mighty sword and bow, and make her a captain. She was unrivaled in her glorious feats in battles. As it was so, now, while many of Yoshinaka's warriors fell or fled, she was among the seven survivors. Yoshinaka wished to find out the whereabouts of Imai no Shirō Kanehira, his retainer and Tomoe's brother, who had been posted at Seta on the southern bank of the lake, so he made his way in that direction. Soon they met, and as Kanehira lifted the banner high, those of Yoshinaka's men who were scattered about nearby hastened to join them, till Yoshinaka had three hundred men about him. Determined to die together, they made their way, fighting desperately with one enemy troop after another, far outnumbered by them, till there were only five of them left. Tomoe was among them. Then Lord Kiso said to her, "You are a woman, so flee from here now. I am going to fight to death. If wounded, I will kill myself. I will not have it said that Lord Kiso had a woman with him in his last fight." Tomoe would not obey her lord's order and continued to follow him. However, as Yoshinaka insisted, she said to herself, "Oh for a worthy enemy, so that I may show my lord for the last time how I can fight." As she waited, there appeared a warrior named Onda no Hachirō Moroshige, who was well known for his strength. He was followed by thirty horsemen. Tomoe rushed into them, came side by side with Onda, and grappling and dragging him down from his horse, held him fast to the front edge of her saddle, and wrung his head off. Then she took off her armor and made her escape eastward.[1] . . . . Finally there were only Yoshinaka and Kanehira left. To Yoshinaka who complained that for the first time he felt the heaviness of his armor, Kanehira said, "You are not yet tired, nor your horse exhausted. Why should you feel the weight of your armor so heavy on you? Maybe it is because you have lost your men and have become diffident. But you have still Kanehira. Though I am the only one you have now, believe me, I am worth a thousand ordinary horsemen. I have seven or eight arrows left. For a while I will cover you with them. The growth of pine trees we see yonder is Pine Grove of Awazu. Kill yourself in that pine grove." As they headed there, a new enemy troop of fifty horsemen appeared. "Go to that pine grove while I cover you," said Kanehira. To him Yoshinaka answered, "I should

---

[1]Later Tomoe became the wife of Yoritomo's retainer Wada no Yoshimori, the *Waki* in *Shichiki-ochi*. Their son, Asahina Saburo, hero of many stories and plays, was a man of legendary strength.

have met my fate in the Capital. Instead I fled so far, all because I wanted to die with you. Rather than to die apart, let us fight to the end." Then he turned his horse to run back with Kanehira. The latter sprang off his horse and holding the reins of his master's horse, he said, "A warrior, whatever his renown for his achievements in many battlefields, will forever disgrace his name if he does not live up to that name at the last moment. You are tired, you have no troops coming to join you. You will be attacked by the enemy, and in grappling with the follower of a worthless man, fall off your horse and have your head severed by him, and if people were to hear a voice call aloud, 'Lord Kiso, whose name is known all over Japan, was slain by one of my retainers,' that would be most regrettable. Do go into that pine grove." Yoshinaka could not but obey him, and ran away.

Imai no Shirō Kanehira, now all alone, ran into the midst of fifty enemy horsemen and challenged them in a thundering voice. Then he let fly the eight arrows left him, throwing eight men off their horses, dead or wounded. After that, he drew his sword and slashed about, darting this way and that. Nobody dared to confront him, and he took many weapons away from the enemy. The enemy surrounded him, shouting, "Let us shoot him down,' and their arrows rained down upon him. However, none of them pierced through his fine armor.

Alone Lord Kiso ran toward the pine grove. It was the twenty-first of January. The sun was setting. Not noticing the thinly iced deep rice paddies before him, he rode into the muddy water, which almost submerged his horse's head. Yoshinaka whipped hard but the horse stood still, unable to move. As he looked back to see what had become of Kanehira, Miura no Jirō Tamehira, who was close behind him, let fly an arrow, aiming at the inside of Yoshinaka's helmet. Yoshinaka fell prostrate against the horse's neck. As Kanehira heard Miura no Jiro calling aloud that he had slain Lord Kiso, he realized that it was no use fighting any more, so, holding the point of his sword in his mouth, he threw himself from his horse and died, pierced by his own sword. Thus ended the battle at Foamy Ford.

The Noh *Kanehira* develops as follows: A traveling monk from Kiso comes to the old battlefield of Awazu (Foamy Ford) by Lake Biwa, to pray for the soul of Kiso Yoshinaka who was slain there. (While the *waki* of a visional Noh is typically a stranger to the *shite* ghost, in most *shura*-Noh he is related to the deceased in some way. In *Kanehira* and *Tomoe*, as well as *Yashima*, he is from the same home place as the *Shite*. Only in three *shura*-Noh including *Tomoakira* and *Yorimasa* the *Shite* and *Waki* are strangers or their encounter is purely casual.) At the ferry of Yabase (Arrow Bridge) he asks an aged boatman to take him across the lake. The boatman at first refuses his request, saying that he is not a ferryman, and his boat only carries brushwood. Finally he takes him to his boat, wishing to do a good turn to a disciple of Buddha. Asked by the monk, the boatman at his pole tells about all the famous places in the landscape they see from the boat: Mt. Hie(i) with its twenty-one Sanno shrines, village houses at the mountainfoot, Enryaku Temple, the head temple of the Tendai sect on the mountain top, and so on. Soon the boat arrives at Awazu and the boatman exits. While the monk is praying for the repose of the souls of those who fell in the battle at Awazu, a figure attired in armor appears and sings, describing the morning scene of Awazu turned into the bloody battlefield of Asura's Hell. To the amazed monk the apparition reveals itself as the ghost of Imai no Shirō Kanehira for whom the monk was praying, and who had appeared to him last evening in the guise of an aged boatman. It is his wish that the boat that had taken the monk across the lake be turned into the sacred vehicle to take Kanehira to yonder shore. The *kuri-sashi-kuse*, accompanied by the *Shite*'s miming, describes Yoshinaka's separation with his only surviving man Kanehira, and his death in the miry rice paddy. During the final section consisting of a *rongi* and a song in *shura-nori*, the *Shite* dances, describing Kanehira's brave fight against fifty enemy horsemen and his self-inflicted death which amazed all who witnessed it.

The Noh *Kanehira* is similar to another *shura*-Noh, *Tomoakira*, in that, besides the *Shite* in the title role, both Noh have an invisible "shadow character," whose fate is deeply involved with that of the *Shite*, who in a way plays the part of the shadow character. In *Tomoakira*, this shadow character is the young hero's father Tomomori, who escapes from the battlefield while the son is fighting to death to cover him. In *Kanehira* the *Shite* fights to cover his master's retreat, and kills himself only when he learns of his lord's death. In the second act of both Noh, the *Shite* actor appearing as the *Shite* character first plays the part of the shadow character in the *kuri-sashi-kuse*, then in the finale, consisting of a *rongi* and a song in *shura-nori*, describes the *Shite* character's own fighting and death in mime and dancing. A similar example is found, to a lesser extent, in *Tomoe*, in which the heroine in the title role plays a role similar to that of the *Shite* in *Kanehira*. This situation is reversed in *Tadanori* (See *Tadanori* in Vol. 2, Book 1) and *Sanemori*. In them a shadow character, an enemy, impersonated by the *Shite* actor, describes the *Shite*'s death. We have another type of role-playing in another *shura*-Noh, *Yorimasa*. The climax of this play is the section where the *Shite*, the ghost of Yorimasa, plays the role of a shadow character, an enemy warrior, urging and giving orders to three hundred horsemen crossing the flooded Uji River. We see on the stage Yorimasa describing the scene, but actually he is absent from that scene. This role-playing is a phase which, like *katari*, constitutes the narrative element of the *shura*-Noh that is largely based on *Heike Monogatari*, which was narrated in chanting by *heike* singers.

It has been pointed out that many *shura*-Noh have deeply sympathetic human interest coloring rooted in human bondages that bind husband and wife, father and son, master and servant, and even mortal enemies, such as Atsumori and Kumagae. *Kanehira* and *Tomoe* are no exceptions. *Tomoe* moves us with the feminine tenderness of heroine whose grief of separation from her lord binds her soul to the earthly world. What makes *Kanehira* a Noh of deep dramatic appeal is the brotherly affection of master and servant. Deeply touching is the ghost Kanehira's appeal to the traveling monk to pray first for his master rather than for himself. It touches us the more, coming, as it does, immediately after the description of the tragic death of Yoshinaka.

The hero of a *shura*-Noh is the ghost of a warrior who seeks deliverance from the torment of Asura's hell through Buddha's mercy. As this is so, the Buddhist element forms a part of the background of *shura*-Noh to varying degrees. In *Kanehira* the Buddhism element plays an important role in intensifying the dramatic effect in many ways: firstly, there is the symbolic treatment of the boat. The old man who has taken the monk to the opposite coast in his boat in the first act reveals himself as the ghost of Kanehira in the second act and asks the monk to pray for him so that the boat may be turned into a holy ship to take him to Buddha's Paradise. Secondly, the deep emotional appeal of the play rooted in the selfless devotion of Kanehira to his lord culminates in Kanehira's entreating the monk to pray first of all for his master rather than for himself. The third phase concerns a section in the first act in which the aged boatman explains to the monk about the celebrated places they see around them, a section technically called *"meisho-oshie,"* (dialog about the celebrated places. Another such example in this book is in *Yorimasa*.) The celebrated places here are the head temple of the Tendai sect on the pinnacle of the sacred Mt. Hiei and its associate temples and shrines. The entire scenery with these edifices of Holy Law symbolizes Buddha's realm with its lake of placid contemplation and mountain of high aspiration, and the old man who is ferrying the monk to the opposite coast is symbolically taking him to the Yonder Shore. This religious coloring enriches the imagery of the scene and intensifies the dramatic appeal.

The description of the celebrated places in *Kanehira* is unusually long, taking up exactly half of the first act. It ends with an *age-uta* having these lines:

| | |
|---|---|
| Itoma zo oshiki sazanami no | No time to lose, rippling waves, |
| Yose yo yose yo iso-giwa no | Roll on, push on, boat, to yonder beach, |
| Awazu ni hayaku tsukinikeri. | At Foamy Ford already the boat has arrived. |

Then the old man simply steps out of the boat and exits, neither hinting at his identity, nor does the Chorus sing a line such as "And the old man disappeared out of sight," which usually accompanies the exit of a ghost in the first act. Throughout the first act, the oldman, the ghost of Kanehira, makes no appeal to the monk to pray for his salvation. He remains to the monk and to the audience an old boatman. His identity is revealed for the first time in the second act when he reappears in the form of an armored warrior and tells his name to the monk, who, his question answered, replies, "No wonder, then, at our first encounter,/ As no ordinary man you appeared to me." This achieves structural unity and intensifies dramatic effect.

Another structural characteristic of *Kanehira*, which generally conforms to the standard form, is found in the ending of the final song:

| | |
|---|---|
| Kanehira ga saigo no shigi | Kanehira's last feat of bravery |
| Me o odorokasu arisama nari | Was watched by all, wide-eyed and in awe, |
| Me o odorokasu arisama | Watched by all, wide-eyed and in awe. |

We realize that the ending is unlike most shura-Noh as well as other ghost Noh in two ways: firstly, it ends with the description of the *Shite*'s death instead of his wish to be saved; secondly a substantive ends the last line with no verb to complete the sentence, which is very exceptional even in prose poetry, or dramatic verse such as in Noh. The only other examples of such endings are in *No-no-Miya* and *Tōru*. The substantive ending is a poetic technic aimed at the lingering effect or suggestiveness, first become popular in the *Shin-Kokin-shū* era. It is successfully used in *Kanehira*.

Season　End of winter.
Scene　Awazu on Lake Biwa, in present Shiga Prefecture.
Characters and costumes:
>*Waki*　A traveling monk in the costume of an ordinary traveling monk, such as the *Waki* in *Yashima*.
>*Waki-tsure*　Two or three attendant monks who sometimes accompany the *Waki*, in the ordinary *waki-tsure*-monk's costume similar to that of the *Waki-tsure* in *Yashima*.
>*Mae-shite*　The ghost of Kanehira in the guise of an old boatman, in the costume of a humble old man, such as the *Mae-shite* of *Yorimasa*, carrying a rowing pole.
>*Nochi-shite*　The ghost of Kanehira in full military attire of a warrior in his prime, which is similar to that of the *Nochi-shite* in *Yashima*, but carrying a "defeated shura" fan, depicting a setting sun, instead of a "victorious-shura" fan with a rising sun pattern.
>*Ai-kyōgen*　A ferryman.

Author:　Attributed to Ze-ami Motokiyo by certain documents.
>*Kogaki　Naga-agura* ("Long Sitting") in Kanze school: Usually the *Nochi-shite* leaves the stool at the end of the *kuse*, but in this *kogaki*, he remains seated till line 256 toward the end of the final song. Also he does not draw his sword, but uses his fan as the sword.

# KANEHIRA

SHIDAI *Waki enters. At nanori-za he turns to the pine tree painted on the back panel.*[1]

Shidai *au*   **WAKI**
On my first trip along Shinano Road,[2]
On my first trip along Shinano Road,
Kiso's memorial site let me enquire.[3]

Jidori *awazu* **JI**
*Waki turns to* On my first trip along Shinano Road,
*face the*  Kiso's memorial site let me enquire.
*audience*

Nanori *spoken* **WAKI**
I am a monk from the mountain land of Kiso.
Now Lord Kiso
Died at Foamy Ford Field in Ōmi Province,
 I am told, so[4]
Wishing to pray for the repose of his departed soul,
Now I hasten to Foamy Ford Field.

Michiyuki *au* Along Shinano Road,
For Kiso's steep mountain foot-paths renowned,[5]
For Kiso's steep mountain footpaths renowned,
The famed one's site to visit, by the wayside,[6]
On the grass of shadowy fields briefly pillowed
Night after night, more and more days passed in
Traveling, before long on the O-omi Road,
At the Bay of Arrow Bridge I have arrived,[7]
At the Bay of Arrow Bridge I have arrived.

*Waki goes to waki-za and sits down. Tsukurimono representing a boat with a bunch of brushwood tied at the prow is placed stage left with the prow foremost.*

ISSEI *Shite enters with a pole in his hand and steps into the stern of the boat.*

Issei *awazu*  **SHITE**
With the worldly chore's

---

[1]When the *Waki* has *Waki-tsure* with him, they sing *shidai, michiyuki* and *machi-utai* together, in the same way as in *Yashima*.

[2]*tabi o shi* (a trip to make) --> Shinano.

[3]Kiso, line 7.  Kiso-dono (Lord Kiso): See the Introduction.

[4]Gō-shiu/shū = Ōmi Province, present Shiga Prefecture.  Awazu-ga-Hara (literally "Foamy Ford Field"), well known for its pine grove, is on the southern coast of Lake Biwa.  "Awazu on a fine windy day" is one of the eight celebrated views around Lake Biwa.

Hajimete tabi o Shinano-ji ya[2]
Hajimete tabi o Shinano-ji ya
Kiso no yukue o tazunen.[3]

Hajimete tabi o Shinano-ji ya
Kiso no yukue o tazunen.                                                                            5

Kore wa Kiso no yamaga yori idetaru sō nite sōrō.
Sate mo Kiso-dono wa
Gōshiu Awazu-ga-Hara nite hate-tamaitaru yoshi
  uketamawari-oyobi sōrō hodo ni[4]
Kano onnato o tomurai-mōsabaya to omoi
Tadaima Awazu-ga-Hara eto isogi sōrō.                                                              10

Shinano-ji ya
Kiso no Kakehashi nanishio-o[5]
Kiso no Kakehashi nanishio-o
Sono ato to-o ya michinobe no[6]
Kusa no kage-no no kari-makura                                                                      15
Yo o kasane-tsutsu hi o soete
Yukeba hodonaku O-omi-ji ya
Yabase no Ura ni tsukinikeri[7]
Yabase no Ura ni tsukinikeri.

Yo no waza no                                                                                       20

---

[5]Kiso no Kakehashi: A steep path along cliffs, one of the district's celebrated places. *Nanishio-o* (name well known) modifies (a) Kiso no Kakehashi, (b) *Sono* (his) in *Sono ato* (his site), which refers to the site where Kiso Yoshinaka died.

[6]Lines 14--15. *Kusa no kage* (grass shade) means "realm of the dead." *kage* (shade) --> *kage-no* (shade/dark field). *kari* (temporary; to cut) in *kari-makura* (temporary pillow, meaning "sleeping on a journey") is an *en-go* (associate word) of *kusa* (grass).

[7]Yabase (literally "Arrow Bridge"): A ferry port on the southeastern coast of the lake. "Sails returning to Yabase" is one of the lake's eight celebrated views.

Bitterness burdened, the brushwood boat[8]
Ere the wood is kindled
Burns to be rowed.

*Waki rises.*  **WAKI**
Mondō *spoken*  You, you boatman, there, take me in your boat.
**SHITE**
This is not a ferryboat of Yamada or Arrow Bridge.[9]
Look, it is a boat that carries brushwood.
I cannot take you in my boat.

**WAKI**
I, too, thought that it was a brushwood boat.  However,
At this moment no other boat is at this ferry.
I am one who has renounced life, so, as a special favor,
*Kakaru*  I beg you to ferry me across.

**SHITE**
Indeed you are one who has renounced life,
*Spoken*  Different from ordinary people.
To be sure, in the sutra it is said, "like finding
a boat for crossing."[10]

*Kakaru*  **WAKI**
A boat waited for comes to the traveler at nightfall.

**SHITE**
A rare encounter by O-omi Lake,[11]

**SHITE** and **WAKI**
Were this a ferryboat of Arrow Bridge,
Then it is only a boat for travelers.

Age-uta *au*  **JI**
But this is a boat
Toiling through the floating world, brushwood laden,
Toiling through the floating world, brushwood laden,
Wet sleeves and a water-soaked pole, an
accustomed sight,[12]

---

[8]Lines 21--23.  *ki* (tree) in *Uki* (sorrow) is an *en-go* of *tsumu* (to pile up) and *shiba* (brushwood).  The verb *tsumu* is used in two ways:  to pile up (a) sorrows on one's person; (b) wood on brushwood boat.  *Kogaru* (to burn; to be rowed) is an *en-go* of *shiba-bune* (brushwood boat).  *Kogaru* also means "to yearn."

[9]Yamada:  A well known ferry port on the eastern coast of the lake.

[10]Lines 34--35.  From *Saddharmpundarīka-sūtra*, Book 23, entitled "The Origin of Yakuō Bosatsu" (Bodhisattva of Medicine):  "This sutra delivers all creatures from afflictions; it benefits them and fulfills their wishes; it heals the thirsty like clean pool water; it is like fire to those who are cold, like clothes to the naked; to have this sutra is like a child's having a mother, like finding a boat at a ferry."

Uki o mi ni tsumu shiba-bune ya[8]
Takanu saki yori
Kogaruran.

Nō, nō, sono fune ni binsen mōsō nō.

Kore wa Yamada Yabase no watashibune nitemo nashi.[9]                    25
Goran sōrae shiba tsumitaru fune nite sōrō hodoni
Binsenna kanai sōrō-maji.

Konata mo shiba-bune to mi-mōshite sōraedomo
Orifushi watari ni fune mo nashi.
Shukke no koto nite sōraeba bechi no on-riyaku ni                        30
Fune o watashite tabi-tamae.

Geni mo geni mo shukke no on-mi nareba
Yo no hito niwa kawari-tamō-beshi.
Geni on-kyō nimo "nyodo tokusen."[10]

Fune machi-etaru ryoko-o no kure                                        35

Kakaru ori nimo O-omi no Umi no[11]

Yabase o wataru fune naraba
Sore wa ryojin no watashi-bune nari.

Kore wa mata
Ukiyo o wataru shiba-bune no                                           40
Ukiyo o wataru shiba-bune no
Hosarenu sode mo minare-zao no[12]

---

[11]*ori ni o-o* (occasion encountered) --> O-omi, the name of the province.
[12]Lines 42--45. *Hosarenu sode* (undried sleeves, sleeves that never get dry) -->
*minare* (familiar with water; familiar to sight), with *mi* meaning "water" and "sight."
--> *minare-zao* (water-familiar pole, a pole that is always in the water) --> *minare-nu
hito* (unfamiliar person, a stranger). In *Nori no hito* (Holy Law's man, a monk), *nori*
(Law; to ride) is an *en-go* of *fune* (ship).

|  | A stranger though you are for me, |
| *Shite makes a* | You, a seeker of Holy Law's vehicle, |
| *kata of poling* | In no way should I grudge my boat to you. |
| *and beckons to* | Lose no time but come aboard, I pray you, |
| *Waki. Waki* | Lose no time but come aboard, I pray you. |
| *steps into the* | |
| *boat and sits down.* | |

*Spoken*

**WAKI**

Boatman, I have something to say.
These coasts and mountains that we see all around, they
    must be celebrated places. Please tell me about them.

*SHITE*

As you say, these are all celebrated places.
Ask me and I will tell you about them.

WAKI

First of all, right in front of us we see a great
    mountain. Is that Mt. Hie?[13]

*SHITE*

*Shite turns to*    Yes, that is none other than Mt. Hiei.
*different*    At its foot twenty-one Sannō Shrines,[14]
*directions as*    The high wooded peak is the site of Hachiōjo Shrine,[15]
*he tells about*    Tozu and Sakamoto with their village houses, we can see
*places.*       even these distinctly.[16]

*WAKI*

And Mt. Hiei lies
To the northeast of the Imperial Palace, doesn't it?[17]

*SHITE*

Yes, indeed, that mountain
Defends the Imperial Palace from the Demon's Quarters,
Driving away the evil spirits. Moreover,
*Kakaru*    As Ekayāna Pinnacle it is known,[18]
To the ancient Holy Eagle Mountain being compared.[19]
And Tendai-san in the temple's name[20]

---

[13]Hiei-san (Mt. Hiei): Lies on the border of Kyoto and Shiga Prefectures, the site
of Enryaku Temple, the head temple of the Tendai sect. "Hiei" is also pronounced
"Hie." We always say "Hie no Yama." (Hie Mountain.)

[14]Twenty-one Sannō shrines: Associate shrines of Hie Shrine at the mountain foot.

[15]Hachiōji: One of the twenty-one shrines.

[16]Tozu and Sakamoto: Villages on the western base of the mountain. Tozu is now
a part of Sakamoto.

[17]Lines 58--60. *Ushitora* (northwest), *kimon* (demons' quarters): In the *Onmyō-dō*
(Yin and Yang Theory), northeast is called "demons' quarters", which are considered

Minarenu hito naredo
Nori no hito nite mashimaseba
Fune oba ikade oshimu-beki.                                    45
Toku toku mesare so-orae
Toku toku mesare so-orae.


Ikani sendō-dono ni mōsu-beki koto no sōrō
Mie-wataritaru urayama wa mina meisho nitezo sōrō-ran
   onnoshie sōrae.

San-zōrō mina meisho nite sōrō                                50
On-tazune-sōrae oshie-mōshi sōrō-beshi.

Mazu mukai ni atatte taisan no miete sōrō wa Hiei-san
   zōrō ka.[13]

San-zōrō are koso Hiei-san nite sōrae.
Fumoto ni Sannō nijiu-issha[14]
Shigeritaru mine wa Hachiōji[15]                              55
Tozu Sakamoto no jinka made nokorinaku miete sōro.[16]


Sate ano Hiei-sanna
Ōjō yori ushitora ni atatte sōrō yo nō.[17]

Nakanaka no koto sore waga yama wa
Ōjō no kimonno mamori                                         60
Akuma o harō nominarazu
Ichibutsujo-o no Mine to mo-osu wa[18]
Tsutae-kiku Washi no Mi-yama o katadoreri.[19]
Mata Tendai-san to go-osuru wa[20]

---

as evil and ominous quarters.
   [18]Ekayāna (one vehicle): The greatest of all the vehicles that lead to enlightenment.
   [19]Holy Eagle Mountain (Grdhrakūta): In Magadha in ancient India, where Sākya-muni preached.
   [20]Lines 64--65. The temple's full name is Tendai-san Enryaku-ji. *Shimei no Hora* (Four-Light Hollows): Originates from the four stone portals facing the four directions, on the top of Mt. Shimei, illuminated by the light of sun and moon. The mountain is to the north of Mt. Tendai on the eastern coast of China and was the center of Chinese Tendai sect.

|              | In Chinese Four-Light Hollows has its origin. |
|--------------|-----------------------------------------------|
| *Spoken*     | Dengyō Daishi, with the Emperor Kanmu as one man,[21] |
|              | During the Enryaku era founded the temple. |
|              | "Where I stand, the wooded hill..." goes his poem, |
|              |     a prayer for[22] |
| *Sings, awazu* | The Central Temple on the summit. |
|              | All clearly we can see. |

*Spoken*

**WAKI**

The Great Shrine is located, I hear, at a place called
    Hashidono.[23]
Is it also in Sakamoto?

**SHITE**

Yes, at the foot of the mountain,
We see a growth of trees,
The Great Shrine stands at Hashidono there.

**WAKI**

Oh, how divine! "All human beings are endowed with
    Buddhahood, to be one with Tathāgata," when thus
    told.[24]
Even for one like me I feel there is promise.

**SHITE**

As you say, Buddha and men are one in entity.
You, holy man,
And, I with no difference,

*Kakaru*     Attain Buddhahood's

**WAKI**

Pinnacle, where Vaiocana's lofty trees grow in thick
    rows,[25]

*Spoken*     **SHITE**

At its foot contemplation's sea brimming spreads.[26]

---

[21]Lines 66--67. Dengyō Daishi = Saichō (767--822), founder of Enryaku Temple.
At nineteen he built a straw hut on Mt. Hiei and there he studied sutras; in 788 he built
Konbon Chūdō and named it Hiei-zan Temple. (See 69). At Emperor Kanmu's order,
he studied Tendai Buddhism in China and laid the foundation of the Tendai sect in
Japan. Kanmu: Reigned 781--806. Enryaku era lasted 782--806.

[22]Lines 68--69. *Waga tatsu soma* (where I stand, the woodland hill): From
Saichō's poem in *Shin-Kokin-shū*: Anokudara/ Sanmyaku sanbodai no/ Hotoke-tachi/
Waga tatsu soma ni/ Myōga arase-tamae (Anuttatara/ Samyaku-sambodhi,/ Holiest
Buddhas!/ Where I stand, the woodland hill,/ Bless and protect it, I pray.) The first
two lines of the poem in Sanskrit means "supreme enlightenment." Saichō wrote this
poem when he was building Konp(b)on Chūdō (literally "fundamental central temple"),
the center of Enryaku Temple.

Shidan no Shimei no Hora o utsuseri.                                    65
Dengyō Daishi Kanmu Tennō to on-kokoro o hitotsu ni shite[21]
Enryaku nenjiu no go-sōsō
"Waga tatsu soma" to eiji-tamaishi[22]

Konbon Chiudo-o no sanjo-o made
Nokorinaku miete so-oro-o.                                              70


Sate sate Ōmiya no go-zaisho Hashidono to yaran mo[23]
Ano Sakamoto no uchi nite sōrō ka.


Sanzōrō fumoto ni atatte
Sukoshi kobukaki kage no mie sōrōo koso
Ōmiya no go-zaisho Hashidono nite onniri sōrae.                         75


Arigata ya "Issai shujō shitsu-u busshō Nyorai" to
   kiku toki wa[24]
Warera ga mi made mo tanomoshiu koso sōrae.


Ōse no gotoku Busshujō tsūzuru mi nareba
O-sō mo
Ware mo hedate wa araji                                                 80
Ichibutsujo-o no


Mine niwa Shana no kozue o narabe[25]


Fumoto ni shikan no umi o tatae[26]

---

[23]Ōmiya (Great Shrine): One of the twenty-one shrines, celebrates God of Miwa Shrine.
[24]From *Daihatsu Nehan-kyō (Mahā-parinibbana-suttanta)*.
[25]*Shana* (Vaiocana) = Dainichi Nyorai (Mahāvaiocana), meaning "Buddha of universal enlightenment and illumination," the principal deity of the Shingon sect of the esoteric Buddhism, identified with Sākya in the Tendai sect.
[26]*shikan* (contemplation): *Shi* = *samatha* (concentration), *kan* = *vipasyanā* (observation), two essential elements in Buddhist discipline preached by the Tendai sect.

*WAKI*

And precepts, contemplation and wisdom, the three
codes, are revealed

*SHITE*

In the edifices named the Three Temples.[27]

*WAKI*

As for men,

*Au*

*JI*

"In a single mind three thousand worlds,"[28]
This truth is embodied
In three thousand priests placed at these temples.
The Law of Fulfilment and Harmony, the pure[29]
Moonlight on Yokawa is shining clearly.
And there at the mountainfoot, the wave-washed[30]
Shiga Karasaki's solitary pine:
Seven shrines' holy palanquins parade[31]
Under its lofty green shade.
The little waves ripple and kiss the pole
Rowing with longing[32]
Till the far away
Yonder shore white-wave lined, and[33]
Foamy Ford's wood now loom at a short distance,
Behind, remote beyond the rippling small waves,[34]
"As of yore Nagara's
Mountain cherries," now green with young leaves,
The image lost in the summer mountain,[35]
A shifting shadow on green lake water,[36]
A brushwood boat, would 'twere oft to be seen,
No time to lose, rippling waves,[37]

---

[27]*Santo-o* (three edifices):  Three centers of Enryaku Temple, namely, To-tō, Saitō
and Yokawa.

[28]From *Tendai Maka Shikan* Vol. 5, by Chih-i (538--597).  The fundamental
teaching of the Tendai sect that mind contains all the phenomena of the universe
represented by the number three thousand.

[29]Lines 90--91.  *kumorinaki* (cloudless) modifies *nori* (the Law) and *tsuki no yo*
(moonlight night).  *yo* (night) --> Yokawa.  For Yokawa, see note to 85.  The moon
here can be purely rhetorical.

[30]Lines 92--93.  *sasanami ya* ("ripple" plus a particle):  *Makura-kotoba* (pillow
word) to Shiga.  Karasaki is in present Ōtsu City on the southern end of the lake.  The
solitary pine in rain, known as "Night rain at Karasaki" is one of the eight celebrated
views.

[31]The seven shrines:  Of the twenty-one shrines, the seven "mid-way" shrines
between the upper and lower shrines on and at the foot of Mt. Hiei.

[32]In *kogare-yuku*, *kogare* means (a) to be rowed, (b) to long or pine for.  See 23.

Mata kai-jo-o-e no sangaku o mise

San-to-o to nazuke[27]                                                         85

Hito wa mata

Ichi-nen san-zen no[28]
Ki o arawashite
Sanzen-nin no shuto o oki
Enniu no nori mo kumorinaki[29]                                               90
Tsuki no Yokawa mo mietari ya.
Sate mata fumoto wa sasanami ya[30]
Shiga Karasaki no hitotsu-matsu
Shichi-sha no shinnyo no miyuki no[31]
Kozue naru-beshi.                                                             95
Sazanami no minare-zao
Kogare-yuku hodo ni[32]
To-okarishi
Mukai no ura-nami no[33]
Awazu no mori wa chikaku narite                                              100
Ato wa to-oki sasanami no[34]
Mukashi-nagara no
Yama-zakura wa aoba nite
Omokage mo natsu-yama no[35]
Utsuri-yuku ya ao-umi no[36]                                                 105
Shiba-bune no shibashiba mo
Itoma zo oshiki sazanami no[37]

---

[33]Lines 99--100. *ura-nami* (coast waves) --> *Awa* (foam) --> Awazu (Foamy Ford).

[34]Lines 101--103. From a poem by Taira no Tadanori (1144--1184) in *Senzai-shū*: Sazanami ya/ Shiga no Miyako wa/ Arenishi o/ Mukashi nagara no/ Yama-zakura kana (Rippling-wave-washed/ Shiga, the old capital,/ Lies in ruins, but/ As in the past Nagara's/ Mountain cherries are in bloom.) In the poem *nagara* (unchanged) is also the name of the mountain at the back of the old capital, present Ōtsu City. See the Introduction to *Tadanori*, p. 93, Vol. 2, Book 1.

[35]*Omokage mo na* (image none) --> *natsu-yama* (summer mountain).

[36]Lines 105--106. *Utsuri-yuku* (to shift, to cast shadow) refers to *natsu-yama* (summer mountain) and *shiba-bune* (brushwood boat). *Shiba-bune* --> *Shibashiba mo* (often). The word opens a sentence, not expressed, to the effect: "It is not often that one visits this place, so time is precious."

[37]Lines 107--109. *sazanami no Yose* (ripples roll to) --> *Yose yo* (Row to the shore), an imperative, with *yose* meaning "to row to." In *iso-giwa* (beach edge), *isogi* means "to hurry." *iso-giwa no Awa* (beachedge foam) --> Awazu (Foamy Ford).

|                        | Roll on, push on, boat, immediate to shore, |
| :--- | :--- |
| *Waki leaves the* | At Foamy Ford already the boat has arrived, |
| *boat and goes* | At Foamy Ford already the boat has arrived. |
| *to waki-za* | |

NAKAIRI *Shite leaves the boat and makes interim exit. The boat is taken out.*

AI-KYŌGEN *Ai-kyōgen, a ferryman, tells the monk about the defeat of Kiso Yoshinaka and the death of Yoshinaka and Kanehira. He thinks that the aged boatman is Kanehira's ghost and exhorts the monk to pray for his soul.*

*Machi-utai au*    **WAKI**
With dew I lie on the mattress of grass,[38]
With dew I lie on the mattress of grass,
Dusk falls and already night creeps over
Foamy Ford Field.  Vanished from life ephemeral,
Hollow shadows, let me pray for their repose,
Hollow shadows, let me pray for their repose.

ISSEI *Nochi-shite enters and stands at jō-za.*

Sashi *awazu*    **SHITE**
White-flashing swords, bones smashed, in agony[39]
Eyes' kernels crush,
Crimson waves sweep shields away,
Arrows quiver, on fishweirs scattering flowers.[40]

Issei *awazu*    Cloud, water,
Foamy Ford Field in the morning wind,

**JI**
War cries resound,
Voices in unison.

**SHITE**
Asura's
Quarters
Tumultuous!

*Kakaru*    **WAKI**
How strange!  To Foamy Ford Field's grass pillow
An armor-clad figure appears.
Who in the world are you?

---

[38]Lines 111--116. The same *machi-utai* is sung in *Tomoe*, lines 84--89. Awazu alliterates with *aware* (foam-like, sad).

[39]Lines 117--119. Cf. *Yorimasa* 115--116.

Yose yo yose yo iso-giwa no
Awazu ni hayaku tsukinikeri
Awazu ni hayaku tsukinikeri.

110

Tsuyu o katashiku kusa-mushiro[38]
Tsuyu o katashiku kusa-mushiro
Hi mo kure yo nimo narishikaba
Awazu no Hara no aware yo no
Naki kage izaya tomurawan
Naki kage izaya tomurawan.

115

Hakujin hone o kudaku kurushimi[39]
Gansei o yaburi
Ko-oha tate o nagasu yoso-oi
Yanagui ni zanka o midasu.[40]

120

Kumo-mizu no
Awazu no Hara no asa-kaze ni

Toki tsukuri-so-o
Koe-goe ni

Shura no
Chimata wa
Sawagashi ya.

125

Fushigi yana Awazu no Hara no kusa-makura ni
Katchiu o taishi mie-tamo-o wa
Ikanaru hito nite mashimasu zo.

130

---

[40]Lines 120--122. *yanagui* means "quiver" and "fishweir." *zanka* (remaining flower) means blood splashed about on the fishweirs. *ka* (flower) --> *kumo* (cloud), from a conventional poetic image, "cloud of flowers" --> *kumo-mizu* (cloud-water), symbol of changeableness --> Awazu (Foamy Ford).

*SHITE*
Unwise is your question.
You have come as far as this place
To pray for my departed soul.
Was this not your intention?
Kanehira comes to you.

*WAKI*
Imai no Shiro-o Kanehira . . .[41]
Imagine, now he is no longer in this life!
Is this then a dream?

*Spoken*       *WHITE*
Not only in the dream that now you see, but
Also actually I am already familiar to you,
        as a pole to water.[42]
You saw me in the boat. The story I told you,
So quickly have you forgotten?

*Kakaru*       *WAKI*
You say I saw you in the boat? Then you are
Arrow Bridge Bay's ferryman . . .

*Spoken*       *SHITE*
That boatman was none other than Kanehira,
With the waking eye you saw him in that form.

*Kakaru*       *WAKI*
No wonder, then, at our first encounter,[43]
As no ordinary man you appeared to me.
So the boatman I saw yesterday

*SHITE*
A boatman he was not

*WAKI*
A fisherman

*SHITE*
He was neither, but[44]

*Age-uta au*   *JI*
A warrior who
At Arrow Bridge Bay as a ferryman,
At Arrow Bridge Bay as a ferryman
Appeared to you, and I was he.

---

[41]Lines 136--137. Imai *alliterates* with *Ima* (now).

[42]*haya mi* (already saw) --> *mi-nare-zao* (water-intimate pole, pole that is always in the water), with *mi* meaning "to see" and "water." --> *fune* (boat).

Oroka to tazune-tamo-o mono kana
Onmi kore made kitari-tamo-o mo
Waga naki ato o towan tame no
On-kokorozashi nite mashimasazu ya.
Kanehira koremade mairitari.                                    135

Imai no Shiro-o Kanehira wa[41]
Ima wa kono yo ni naki hito nari.
Sate wa yume nite aruyaran.

Iya ima miru yume nomi ka
Utsutsu nimo haya minare-zao no[42]                             140

Fune nite mimieshi monogatari
Hayaku mo wasure-tamaeri ya.

Somoya fune nite mimieshi towa
Yabase no Ura no watashimori no

Sono funabito koso Kanehira ga                                  145
Utsutsu ni mimieshi sugata nare.

Sareba koso hajime yori[43]
Yo-o aru hito to mietsuru ga
Sate wa kino-o no funabito wa

Funabito nimo arazu                                            150

Gyofu nimo

Aranu[44]

Mononofu no
Yabase no Ura no watashimori
Yabase no Ura no watashimori to                                155
Mieshi wa ware zo kashi.

---

[43]Lines 147--148. *yori* (from) in "from the beginning," "at first sight" and *Yō aru* (significant, unordinary) are in alliteration.
[44]Lines 152--154. *Aranu mono* (not the one = one who is not a fisherman) --> *Mononofu* (warrior) --> *Ya* (arrow) --> Yabase (Arrow Bridge).

It is my wish that that boat
Into the Holy Law's ship be turned so that[45]
I in my turn to yonder shore may be
Rowed across by the grace of your prayer.

Kuri *awazu*
*Shite sits on a*
*stool center*
*stage.*

Phantasmal world of life and death,
Where men come and are quickly gone,
Young or old, never in due order,
Dream, vision, bubbles, shadows,[46]
To which comparable?

Sashi *awazu*

SHITE
No more than a hibiscus in a single day's glory.[47]

JI
In the cavaliers' homes dwelt clear-shining the moon,[48]
Her orb waning, there remained but few warriors,
To seven horsemen reduced, Lord Kiso and his men,
Down this O-omi Road they made their way.

SHITE
Kanehira from Seta joined them,[49]

JI
And now there were more than three hundred horsemen.

SHITE
Then we fought one battle after another
Till save my lord and myself, only two, all fell fighting.

JI
"Now we can do no more.
To yonder pine grove make your retreat
And end your life with your own sword,"
Kanehira thus urged his lord.
Helpless and lonely, master and servant, two horsemen,
Toward Foamy Ford's pine grove made their retreat.

Kuse *au*
*Shite mimes the*
*action to the*
*end of kuse,*

Kanehira said to his lord,
"From behind us comes the enemy
In great number, running after us.
With my arrows I will cover your retreat,"
And he turned his horse toward the enemy.

---

[45]Lines 158--159. *Minori no fune* (Holy Law's boat): The boat that takes the dead to *kano kishi* (yonder shore) the land of Buddha's Paradise.

[46]From *Kongō-hannyaharamitsu-kyō (Vajracchedikā-prajñāpāramitā-sūtra)*: "All phenomena are like dream, vision, foam or shadow."

[47]From a poem by Po Chü-i (771--846) in *Wakan Rōei-shū*: "The pine after a thousand years finally decays; the hibiscus for a single day fully enjoys life." See *Senju* 84, Vol. 3, Book 3.

Onajikuwa kono fune o
Minori no fune ni hikikaete[45]
Ware o mata kano kishi ni
Watashite tabase tamae ya.                               160

Geni ya ui sho-oji no chimata
Kitatte saru koto hayashi.
Ro-osho-o motte zengo fudo-o
Mugen ho-oyo-o[46]
Izure naran.                                            165

Tada kore kinka ichi-jitsu no ei[47]

Kiuba no ie ni sumu tsuki no[48]
Wazukani nokoru tsuwamono no
Shichi-ki to narite Kiso-dono wa
Kono O-omi-ji ni kudari-tamo-o.                          170

Kanehira Seta yori mairi-aite[49]

Mata sanbyaku-yo-ki ni narinu.

Sono nochi kasen tabitabi nite
Mata shiujiu ni-ki ni uchinasaru.

Ima wa chikara nashi                                    175
Ano matsubara ni ochi-yukite
On-hara mesare so-orae to
Kanehira susume-mo-oseba
Kokorobosoku mo shiujiu ni-ki
Awazu no matsubara sashite ochi-tamo-o.                  180

Kanehira mo-osu yo-o
Ushiro yori on-kataki
O-ozei nite okkaketari.
Fusegi-ya tsukamatsuran tote
Koma no tazuna o kaeseba                                 185

---

[48]In *Kiu-ba no ie ni sumu* (bow-and horse house to live in = to be a warrior), *sumu* (to live; to shine clearly) leads to *tsuki* (the moon) --> *Wa* (orb, rim) --> *Wazuka* (very little; few). In *Wazuka ni nokoru* (very few/little remain(s)), there is an image of a waned moon.

[49]Seta. On the southern end of the lake.

Lord Kiso, having heard Kanehira's words, said,
"Fighting with many a foe I made my escape,
Only to be united with you
Was the sole wish that was left to me,"
With these words, he, too, turned to go back.
Kanehira again spoke to his lord,
"How regrettable, to hear you speak thus!
If such a man as Lord Kiso
Were to succumb to an enemy's sword,
Everlasting shame would be on his name.
You ought to end your life with your own hand.
Imai, too, in no time will accompany you."
By Kanehira thus admonished,
Again his lord turned his horse and went away.
Having parted with his man, Lord Kiso,
Full of misgivings, rode all alone,
Past Foamy Ford Field and beyond it,
Toward the pine grove he made his retreat.

   *SHITE*
It was the end of the first month of the year,

   *JI*
With signs of spring in the air, but icy cold
Down Hie Mountain blew winds,
Clouds drifted in the twilight sky, weaving[50]
Dazzling motley.  An evasive path
Led he knew not whither.  White snow froze in thin ice[51]
On rice paddies, into this miry depths his horse fell
And could neither get out
Nor move, however pulled and whipped, till the mire[52]
Closed in over the horse, hiding its head.
"Ah, curse on me, am I to die like this?"
Helpless and stupefied out of his wits,
He decided to kill himself there and then.
As he put his hand on the sword to draw,
He thought about Kanehira.
Wondering how he is faring, far away
Behind him he turned his gaze.  As he did so,

---

[50]Lines 207--208.  *sora mo kure* (the sky darkens) --> *kure-hatori* (Wu weavers), who came to Japan in ancient times, a pillow word to *Aya* (silk textile with colorfully woven patterns).  The words adds to the imagery of sunset sky --> *Ayashi* (strange, uncertain, suspicious).

Kiso-dono gojo-o arikeru wa
O-oku no kataki o nogareshi mo
Nanji issho ni narabaya no
Shozon aritsuru yue zo tote
Onajiku kaeshi-tamaeba                                    190
Kanehira mata mo-osu yo-o
Kowa kuchioshiki gojo-o kana
Sasugani Kiso-dono no
Hitode ni kakari-tamawan koto
Matsudai no on-chijoku                                    195
Tada on-jigai aru-beshi
Imai mo yagate mairan tono
Kanehira ni isamerare
Mata hikkaeshi ochi-tamo-o.
Sate sono nochi ni Kiso-dono wa                           200
Kokorobosoku mo tada ikki
Awazu no Hara no anata naru
Matsubara sashite ochi-tamo-o.


Koro wa mutsuki no sue-tsu-kata


Harumeki nagara sae-kaeri                                 205
Hie no yama-kaze no
Kumo yuku sora mo kurehatori[50]
Ayashi ya kayoi-ji no
Sue-shira-yuki no usu-go-ori[51]
Fukada ni nma o kake-otoshi                               210
Hikedomo agarazu
Utedomo yukanu Mochizuki no[52]
Koma no kashira mo mieba koso
Kowa nani to naran mi no hate
Senkata mo naku akire-hate                                215
Kono mama jigai sebaya tote
Katana ni te o kake-tamaishiga
Sarunitemo Kanehira ga
Yukue ikani to ochikata no
Ato o mikaeri-tamaeba                                     220

---

[51]*sue shira* (ahead unknown) --> *shira-yuki* (white snow) --> *usu* (thin) --> *usu-go-ori* (thin ice). *usu-go-ori* (thin ice) and *Fuka-da* (deep paddy) in 210 are antonyms.
[52]Lines 212--213. Mochizuki: In Shinano Province, present Nagano Prefecture, famous for its fine horses. Here the word is used as a sort of pillow word to *Koma* (horse). *Mochi-zuki* means "full moon."

*SHITE*
There was no knowing from where it came,

*JI*
But what proved deadly, launched from a
  zelkowa bow,[53]
An arrow flew and struck his helmet's inner side
With a clatter,
Inflicting a mortal injury.
Unable to sit in the saddle, from his mount

*Shite kneels*

He fell, far from home to lie in dust[54]
At this very place.  Rather than for myself

*Shite rises,*

But for my lord's departed soul
First of all say prayers, I beseech you.

*Rongi au*

Ah, most pathetic story, indeed!
Kanehira, too, lost his life there.
In what way did the warrior meet his death?

*Shite dances to
the end, describ-
ing the action.*

*SHITE*
  Kanehira, of what had happened
Unaware, fought with the foe, all the while,
To follow his lord on the last journey . . .
His mind was set on no other thought than this.

*JI*
While he was thus engaged, taking him by surprise,
From among the enemy a voice cried out,

*SHITE*
"Lord Kiso has fallen at our hand,"

*JI*
Aloud shouted thus the voice.  Hearing this,

*SHITE*
"Now what is there to set my mind on?  None!"

*JI*
Thus concluded Kanehira and

*SHITE*
To make his last proud address to the enemy,

*JI*
Standing up in the stirrups,

---

[53]*inochi wa tsuki* (life expires) --> *tsuki-yumi* (zelkowa bow).

Izuku yori kitariken

Ima zo inochi wa tsuki-yumi no[53]

Ya hitotsu kitatte uchi-kabuto ni
Karari to iru.
Itade nite mashimaseba                              225
Tamari mo aezu basho-o yori
Ochi-kochi no tsuchi to naru[54]
Tokoro wa koko zo ware yori mo
Shukun no onnato o
Mazu tomuraite tabi-tamae.                          230

Geni itawashiki monogatari
Kanehira no go-saigo wa
Nanitoka narase-tamaikeru.

Kanehira wa kaku zo tomo
Shirade tatako-o sono hima nimo                     235
Go-saigo no on-tomo o
Kokoro ni kakuru bakari nari.

Sate sono nochi ni omowazu mo
Kataki no kata ni koe tatete

Kiso-dono utare-tamainu to                          240

Yobawaru koe o kikishi yori

Ima wa nani oka gosu-beki to

Omoi-sadamete Kanehira wa

Kore zo saigo no ko-ogen to

Abumi funbari                                       245

---

[54]*Ochi* (to fall) --> *Ochi-kochi* (far and near), a set phrase leading to *ochi-kochi no tsuchi* (far and near dust = far and near lands' dust), *kochi* (near) being purely rhetorical here.

                    *SHITE*
            In thundering voice he shouted, "Lord Kiso's
            Retainer, Imai no Shiro-o

*Shura-nori*        *JI*
            Kanehira!"  Having thus called out his name,
            He plunged among the numerous foe,
            A warrior who could fight against a thousand,
            Yielding every secret art of battle the mighty foe
            As far as Foamy Ford's beach he drove,
            To the shore like wave-dashed seaweed thrusting them,[55]
            Crisscross now, now in radial
            Breaking through them and darting across,
            Then, "Watch how a warrior kills himself!" he shouted,
            Thrusting his sword into his mouth,
            Fell headlong from his horse
            And pierced by his sword he expired.
            Kanehira's last feat of bravery
            Was watched by all, wide-eyed and in awe,
            Watched by all, wide-eyed and in awe.

---

[55]*makuri-giri* (striking about with a sword in quick succession) contains *makuri*, a seaweed, which adds to the wave imagery.

Daionnage Kiso-dono no
Miuchi ni Imai no Shiro-o

Kanehira to nanorikakete
O-ozei ni watte ireba
Motoyori ikki to-osen no                                    250
Hijutto arawashi o-ozei o
Awazu no migiwa ni ottsumete
Iso utsu nami no makuri-giri[55]
Kumode jiumonji ni
Uchi-yaburi kake-to-otte                                    255
Sononochi jigai no tehonnyo tote
Tachi o kuwae-tsutsu
Sakasama ni ochite
Tsuranukare usenikeri.
Kanehira ga saigo no shigi                                  260
Me o odorokasu arisama nari
Me o odorokasu arisama.

# TOMOE

頼もしや あらありがたや

Full of promise, full of promise,
Oh, what bliss!

Tanoshimi ya, tanoshimi ya
Ara arigata ya

-Lines 102-103

# INTRODUCTION

The source and background of the Noh *Tomoe* are explained in the Introduction to *Kanehira*. *Tomoe* is the only *shura*-Noh in which the *Shite* is the ghost of a female warrior. The heroine Tomoe, Kanehira'a sister, followed her lord Minamoto no Yoshinaka, also called Kiso Yoshinaka, in his victorious battles against the Heike, to his final defeat and death at Awazu no Hara (Foamy Ford Field) by Lake Biwa. Yoshinaka did not allow Tomoe, a woman, to die with him, and bade her flee from the battlefield. The earthly attachment that binds her after her death, caused by her grief at being abandoned by her lord, is the theme of the Noh. Although there is a great difference between *Kanehira* and *Tomoe* -- the first act of *Kanehira* is characterized by unique structural features, while that of *Tomoe* is brief and conforms to the standard form -- in many respects they are similar to each other: the scene of both Noh is Awazu no Hara; the *Waki* is a monk from Kiso, the home of the two protagonists and of Yoshinaka. In both the tragic death of Yoshinaka and the loyalty and bravery of his two followers constitute the major features of the second act. The Noh *Tomoe* develops as follows;

The *Waki*, a traveling monk from Kiso, who has come to Awazu no Hara, sees a woman, the *Shite*, praying in tears before a shrine in the shade of pine trees, and asks her why she is weeping. The woman answers, quoting a poem by an ancient priest, who was moved to tears as he knelt before Usa Hachiman Shrine in Kyushu. The monk is deeply impressed by the woman's reply which reflects her urbane elegance. The woman, on hearing that the monk is from Kiso, tells him that the shrine celebrates the spirit of Kiso Yoshinaka, his fellow provincial, and urges him to worship the deity. This exchange between the woman and the monk is followed by an *age-uta* which, singing for the woman, extolls Yoshinaka who as deity protects the land, exhorts the monk to read the sutra all night to console divine suffering, and expresses joy at the blissful encounter with a man of Holy Law. The song ends with a description of the sun setting behind the mountain and tolling of the evening bell. The woman makes her interim exit, saying that she is really a ghost, and her identity may be known on asking a villager.

In the second act, while the monk is praying for the repose of the departed soul, the *Nochi-shite*, the ghost of Tomoe, appears in a costume representing military attire, halbert in hand, and rejoices at the prayer which will deliver her from the torture of her karma. In the exchange between the *Shite* and *Waki*, and the *age-uta* after it, the *Shite* reveals her identity as the ghost of Tomoe, and expresses her grief at being abandoned by her lord at his death. A short *kuse* follows, which briefly relates Yoshinanka's brilliant military achievement, the decline of his fortune and his death at Awazu Field. Then the ghost begs the monk to say prayer for her lord.

The rest of the second act can be divided into three sections: in the first, the *Shite* describes Yoshinaka mired in the rice paddy, whom Tomoe helps onto a second horse and leads to a pine grove, where she urges him to kill himself, herself wishing to die with him. Yoshinaka tells her to flee, taking his talisman and robe home as mementos, with a warning that, should she disobey his words, he will forever disown her. The second section is a description of Tomoe's fight with enemy warriors who came in pursuit. She fights bravely, brandishing her halbert, and drives the enemy away. In the last section, Tomoe, returning to her lord, finds he has fallen on his sword. She doffs her armor, bids farewell to her dead lord, and returns to Kiso, carrying Yoshinaka's mementos with her. The plot of the Noh *Tomoe* outlined above deviates from its source in that Yoshinaka kills himself, whereas actually he was slain by his foe, as described in *Kanehira*.

The *shura-nori* rhythm which typically comes in the final song of a *shura*-Noh describing fighting action, occurs twice in *Tomoe*, first briefly in the section when Yoshinaka struggles in the rice paddy (149 -- 154); secondly when the *Shite* fights with halbert (163 -- 191). However, the concluding section is quiet *hira-nori* (ordinary rhythm) sung, not in the *tsuyo-gin* (strong singing) which is usual in *shura*-Noh, but in the soft *yowa-gin* (gentle singing) appropriate to the pathetic scene where Tomoe flees from the battlefield, all alone, leaving her dead lord behind. Accompanied by the *Shite*'s miming and dancing describing the shifting dramatic situations, rhythm changes from slow to quick and to slow, with the progression of the emotional moods of the heroine, who is at the same time an Amazon and a woman of tender love and devotion.

Season   January by the lunar calendar.
Scene   Awazu on Lake Biwa, in present Shiga Prefecture.
Characters and costumes
   *Waki*  A traveling monk in the costume of an ordinary traveling monk, such as the *Waki* in *Yashima*.
   *Waki-tsure*  Two or three attendant monks, in costumes similar to those of the *Waki-tsure* in *Yashima*.
   *Mae-shite*  The ghost of *Tomoe* appearing as an ordinary woman in the costume of an ordinary (young) *mae-shite* woman consisting of a *karaori* robe in bright/subdued colors, worn in the *kinagashi* style

over a *surihaku kitsuke*, wearing a young/middle-aged-woman mask.

*Nochi-shite*    The ghost of *Tomoe* in *zō* or *masugami* mask, the costume representing military attire, consisting of a *nashiuchi eboshi* hat, *karaori* worn in the *tsubo-ori* style over *surihaku kitsuke* and white or colored, or patterned *ōkuchi* divided skirt, wearing a sword and carrying a halbert.

*Ai-kyōgen*    A villager.

The author:  Not identified.

SHIDAI   *Waki and Waki-tsure enter and stand center stage, Waki on the right, Waki-tsure on the left, facing each other.*

Shidai *au*

**WAKI** and **WAKI-TSURE**
Traversing deep mountains light of steps and quick,[1]
Traversing deep mountains light of steps and quick,
Along the Kiso Road let's start on a journey.

Jidori *awazu*

**JI**
Traversing deep mountains light of steps and quick,
Along the Kiso Road let's start on a journey.

Nanori *spoken*

**WAKI**
I am a monk from the mountain village of Kiso.
I have not yet seen the Capital, so
Now I have decided to make a trip there.

Michiyuki *au*

**WAKI** and **WAKI-TSURE**
In traveling robe[2]
Kiso Pass and further away beyond it.
Kiso Pass and further away beyond it,
We go, our lives may end at Mino, Owari,
Changing our lodging place every evening,
Night piling on night and days' number increasing
We travel on, and shortly by O-omi Road
Lake of Little Grebes now lies before our eyes,[3]
Lake of Little Grebes now lies before our eyes.

Tsuki-zerifu *spoken*   **WAKI**
Having hurried,
We have arrived at a place named Foaming Ford Field
in Omi Province.[4]
Let us rest here for a while.

---

[1]Lines 1--3.  *mi-yama* (deep mountain) --> *asa* (shallow), an antonym of *mi* (deep) --> *asamoyoi*, a *makura kotoba* (pillow word) to *Ki* in *Kiso-ji* (Kiso Road). The exact meaning of *asamoyoi* is not clear. *Asa* means "linen; morning," *mo*, "skirt; too" and *yoi*, "good," so that *asa-mo* in the sense of "linen skirt" is an *en-go* (associate word) of *Ki* in the sense of "to wear." The phrase in the sense of "morning, too, is good" implies the pleasant mood of journey.

Yukeba mi-yama mo asamoyoi[1]
Yukeba mi-yama mo asamoyoi
Kiso-ji no tabi no ijo-o yo.


Yukeba mi-yama mo asamoyoi
Kiso-ji no tabi no ijo-o yo.                                              5


Kore wa Kiso no yamaga yori idetaru sō nite sōrō.
Ware imada Miyako o mizu sōrō hodoni
Konotabi omoitachi Miyako ni nobori sōrō.


Tabi-goromo[2]
Kiso no Misaka o harubaru to                                            10
Kiso no Misaka o harubaru to
Omoitatsu hi mo Mino Owari
Sadamenu yado no kure-goto ni
Yo o kasane-tsutsu hi o soete
Yukeba hodonaku O-omi-ji ya                                             15
Nio no Umi towa kore katoyo[3]
Nio no Umi towa kore katoyo.


Isogi sōrō hodoni
Gōshiu Awazu no Hara to yaran ni tsukite sōrō.[4]


Kono tokoro ni shibaraku yasurawabaya to omoi sōrō.                     20

---

[2]Lines 9--14. *Tabi-goromo* (travel robe) --> *Ki* (to wear) --> *Ki, haru* (to wash and full) in *harubaru* (far), *tatsu* (to cut) in *omoi-tatsu* (to think of doing something), *hi mo* (days, too; string), *mi* (body part of a robe), and *kasane* (to pile one on another) are *engo* of *tabi-goromo* (travel robe). Kiso no Mi-saka: an *uta-makura* (poetic place), also called Magome-tōge (Magome Pass), in the southwestern part of Nagano Prefecture, at the southern end of Kiso Highway. Mino, Owari: the old names of present Gifu and Aichi Prefectures, In Mino, *mi* can mean "one's self, being," *no* is a particle; Owari has a sense "end" so that the name of the two provinces can mean "one's end" with a suggestion of a traveler's pessimism.
[3]Nio no Umi (Little Grebes Lake) = Lake Biwa.
[4]Awazu no Hara, also Awazu-ga-Hara: See *Kanehira*, 8.

*Waki sits at waki-za, Waki-tsure sit to his right.*
ASHIRAI  *Shite enters and stands at jō-za.*

Sashi *awzau*

**SHITE**
Ah, enthralling, Little Grebes Lake rippling quiet!
In foaming Ford Field's pine shade,

*Shite makes kata*    Diety is honored with festive rite.
*of weeping.*    Indeed, the divine response full promising!

Mondō *spoken*

**WAKI**
How strange!  Here a woman has come to the shrine
    and, as she prays,
Tears flow down her cheeks.
It is most strange indeed.

**SHITE**
You, holy man, are you talking about me?

**WAKI**
That is right.  You worship god, shedding tears while
    praying.  I thought it most strange.

**SHITE**
It is senseless that you should think this strange.
We are told that Reverend Gyōkyō,[5]
On visiting Usa Hachiman Shrine,
Composed this poem:

*Awazu*
"What holy being is enshrined in this place I know not,
    and yet,[6]

*Spoken*
Divine presence moves me so, tears flow down from my
    eyes."
The recitation of this poem
Must have impressed the deities,
On the sleeve of the holy man's robe they revealed their
    images.
Since then they are enshrined on Otokyo-yama near the
    Capital, promising

*Kakaru*
To safeguard the country.
You wonder in ignorance.

**WAKI**
Oh, how elegant!  You are only a woman.  However, this
    village

---

[5]Lines 31--39. Usa Hachiman Shrine in Kyushu celebrates Emperor Ōjin, Empress
Jingū and an ancient goddess Tamayori-hime.  It is said that when Gyōkyō, head priest
of Daian Temple in Nara, visited the shrine, he was told by an oracle to celebrate the
shrine deities in Kyoto, so in 859 he founded Iwashimizu Hachiman Shrine at Otoko-
yama in Kyoto Prefecture.

Omoshiro ya Nio no ura-nami shizukanaru
Awazu no Hara no matsu-kage ni
Kami o io-o ya matsurigoto
Geni shinkan mo tanomoshi ya.

Fushigi yana kore naru nyoshō no kami ni mairi        25
Namida o nagashi-tamō koto
Kaesu gaesu mo fushin ni koso sōrae.

On-sō wa mizukara ga koto o ōse sōrō ka.

Sanzōrō kami ni mairi namida o nagashi-tamō koto
  o fushin mōshite sōrō.

Oroka to fushin shi-tamō ya.        30
Tsutae-kiku Gyōkyō Kashō wa.⁵
Usa Hachiman ni mōde-tamai
Isshu no uta ni iwaku:
"Nanigoto no owashimasu towa shiranedomo⁶

Katajikenasa ni namida koboruru" to        35

Kayō ni eiji-tamaishikaba
Kami mo aware toya oboshimesareken
On-koromo no tamoto ni mi-kage o utsushi

Sore yori Miyako Otoko-yama ni chikai o shimeshi-tamai

Kokudo ansen o mamori-tamo-o.        40
Oroka to fushin shi-tamo-o zoya.

Yasashi yana nyosho-o naredomo kono sato no

---

⁶Lines 34--35. No record exists attributing the poem to Gyōkyō. The poem is popularly attributed to the poet monk Saigyō (1118--1190), although it is not in *Sanka-shū*, the anthology of his poems, except in the printed editions of later days.

To the Capital lies close.  Living there as you do,
Renowned urban elegance is even in your words.[7]

*Spoken*

**SHITE**
And your dwelling place, you holy man,
In what province can it be?

**WAKI**
I am from a mountain village of Kiso in Shinano
Province.

**SHITE**
If you are from a mountain village of Kiso,
The name of the god of Foaming Ford Field,
Without asking how should you know?
The very place you come from is[8]
Kiso Yoshinaka's homeland.  Here enshrined,
As deity he is celebrated.
Worship him, you traveler.

*Kakaru*

**WAKI**
How strange!  Then Yoshinaka
As god reveals himself, at this place
Enshrined.  Oh, how divine!

*Waki makes kata*  Turning toward the shrine, I join my hands in
*of prayer.*  prayer.

*Age-uta au*

**JI**
Of the time long gone,
This is none other than the lord whose name even now,[9]
This is none other than the lord whose name even now

*Shite goes to*  Remains, the moon at dawn, Yoshinaka.
*center stage*  As Buddha he reveals himself, and as god
*and sits down.*  He protects the land and men,
True to his divine pledge.  Oh, what bliss!
Traveler, the same tree's shade draws us together,[10]
Our former lives' karma leading us.  As it is,
At the foot of this pine tree pass the night,
And all night long recite the holy scripture,
The immortal in five-fold ailments giving comfort.[11]

---

[7]*Na-ni-shi-oitaru* (a. "name one has," b. "renowned") 43--44.  See note to
*Yorimasa* 62.

[8]Lines 51--52.  *Omni no sumi-tamō Kiso* (the place where you live, Kiso) --> Kiso
Yoshinaka.

[9]Lines 60--62.  *na wa ima mo Ari* (name even now exists) --> *Ariake-zuki* (dawn
moon) --> *tsuki (zuki) no yo* (moonlight night) --> Yoshinaka.

Miyako ni chikaki sumai tote
Nanishioitaru yasashi-sa yo.[7]


Sate sate o-sō no sumi-tamō           45
Zaisho wa izuku no kuni yaran.


Kore wa Shinano no Kuni Kiso no yamaga no mono nite sōrō.


Kiso no yamaga no hito naraba
Awazu no Hara no kami no on-na o
Towazuwa ikade shiri-tamō-beki.          50
Kore koso onmi no sumi-tamō[8]
Kiso Yoshinaka no on-zaisho
Onajiku kami to iwaware-tamō.
Ogami-tamae ya tabibito yo.


Fushigi ya satewa Yoshinaka no          55
Kami to araware kono tokoro ni
Imashi-tamo-o wa arigatasa yo to
Shinzen ni mukai te o awase


Inishie no
Kore koso kimi yo na wa ima mo[9]        60
Kore koso kimi yo na wa ima mo
Ariake-zuki no Yoshinaka no
Hotoke to genji kami to nari
Yo o mamori-tamaeru
Chikai zo arigatakarikeru.          65
Tabibito mo ichi-ju no kage[10]
Tasho-o no en to oboshimeshi
Kono matsu-ga-ne ni tabi-i shi
Yomosugara kyo-o o dokuju shite
Gosui o nagusame-tamo-obeshi.[11]      70

---

[10]Lines 66--67. According to Buddhism, even a casual encounter, such as strangers' taking shelter together under a tree, is predestined by their former lives' karma. The phrase frequently occurs in Noh.

[11]*Go-sui* (five-fold weakening): Five symtoms that appear at the death of a heavenly being: withering of the flowers on the crown; perspiration in the armpits; failing of eyesight; staining of heavenly robe; impossibility to enjoy heavenly state. In a number of Noh there are references to an immortal suffering from the five-fold weakening, seeking deliverance by Buddhist prayer.

Blessed is this encounter most rare,
Blessed indeed is this encounter most rare.
But time passes on,
The day's light fades, the sun behind the mountain ridge
Sinking.  Curfew begins to toll,[12]
O'er the lake's rippling water its echoes spreading.
The entire landscape desolate and ghastly.
I, too, am a phantom come before you.
If to what name it answers
Be unknown to you, of some one of this village
Pray enquire, having thus spoken, darkling,[13]

*Shite rises.*    Into the grass mound the shade faded away,[14]
Into the grass mound the shade faded away.

NAKAIRI  *Shite makes interim exit.*
AI-KYŌGEN  *Ai-kyōgen, a villager, who has come to worship at the shrine, tells the Waki how Tomoe followed her defeated lord to this place, where she had to leave him to his fate.  The villager also tells about the shrine which enshrines Yoshinaka.  He thinks that the woman who has just appeared must be Tomoe's ghost and urges the Waki to pray for her soul.*

Machi-utai *au*     WAKI and WAKI-TSURE
With dew we lie on the mattress of grass,[15]
With dew we lie on the mattress of grass.
Dusk falls and already night creeps over
Foamy Ford Field.  Vanished from life ephemeral,
Hollow shadows, let us pray for their repose,
Hollow shadows, let us pray for their repose.

ISSEI  *Nochi-shite enters with a halbert in hand, and stands at jō-za, or by the first pine on the hashigakari during the first three lines.*

Sashi *awazu*     SHITE
A flower falls, knowing that all is vain;[16]
Water flows insentient, but by nature
Pure-hearted, in contentment,

---

[12]*Iri* (to set) --> *Iriai* (evening, sunset).  Five "n" sounds in a short line.
[13]*iu* (to say) --> *iugure* (evening, evening dusk).
[14]*Kusa no ha* (grass leaves) --> *hatsuka* (dim), which contains *tsuka* (mound).
*Kusa no hatsuka ni*: Cf. Kasuga-no no/ Yukima o wakete/ Moede-kuru/ Kusa no hatsuka ni/ Mieshi kimi wamo (In Kasuga Field/ Where snow still lies in patches,/ Grass begins to grow./ Like that grass ephemeral/ Was the sight I had of you!) by Mibu no Tadamine in *Kokin-shū*.

Arigataki chigu-u kana
Geni arigataki chigu-u kana.
Saruhodo ni
Kurete yuku hi mo yamanoha ni
Iriai no kane no ne no[12]                         75
Urawa no nami ni hibiki-tsutsu
Izure mo monosugoki orifushi ni
Ware mo mo-oja no kitaritari.
Sono na o izure tomo
Shirazuwa kono satobito ni                          80
Towase-tamae to iugure no[13]
Kusa no hatsuka ni irinikeri[14]
Kusa no hatsuka ni irinikeri.

Tsuyu o katashiku kusa-mushiro[15]
Tsuyu o katashiku kusa-mushiro                      85
Hi mo kure yo nimo narishikaba
Awazu no Hara no aware yo no
Naki kage izaya tomurawan
Naki kage izaya tomurawan.

Rakka munashiki o shiru[16]                         90
Riusui kokoro no-oshite onozukara
Sumeru kokoro wa tarachine no

---

[15]Lines 84--89. The *machi-utai* is exactly the same as that in *Kanehira* (111--116). In translation, the personal pronoun, which is absent in the original, is plural in *Tomoe* and singular in *Kanehira*.

[16]Lines 90--91. From a poem by Po Chü-i (772--846) in *Wakan Rōei-shū*: "Flowers fall in silence, leaving the tree in vain; Water flows without thinking, pouring itself into a pond." The poet wrote this poem on passing by the house of a friend who was dead.

*Noru*

**JI**
Sins and retributions,
Karma-bound bitter torments,
Now will be absolved
By the divine Law's virtue,
Grasses and trees, all things on earth,[17]
Attain Buddhahood.
Still more so those endowed with life.
Straight to the Way leads them the prayer.
In all and every way
Full of promise, full of promise,
Oh, what bliss!

*Kakaru*

**WAKI**
How strange! By the Foamy Ford Field's grass-pillow
I see a woman, the same woman who appeared before,
But now clad in armor. It is most strange!

*Spoken*

**SHITE**
You wonder with reason.   Tomoe was my name, a
   woman warrior,
A woman to his death
My lord did not allow to follow him. My grief

*Kakaru*

**WAKI**
Become an attachment, still remains. Even to this day

**SHITE**
Although I wait on my lord

**WAKI**
This grief still now[18]

**SHITE**
Lies, wild sea and deep

Age-uta *au*

**JI**
At Foamy Ford, close to the beach,
Wave-beaten, fighting to death, to his end
I should have followed my lord. However,
A woman as I was, at his death

*Shite makes kata* I was abandoned by him. Ah, I take it hard indeed!
*of weeping, and* One dies for one's benefactor,[19]
*sits center stage.* One's life is bound to what one owes. This truth
Ignores any who handles a white-spindle-tree bow?[20]

---

[17]Lines 97--98. From a Buddhist text in verse, frequently found in Noh.
[18]Lines 112--113. *nao mo Ari* (still exits) --> *Ari-so-umi* (wild-beach sea) -->
*Awa* (foam) --> (Foamy Ford). *Nami no uchi* (waves strike) --> *uchijini su* (fall in
battle + verbal ending) --> *sue* (the end, death).

Tsumi mo mukui mo
Inga no kurushimi
Ima wa ukaman                                                95
Mi-nori no kuriki ni
So-omoku kokudo mo[17]
Jo-obutsu nareba
Iwannya sho-oaru
Jikido-o no tomurai                                          100
Kare kore izure mo
Tanomoshi ya, tanomoshi ya
Ara arigata ya.


Fushigi yana Awazu-ga-Hara no kusa-makura o
Mireba aritsuru nyosho-o naru ga                             105
Katchiu o taisuru fushigi-sa yo.


Nakanaka ni Tomoe to iishi onna musha


Onna tote go-saigo ni
Meshi-gusezarishi sono urami


Shiushin nokotte ima made mo                                 110


Kunpen ni tsukae-mo-osedomo


Urami wa nao mo[18]


Ariso-umi no


Awazu no migiwa nite
Nami no uchijini sue made mo                                 115
On-tomo mo-osu-bekarishi o
Onna tote go-saigo ni
Suterare-mairaseshi urameshi ya.
Mi wa on no tame[19]
Mei wa gi ni yoru kotowari                                   120
Tare ka shira-mayumitori no mi no[20]

---

[19]Lines 119--120. From "Life of Chu Mu" in *History of Later Han*.
[20]*Tare ka shira* (who does not know?) --> *shira-mayumi* (white spindletree) -->
*yumi-tori* (bow-taker, warrior).

Facing death, the name he is leaving behind,
Who will not think dearly of it?

Kuse *au*        At the time when Yoshinaka
From Shinano departed on his expedition,
Over fifty-thousand horsemen with him
In dense array rode, fighting all the way.
Tonami Mountain, Kurikara,[21]
Shio, in one and every battle they fought,
Trophies seized, feats of bravery without number,
Were by no one to be surpassed,
To any was her behavior inferior?[22]
No longer in life, in folk tales
The name she would leave stood first in her thought.[23]

> **SHITE**
> However, the fatal moment had come.

> **JI**
> Fortune's string snapped, and the zelkova bow's.  To
>    draw back[24]
> No way by the beach.  In Foaming Ford Field's
> Grass, as dew and frost vanish, he passed away
> Here at this very place.  You, holy one,
> Who come from the same home place, are with him
> By former lives' karma bound.  Pray for his repose.

Rongi *au*      So here in this field the battle was fought and
*Shite mimes*     Defeated to death was Yoshinaka.
*action, sitting*   About his end pray tell me, I beg you.
*on the stool.*

> **SHITE**
> As it was in the first month of the year,

> **JI**
> Snow melting in patches still lay on the ground,
> The only passage open.  Along it toward the coast,
> His horse as his guide he fled.  However, the horse

*Shura-nori*   Rushed into a thinly iced rice paddy, a deep mire.
On the left and right his stirrups were sinking,
To dismount, there was no solid ground to set feet.

---

[21]Lines 128--129. Tonami: In present Toyama Prefecture. Kurikara Pass goes through this mountain. Shio is in present Ishikawa Prefecture.

[22]Lines 132--133. *furumai no Naki* (behavior none) --> *Naki yo* (no more in life, posthumous) --> *yo-gatari* (folk tale). *Naki yo-gatari* is a contraction of *naki yo no yo-gatari*, meaning "to be posthumously talked about in folk tales."

Saigo ni nozonde ko-omei o
Oshimanu mono ya aru.

Sate mo Yoshinaka no
Shinano o idesase-tamaishi wa             125
Go-man yoki no on-sei
Kutsubami o narabe seme-noboru
Tonami-yama ya Kurikara[21]
Shio no kasen ni oite mo
Bundori ko-omyo-o no sono kazu           130
Tare ni omote o kosare
Tare ni otoru furumai no[22]
Naki yogatari ni
Na o-o shi omo-o kokoro kana.[23]

Saredomo jikoku no to-orai             135

Un-tsuki-yumi no hiku kata mo[24]
Nagisa ni yosuru Awazu-no no
Kusa no tsuyu-shimo to kie-tamo-o
Tokoro wa koko zo o-so-o-tachi
Do-osho no hito nareba            140
Junnen ni towase-tamae ya.

Sate kono hara no kasen nite
Utare-tamaishi Yoshinaka no
Saigo o katari owashimase.

Koro wa Mutsuki no sora nareba         145

Yuki wa mura-gie ni nokoru o
Tada kayoiji to migiwa o sashite
Koma o shirube ni ochi-tamo-oga
Usu-go-ori no fukata ni kakekomi
Yunde mo mete mo abumi wa shizunde     150
Ori-tatan tayori mo nakute

---

[23]*Na o-o shi*: Actually *"Na o shi."* *"o"* is printed in two syllables as it is sung.
[24]Lines 136--138. *Un tsuki* (fortune runs out) --> *tsuki-yumi* (zelkova bow) -->
*hiku* (to draw; withdraw). *na* (none), that is, no way to draw a bow/withdraw -->
*Nagisa* (beach) --> *yosuru awa* (rolling foam) --> Awazu-no (Foamy Ford Field) -->
*kusa* (grass) --> *tsuyu-jimo* (dew and frost) --> *kie* (to vanish).

|              | Clinging to the reins he whipped his horse.  However, |
|              | To pull himself out, there was no way by the beach |
|              | sands.[25] |
|              | Not knowing what to do, he sat still on his horse, |
| *Hira-nori*  | At a loss, in consternation. |

| *Shite rises, then* | While my lord was in this plight, I |
| *kneels front,*     | Sped my horse and approaching saw |
| *center stage.*     | That he was severely wounded. |
|                     | I helped him onto a new horse and |
|                     | As far as this pine grove I accompanied him. |
|                     | "Now, without delay you must take your own life. |
| *Shite bows.*       | Tomoe, together, will die with you," I said.[26] |
|                     | At this, however, Yoshinaka spoke thus to me: |
|                     | "Since you are a woman, |
|                     | A place of hiding you will find for yourself. |
|                     | Here is my talisman, and this, my under-robe. |
|                     | Take them to Kiso to my people.  Should you |
|                     | Disobey, master and servant's[27] |
|                     | Three-live long bond binding us will break, |
|                     | Forever I will disown you."  As he thus spoke, |
| *Shite bows and*    | Tomoe uttered not a word,[28] |
| *makes kata of.*    | In floods of tears choking she could only weep. |
| *weeping.*          | |

| *Shura-nori*   | Then leaving her lord, as she rose to go, |
| *Shite dances,* | She saw enemies in great number, |
| *miming her*   | "Is that Tomoe, the female warrior? |
| *fighting.*    | Let us get her, don't let her escape!" |
|                | Shouting thus, they fell on her in a dense throng. |
|                | "Now for retreat there would be no way out," she |
|                |     thought, |
|                | "Then let them come.  One more combat, oh, what joy!" |
|                | Tomoe, not in the least disturbed, |
|                | Deliberately, to lure the enemy to her, |
|                | Held her halbert drawn close to her, |
|                | Recoiling a little in fear she seemed. |
|                | The enemy, losing no time, struck at her. |
|                | With her halbert thrust at full length into them, |
|                | She slashed them about in every direction, |
|                | Sweeping them down all together like so many leaves, |
|                | In the stormy wind like flowers falling in cataract. |

---

[25]*Hiku kata mo nagisa.* See 136--137.

[26]Tomoe alliterates with *tomo* (together)

[27]Lines 168--169. According to Buddhism, the bonds of parent and child, husband and wife, and master and servant last respectively for one life, the present; two lives,

Tazuna ni sugatte muchi o utedomo
Hiku kata mo nagisa no hama nari[25]
Zengo o bo-ojite hikae-tamaeri.
Kowa ika ni asamashiya.                                155

Kakarishi tokoro ni mizukara
Kake-yosete mi-tatematsureba
Omode wa oi-tamainu
Norigae ni mesase-mairase
Kono matsubara ni on-tomo shi                          160
Haya on-jigai so-orae
Tomoe mo tomo to mo-oseba[26]
Sono toki Yoshinaka no o-ose niwa
Nanji wa onna nari
Shinobu tayori mo aru-beshi.                            165
Kore naru mamori kosode o
Kiso ni todoke yo kono mune o
Somukaba shiujiu[27]
San-ze no chigiri tae-hate
Nagaku fukyo-o to notamaeba                             170
Tomoe wa tomokaku mo[28]
Namida ni musebu bakari nari.


Kakute gozenno tachiagari
Mireba kataki no o-ozei
Are wa Tomoe ka onna-musha                             175
Amasu na morasu na to
Kataki teshigeku kakareba
Ima wa hiku tomo nogarumaji

Ide hito-ikusa ureshi ya to
Tomoe sukoshimo sawagazu                               180
Wazato kataki o chikaku nasan to
Naginata hiki-sobame
Sukoshi osoruru keshiki nareba
Kataki wa etarito kitte kakareba
Naginata e nagaku ottori-nobete                        185
Shiho-o o haro-o happo-o-barai
Issho ni ataru o konoha-gaeshi
Arashi mo otsuru ya hana no taki-nami

---

present and future; and three lives, past, present and future.
[28]Lines 171--172. Tomoe alliterates with *tomokaku* (this and that). *tomokaku mo na* (this or that, no = cannot say anything, speechless) --> *Namida* (tears).

Thus she fought, felling the enemy one after another
Till in one direction they were all driven back
And fled away, leaving no trace behind,

*Hira-nori*    And fled away, leaving no trace behind.

*Shite discards*     **SHITE**
*halbert, kneels*   Now it is all over, thinking thus,
center stage.

       *JI*
She returned to where she had left her lord,
There to be greeted by a piteous sight.
Already he had killed himself and
Here at the foot of this pine tree he lay.
Close to his head were the under-robe
And the talisman which he had laid there.
Tomoe, weeping, picked her lord's keepsakes up,

*Shite bows and*   To the lifeless body made the last farewell.
*rises. Makes*    And rose to go, but alas, could hardly move on,
*kata of weeping.* Her lord, how could she part with him and go?
And yet the words he insistently repeated
At his death sadly she had to obey,
So to the Foamy Ford's beach she went,

*She kneels,*     And cutting the sash, her armor
*takes off sword*  Quietly she discarded, there letting it lie,
*and hat.*        The fighting hat in the same manner
She doffed and left at the same place.
His under-robe she pulled over her head,

*Shite picks up*   What he wore with the sword to his death,
*the sword and*   The dagger she hid in the folds of her robe,
*holds it in one*   And from here, the Province of O-omi,
*arm, rises.*     A Shigaraki hat covering her head, to Kiso,[29]
But for her tears, Tomoe, all alone,[30]
Escaped, her bitter remorse still remains as
Earthly attachment. Absolve it with your prayer,
Earthly attachment. Absolve it with your prayer.

---

[29]*Shigaraki-gasa* (Shigaraki hat): A hat made in Shigaraki, a district to the south of Lake Biwa --> *ki* (to wear) --> Kiso.

Makura o tatande tatakaikereba
Mina ippo-o ni kiritaterarete
Ato mo harukani miezarikeri                                    190
Ato mo harukani miezarikeri.


Ima wa koremade nari to


Tachikaeri waga kimi o
Mi-tatematsureba itawashi ya                                   195
Haya on-jigai so-oraite
Kono matsu-ga-ne ni fushi-tamai
On-makura no hodo ni on-kosode
Hada no mamori o oki-tamo-o.
Tomoe naku-naku tamawarite                                     200
Shigai ni onnitoma mo-oshi-tsutsu
Yukedomo kanashi ya yukiyaranu
Kimi no nagori o ikani sen.
Towa omoedomo kuregure no
Go-yuigon no kanashi-sa ni                                     205
Awazu no migiwa ni tachiyori,
Uwa-obi kiri mononogu
Kokoro shizuka ni nugi-oki
Nashiuchi eboshi onajiku
Kashiko ni nugi-sute                                          210
On-kosode o hiki-kazuki
Sono kiwa made no haki-zoe no
Kodachi o kinu ni hiki-kakushi
Tokoro wa koko zo O-omi naru
Shigaraki-gasa o Kiso no sato ni[29]                           215
Namida to Tomoe wa tada hitori[30]
Ochi-yukishi ushirometa-sa no
Shiushinno toite tabi-tamae
Shiushinno toite tabi-tamae.

---

[30]*Namida to tomo* (tears together, in tears) --> Tomoe. *Ochi* (to escape; to fall) is an *en-go* (associate word) of *namida* (tears).

## Table 1. Dance Actions in *Shura*-Noh

| | Kuse dance | Kakeri | Chū-no-mai | Kiri | Number of dances | Katari |
|---|---|---|---|---|---|---|
| **1. Dance and Song Type** | | | | | | |
| Two Act Noh with *Kuse* in act two | | | | | | |
| *Atsumori* | + | - | + | + | 3 | - |
| One act Noh with *kuse2* | | | | | | |
| *Ikuta Atsumori* | + | - | + | + | 3 | - |
| *Shunzei Tadanori* | + | + | - | + | 3 | - |
| *Tsunemasa* | + | + | - | + | 3 | - |
| *Kiyotsune* | +[1] | - | - | + | 2 | - |
| Two act Noh with variation of *kuse* | | | | | | |
| *Tadanori* | + | +[2] | - | + | 3 | - |
| **2. Narrative type** | | | | | | |
| Two act Noh with *kuse* in act two | | | | | | |
| *Tomoakira* | - | - | - | + | 1 | + |
| *Yashima* | - | + | - | + | 2 | + |
| *Yorimasa* | - | - | - | - | 0 | + |
| *Kanehira* | - | - | - | + | 1 | + |
| *Michimori* | - | + | - | + | 2 | - |
| *Tomoe* | - | - | - | +[3] | 1 | - |
| *Tomonaga* | - | - | - | - | 0 | + |
| Two act Noh with *kuse* in act one | | | | | | |
| *Ebira* | - | + | - | + | 2 | + |
| **3. Between Types 1 and 2** | | | | | | |
| Two act Noh with dance in *kuse* and with *Katari* | | | | | | |
| *Tamura* | +[4] | + | - | + | 3 | + |
| *Sanemori* | + | - | - | + | 2 | + |

1  *Kiyotsune* has a long *kuse*
2  In *Tadanori* the *Kanze* school has a *tachimawari* instead of a *kakeri*
3  *Tomoe* has a long *kiri*
4  In *Tamura* there is a *kuse* in acts one and two

## Table 2. *Shura*-Noh by Type of *Shite* and Other Criteria

| Play | Clan | *Shite* in First Act | *Waki*[1] | Remarks |
|------|------|---------------------|-----------|---------|
| **Kindachi mono (Young Nobleman)** | | | | |
| *Atsumori*[2] | Heike | Grass-cutter maskless[3] | Monk who killed *Shite* in battle | 3-4 Mae-tsure appear as *Shite*'s companions |
| *Ikuta Atsumori* | Heike | One Act | Monk or layman who attends *Shite*'s son | *Kokata* appears as *Shite*'s son. Largely fiction |
| *Kiyotsune* | Heike | One Act | Servant to *Shite* | *Tsure* appears as *Shite*'s wife |
| *Michimori* | Heike | Old fisherman | Monk who prays for the souls of the Heike | *Tsure* appears as *Shite*'s wife |
| *Shunzei Tadanori* | Heike | One Act | Warrior who killed *Shite* in battle | *Tsure* appears as *Shite*'s friend |
| *Tadanori* | Heike | Old fisherman | Monk who was servant to *Shite*'s friend | |
| *Tomoakira* | Heike | Villager, maskless | Monk, a stranger | |
| *Tomonaga*[4] | Genji | A woman | Monk who was *Shite*'s servant | *Shite* in Acts 1 and 2 different characters |
| *Tsunemasa* | Heike | One Act | Priest of a temple where *Shite*, as a boy, waited on the abbott | |

1 Unlike other visional Noh, *waki* in most *shura*-noh is not a total stranger to *shite*
2 Main source for all *Shura*-Noh except *Tomonaga*, *Ikuta Atsumori* and *Tamura* is *Heike Monogatari*
3 Maskless: a character without a mask is an ordinary male neither old nor very young
4 Source: *Heiji Monogatari*

**Table 2.** *Shura*-Noh by Type of *Shite* and Other Criteria (cont.)

| Play | Clan | *Shite* in First Act | *Waki*[1] | Remarks |
|------|------|----------------------|-----------|---------|
| *Heida-mono* (Brave warrior wearing *heida* mask) | | | | |
| *Ebira*[5] | Genji | Villager, maskless | Monk, stranger | Sometimes *Shite* wears a *kindachi* mask and costume |
| *Yashima* | Genji | Old fisherman | Monk from Kyoto as is *Shite* | *Tsure* appears as young fisherman |
| *Tamura*[6] | | A boy servant of the temple | Monk, stranger | |
| *Kanehira* | Genji | Old ferryman | Monk from same province as *Shite* | |
| *Ro-musha-mono* (Old Warrior) | | | | |
| *Sanemori* | Heike | Old man | Monk, a stranger | |
| *Yorimasa* | Genji | Old man | Monk, a stranger | |
| *Onna-musha-mono* (Female Warrior) | | | | |
| *Tomoe* | Genji | A young woman | Monk from same province as *Shite* | |

5  *Ebira, Yashima,* and *Tamura* are *kachi* (victorious) *shura*, all others are *make* (defeated) *shura*

6  Main source: *Konjaku Monogatari*

187

**Table 3.** *Shura*-Noh Currently in the Repertories of Five Noh Schools

| Title | | In the repertories of |
|---|---|---|
| *Atsumori* | 敦　盛 | All schools |
| *Ebira* | 箙 | All schools |
| *Ikuta Atsumori* * | 生田敦盛 | All schools except Kita |
| *Kanehira* | 兼　平 | All schools |
| *Kiyotsune* | 清　経 | All schools |
| *Michimori* | 通　盛 | All schools |
| *Sanemori* | 実　盛 | All schools |
| *Shunzei Tadanori* | 俊成忠度 | All schools except Konparu |
| *Tadanori* | 忠　度 | All schools |
| *Tamura* | 田　村 | All schools |
| *Tomoakira* | 知　章 | All schools except Hōshō |
| *Tomoe* | 巴 | All schools |
| *Tomonaga* | 朝　長 | All schools |
| *Tsunemasa* | 経正 (政) | All schools |
| *Yashima* | 屋 (八) 島 | All schools |
| *Yorimasa* | 頼　政 | All schools |

*Ikuta* in the Konparu school

Remarks: *Ikarikazuki*, which is not treated as a *shura*-Noh in this book, is in the repertories of only the Kanze and Kongō schools. It is classified as *shura*-Noh in the former, but as *yonban-me-mono* (fourth-category piece) in the latter.

# CHRONOLOGY

Fifteen out of the sixteen *shura*-Noh have as their protagonists the members of the Heike or Genji who fought in the battles involving these two clans. This chronology and the genealogical charts on the following pages provide a historical background for the stories in these *shura*-Noh.

| Emperor and Ex-Emperor | Historical events |
| --- | --- |

Emp. Goshira-kawa

Ex. Sutoku

**1156, Hōgen 1[1], July 10-29**

Hōgen no Ran (Hōgen Rebellion): Ex-Emperor (*Shite* of *Matsuyama Tengu*) raised an army against the Emperor and was defeated by Taira no Kiyomori, MINAMOTO NO YORIMASA[2] (*Shite* of *Yorimasa*) and Minamoto no Yoshitomo.[3] Yoshitomo's father, Tameyoshi, who supported Sutoku, as well as his four infant sons, were executed by Yoshitomo. His older sons who fought under him were either beheaded or exiled.

Emp. Nijō

Ex. Goshiraka-wa

Ex. Sutoku

**1159, Heiji 1, Dec. 9--26**

Heiji no Ran (Heiji Rebellion): Minamoto no Yoshitomo sided with the traitor Fujiwara no Nobuyori and was defeated by Taira no Kiyomori. With three of his sons he fled to Ōhaka (in present Gifu Prefecture) and stayed at the hosue of CHŌJA (an owner of a post-town inn, who kept courtesans to entertain her guests; *Mae-shite* of *Tomonaga*). Her daughter was Yoshitomo's mistress. TOMONAGA (the *Nochi-shite*), one of Yoshitomo's three sons who fled with him, had been badly wounded and died there at his father's hand. The eldest son Yoshihira[3] was captured and executed. Yoritomo,[3] (*Tsure* in *Shichiku-ochi* and *Kokata* in *Daibutsu-Kuyō*) the youngest of the three, was lost on the way. He was captured and then exiled to Izu (in present Kanagawa Prefecture. Later he became the leader of the Genji clan and destroyed the Heike.) Yoshitomo then went to Owari (present Aichi

189

Prefecture), where he was assassinated with his retainer Kamata no Masakiyo[3] by the latter's father-in-law Osada no Tadamune.[3] Another mistress of his, Tokiwa, was captured with her three young sons, but their lives were saved on condition that Tokiwa should become Kiyomori's mistress. The youngest boy, Ushiwaka, became known as YOSHITSUNE (*Shite* of *Yashima*, *Tsure* or *Kokata* in a number of Noh). He destroyed the Heike clan for his brother Yoritomo, only to be killed by the latter.

**1160, Eiryaku 1, August**

As a reward for his military services, Kiyomori was promoted to a higher court rank and his sons were given important government posts.

**1161, Ōho 1**

During the Ōho era, MINAMOTO NO YORIMASA shot down a *nue*, a monstrous night bird that had nightly tormented the Emperor. (The Noh *Nue* is about this episode.)

Emp. Rokujō **1167, Nin-an 2, Feb. 11**

Kiyomori was made Grand Minister of State.

Emp. Takakura **1171, Shōan 1**
Ex. Goshiraka-
wa
Ex. Rokujō

Kiyomori's daughter Tokuko, aged fifteen, became an Imperial consort and the next year became Chūgū (equivalent to an Empress). Later she gave birth to a boy who became Emperor Antoku.[4] Tokuko became the Empress Dowager with the title Kenreimon-in (*Shite* of *Ohara Gokō*).

**1177, Jishō 1, May 29--June**

A conspiracy against the Heike, supported by Goshirakawa[5] was discovered, and the conspirators were subsequently punished.

**1179, Jishō 3, November**

Kiyomori effected a *coup d'état*, suspended Goshirakawa's *insei* (administration by a retired emperor, first introduced by Ex-Emperor Shirakawa, Goshirakawa's great grandfather), moved him to the Toba Detached Palace and kept him there under guard.

**1180, Jishō 4, Feb. 21**

Kiyomori dethroned Emperor Takakura, his daughter's husband, and enthroned his two-year old son, later known as Emperor Antoku.

Emp. Antoku **April 9--May 26**
Ex. Goshiraka-
wa
Ex. Takakura

MINAMOTO NO YORIMASA persuaded Prince Mochihito, Goshirakawa's son,[7] to revolt against the Imperial court and the Heike, and distributed the prince's letters among the Genji clansmen. The conspiracy came to light, the prince was killed as he fled to Nara, and YORIMASA committed suicide. (The Noh *Yorimasa* is about this incident.)

**June 2**

Kiyomori made Fukuhara (in present Hyogo Prefecture), the site of his detached palace, the new capital. The Emperor and the Ex-Emperors moved there, followed by their courtiers.

**June 24**

Minamoto no Yoritomo, on receiving Prince Mochihito's letter, raised his forces in the eastern districts against the Heike (at Goshirakawa's order, according to *Heike Monogatari*).

**September 7**

Minamoto no Yoshinaka,[8] Yoritomo's cousin, revolted against the Heike and raised an army in Kiso (in present Gifu prefecture).

**Oct. 20**

Yoritomo's forces met the Heike army by the Fuji River (in present Shizuoka Prefecture). The Heike, led by Taira no Koremori and TADANORI (*Shite* of *Tadanori*), fled without fighting, frightened by the sudden sound of numerous ducks flying up at night. Among the Heike warriors was SAITŌ BETTŌ SANEMORI, the aged warrior, the *Shite* of *Sanemori*.

**Nov. 26**

The men of the Heike and the Imperial court followed the Emperor and Ex-Emperors back to Kyoto, which again was made the capital.

**Dec. 28**

Kiyomori sent an army to Nara, led by his son Shigehira,[9] to subdue the rebellious monks of Tōdai and Kōfuku Temples. In the battle, the temples were burnt and many people died.

**1181, Yōwa 1, Jan. 14:** The death of Ex-Emperor Takakura.

**Feb. (Inter-calary) 4:** The death of Kiyomori

**24:** Goshirakawa was freed from Toba palace where he had been confined.

**1183, Juei 2, April 17--May 11**

The Heike forces attacked Minamoto no Yoshinaka headquartered at Kiso in the present Gifu Prefecture, but were defeated at Kurikara Tōge (a mountain pass on the borderline between Ishikawa and Toyama Prefectures) and fled with heavy casualties.

**May 12**

Yoshinaka defeated the Heike at Shinohara. SAITŌ

BETTŌ SANEMORI fell in the battle.

**July 22**

Having defeated the Heike in the subsequent battles, Yoshinaka arrived at Mt. Hiei, the site of Enryaku Temple, northwest of Kyoto.

**July 24**

The Heike fled to Fukuhara with the boy Emperor and his mother. They also tried to take Goshirakawa, but he had escaped to Enryaku Temple.

**In July**

From Fukuhara the Heike sailed to Dazaifu in Kyushu.

**July 28**

Kyoto was occupied by Yoshinaka.

Emp. Antoku
Emp. Gotoba
Ex. Goshiraka-
wa

**August 20**

In the absence of the boy Emperor, one of his younger brothers was made a new Emperor (later named Emperor Gotoba) by Goshirakawa.

**Oct. 20**

Driven from Dazaifu by local leaders, the Heike fled to Yamaga Castle, and then by ship to Yanagi-ga-Ura (Willow Bay). En route TAIRA NO KIYOTSUNE (Kiyomori's grandson, *Shite* of *Kiyotsune*) threw himself overboard and was drowned.

**During October**

The Heike settled at Yashima in Shikoku.

**Nov. 29--21**

Yoshinaka attacked Goshirakawa's palace and effected a *coup d'état*.

**December**

To attack Yoshinaka, Yoritomo sent an army led by his younger brothers, Noriyori[4] and YOSHITSUNE.

**1184, Juei 3=Genryaku 1, Jan. 20**

YOSHITSUNE and Noriyori entered Kyoto after they had beaten Yoshinaka, who fled from Kyoto and was killed in a skirmish at Awazu by Lake Biwa. Among those who followed him were IMAI NO KANEHIRA (*Shite* of *Kanehira*) and TOMOE (a female warrior, *Shite* of *Tomoe*).

**January**

The Heike forces came to Fukuhara and were headquartered at Ichinotani.

**Feb. 7**

The battle of Ichinotani. The Heike escaped to Yashima by ship. Many Heike leaders were killed, among them the *Shite* in the title roles of *Atsumori*, *Michimori*, *Tadanori*, *Tomoakira*, and *Tsunemasa*. KAJIWARA GENDA KAGESUE, a Genji warrior (*Shite* of *Ebira*), fought with

a branch of plum blossoms in his quiver (*ebira*).
**March 28**
Koremori, the heir of Kiyomori's deceased eldest son, left Yashima to visit the Kumano Shrine. Then he threw himself into the sea and was drowned.
**1185 Juei 4=Genryaku 2, Feb. 19**
YOSHITSUNE defeated the Heike in the battle of Yashima.
**March 24**
YOSHITSUNE destroyed the Heike in the battle of Dan-no-Ura. The boy Emperor Antoku was drowned when his grandmother, Ni-i no Ama (Kenreimon-in's mother)[4] leapt into the sea with him.

---

[1] Hōgen etc.: Name of a "year period." In Japan, years are counted by "year period," a system of Chinese origin. A year period was formerly changed at the occurrence of a disaster or a propitious omen, but in modern times, year periods have coincided with the reigns of Emperors.

[2] The names of *Shite* characters in *shura*-Noh are written in capital letters.

[3] Mentioned in *Tomonaga*.

[4] Mentioned in *Ohara Gokō*.

[5] A *Tsure* in *Ohara Gokō*.

[6] Mentioned in *Kogō*

[7] Mentioned in *Yorimasa*.

[8] A *Tsure* in *Kiso*; Mentioned in *Kanehira* and *Tomoe*.

[9] The *Tsure* in *Senju*.

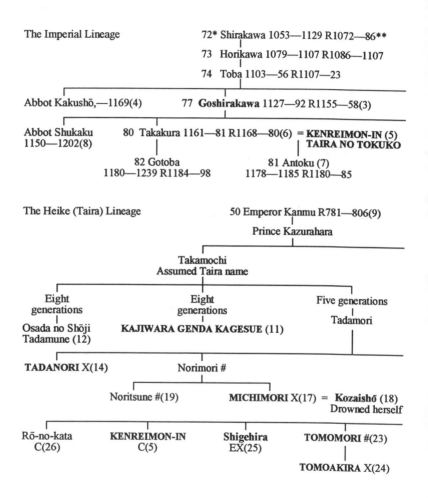

The Imperial Lineage

72* Shirakawa 1053—1129 R1072—86**

73 Horikawa 1079—1107 R1086—1107

74 Toba 1103—56 R1107—23

Abbot Kakushō,—1169(4)    77 **Goshirakawa** 1127—92 R1155—58(3)

Abbot Shukaku    80 Takakura 1161—81 R1168—80(6) = **KENREIMON-IN (5)**
1150—1202(8)                                              **TAIRA NO TOKUKO**

82 Gotoba              81 Antoku (7)
1180—1239 R1184—98    1178—1185 R1180—85

The Heike (Taira) Lineage

50 Emperor Kanmu R781—806(9)

Prince Kazurahara

Takamochi
Assumed Taira name

Eight                    Eight                    Five generations
generations              generations
                                                  Tadamori
Osada no Shōji    **KAJIWARA GENDA KAGESUE (11)**
Tadamune (12)

**TADANORI** X(14)    Norimori #

Noritsune #(19)    **MICHIMORI** X(17) = **Kozaishō** (18)
                                          Drowned herself

Rō-no-kata    **KENREIMON-IN**    **Shigehira**    **TOMOMORI** #(23)
C(26)         C(5)                EX(25)

**TOMOAKIRA** X(24)

* 72 = 72nd Emperor; ** R 1072-86 = Span of Reign.

Numbers in parentheses refer to names listed under the Genji Genealogy, following

X = Killed at Ichinotani. # = Killed at Dan-no-Ura.

C = Captured. EX = Captured and executed

Many other important Heike members were killed in battle or executed

Names in boldface are Noh characters, those in capitals being *Shite* roles

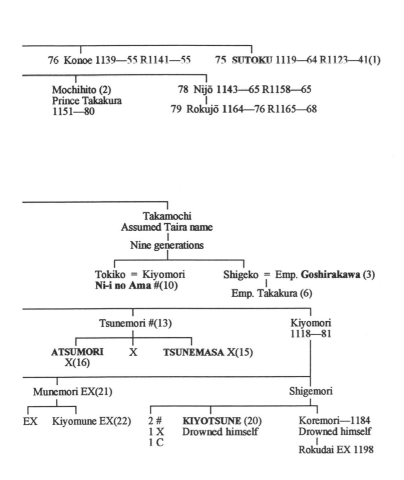

76 Konoe 1139—55 R1141—55      75 **SUTOKU** 1119—64 R1123—41(1)

Mochihito (2)
Prince Takakura
1151—80

78 Nijō 1143—65 R1158—65
79 Rokujō 1164—76 R1165—68

Takamochi
Assumed Taira name
Nine generations

Tokiko = Kiyomori
**Ni-i no Ama** #(10)

Shigeko = Emp. **Goshirakawa** (3)
Emp. Takakura (6)

Tsunemori #(13)

Kiyomori
1118—81

**ATSUMORI**    X    **TSUNEMASA** X(15)
X(16)

Munemori EX(21)

Shigemori

EX   Kiyomune EX(22)

2 #   **KIYOTSUNE** (20)
1 X   Drowned himself
1 C

Koremori—1184
Drowned himself

Rokudai EX 1198

Note: In these lineages, from right to left in any generation, is from elder to younger

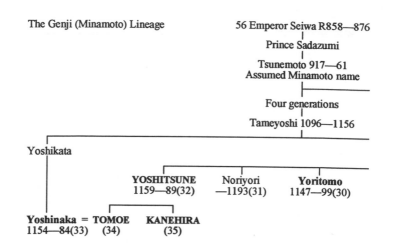

The Genji (Minamoto) Lineage

56 Emperor Seiwa R858—876
Prince Sadazumi
Tsunemoto 917—61
Assumed Minamoto name

Four generations
Tameyoshi 1096—1156

Yoshikata

YOSHITSUNE 1159—89(32)    Noriyori —1193(31)    Yoritomo 1147—99(30)

Yoshinaka = TOMOE    KANEHIRA
1154—84(33)   (34)      (35)

In the list below, "M" indicates mentioned in a Noh play

1 **SUTOKU**: in *Matsuyama Tengu*
2 Mochihito: M. *Yorimasa*
3 **Goshirakawa**: in *Ohara Gokō*; M. *Tadanori, Tomonaga*
4 Kakushō: M. *Tsunemasa*
5 **KENREIMON-IN**: in *Ohara Gokō*
6 Takakura: M. *Kogō*
7 Antoku: M. *Kiyotsune, Ohara Gokō*
8 Shukaku: M. *Tsunemasa*
9 Kanmu: M. *Funa-Benkei; Kanehira*
10 **Ni-i-no-Ama**: in *Ikari Kazuki*; M. *Ohara Gokō* and others
11 **KAJIWARA GENDA KAGESUE**: in *Ebira*
12 Osada no Shōji: M. *Tomonaga*
13 Tsunemori: M. *Atsumori*
14 **TADANORI**; in *Tadanori*
15 **TSUNEMASA**: in *Tsunemasa*
16 **ATSUMORI** in *Atsumori*
17 **MICHIMORI**: in *Michimori*
18 **Kozaishō**: in *Michimori*
19 Noritsune: M *Ohara Gokō, Yashima, Ikari Kazuki, Michimori*

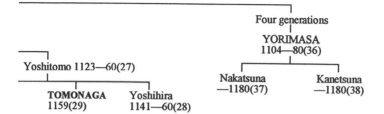

20 **KIYOTSUNE**: in *Kiyotsune*
21 Munemori: in *Yuya*; M in *Tomoakira*
22 Kiyomune: M. in *Tomoakira*
23 **TOMOMORI**: in *Funabenkei*, *Ikari Kazuki*; M. in *Ohara Gokō*, *Tomoakira*
24 **TOMOAKIRA**: in *Tomoakira*
25 **Shigehira**: in *Senju*
26 Rō-no-Kata: her mother, **TOKIWA**, in *Fue no Maki*, was Yoshitsune's mother
27 Yoshitomo: M. *Tomonaga*
28 Yoshihira: M. *Tomonaga*
29 **TOMONAGA**: in *Tomonaga*
30 **Yoritomo**: in *Shichiki-ochi*, *Daibutsu Kuyō*; M. *Tomonaga* and others
31 Noriyori: M. *Ohara Gokō*
32 **YOSHITSUNE**: in *Yashima*, *Settai*, *Shōzon* among others
33 **Yoshinaka**: in *Kiso*; M. *Kanehira*, *Tomoe*
34 **TOMOE**: in *Tomoe*
35 **KANEHIRA**: in *Kanehira*
36 **YORIMASA**: in *Yorimasa*, M. *Nue*
37 Nakatsuna: M. *Yorimasa*
38 Kanetsuna: M. *Yorimasa*

# GLOSSARY OF TECHNICAL TERMS
## USED IN THIS BOOK

For the terms about the Noh stage, refer to the stage plan, p. ix.

AGE-UTA (high-pitched song)  General term for high-pitched songs in *hira-nori*. *Michiyuki*, *rongi*, and the latter part of the *kuse*, among others, are *age-uta* type songs.

AI-KYŌGEN, also AI
   1. Interlude between the first and second acts, performed by *kyōgen-kata* (comedian). Sometimes *ai-kyōgen* comes at the beginning of a Noh.
   2. *Kyōgen-kata* who perform *ai-kyōgen*. In a number of Noh *ai-kyōgen* play minor roles with other actors during the main performance.

ASAKURA-JŌ  A mask for a humble old man.

ASHIRAI ("taking part")  Incongruent instrumental accompaniment, quiet music performed by flute alone, or by *daishô*, or by flute and *daishô*. Typically *ashirai* accompanies *sashi*-style singing. Example: *sashi*-song in *kuri-sashi-kuse*; quiet entrance of a graceful *shite* woman. Example: *Yuya*, *Hajitomi*; entrance from the *hashigakari* onto the main stage of *shite* and *tsure* after they have sung *issei*. Example: *Takasago*, *Yashima*.

ATSUITA ("thick board")  A type of *kitsuke* (kimono) made of *atsuita-mono* (thick board type), a type of silk cloth so named because it is thick and comes folded flat about *atsu-ita* (thick board), instead of thin board or in a roll as in the case of soft cloth. *Atsuita kitsuke* is primarily worn by male characters. One with bold patterns is worn by warriors in full battle attire or by demons; one with bold horizontal stripes in red and white, by young *waki*-Noh gods; a plaited one, by dignified old men and high-ranking priests. *Atsuita* is also worn by special types of humble old men and *yamabushi* priests,

ATSUITA KARAORI  Colorful, gorgeous *karaori*, which is primarily a woman's outer robe, is referred to as *atsuita karaori* when worn by a male character as *kitsuke*. In color and pattern, an *atsuita karaori* is more masculine than an ordinary *karaori*. See KARAORI.

AU, or more properly, AI  (In *hira-nori* rhythm)  In this series, the first term is used in the texts because the second term is like *ai* in the sense of interlude performance and its players.

199

AWAZU (In free rhythm)

CHŌKEN ("long silk") A robe made of transparently woven thick silk named *chōken*, with elegant patterns in gold and silver, used as the dancing robe of heavenly maidens, female spirits and ghosts. It is also worn by elegant male characters, among them, the young warrior ghosts of *shura*-Noh in full battle attire. Examples: *Michimori* and *Tomoakira*.

DAISHŌ ("large and small") Large and small hand drums.

DAN-ATSUITA (*atsuita* with horizontal stripes) A type of *atsuita kitsuke* (See ATSUITA) with gorgeous patterns in two-tone color arrangement forming thick horizontal stripes (*dan*), worn by brave warriors, mighty deities and supernatural beings.

DAN-NOSHIME See NOSHIME.

DEHA A type of music by *daishō* and *taiko* in *ō-nori* rhythm, with the flute accompaniment in free rhythm, performed at the entrance of certain types of deities, demons, spirits, heavenly maidens and ghosts. Among *shura*-Noh, *deha* is performed in *Michimori*, *Sanemori* and *Tomonaga*.

FIRST PINE Of the three pines planted along the *hashigakari*, the first pine is nearest the main stage, close to the *shite* pillar.

HANGIRE or HANGIRI A type of divided skirt made of gorgeous brocade with bold patterns, worn by powerful deities, demons and warriors.

HAPPI A long- and wide-sleeved brocade robe with large colorful patterns. Lined *happi* with bold patterns are sworn by demons and mighty warrior ghosts; unlined ones with elegant patterns, by young warrior ghosts in place of *chōken*.

HASHIGAKARI (bridgeway) The passage leading from *kagami-no-ma* (mirror room) to the main stage. Besides serving for entrances and exits, it is also often used as an extension of the main stage.

HEIDA or HEITA A male mask for *shura*-Noh ghost warriors in their prime. Heida is a common samurai name meaning "the first son of a Heike-descendant family," with "Hei" meaning Taira or Heike, and "da(ta)" meaning the first son, short for "Tarō."

HIRA-NORI (ordinary rhythm) In this rhythm, 12-syllable lines in a song are divided into eight beats, For example:

|    | 1 |    | 2 |    | 3 |    | 4 |    | 5 |    | 6 |    | 7 |    | 8 |
|----|---|----|----|----|----|----|----|----|---|----|----|----|----|----|---|
| Wa | ˂ ga | ná | o | ˂ na | ní to | ˂ | i | ú na | mí no | ˂ |
| Hi | - ku | ya yo | - ji | o | mo | - a | sa ku | ra ya | ˂ |

"My name . . . but what name? Evening waves
Ebb with nocturnal tide, not deep yet the dawn's glow,"
*Yashima* 157--158

HITOE-HAPPI (unlined *happi* robe) See HAPPI.

ISSEI
1. A type of music by flute and *daishō*, played at the entrance of a character who first sings a song in free rhythm such as *issei* or

*sashi*. Examples: At the entrance of *Mae-shite* and *Tsure*, and of *Nochi-shite* in *Yashima*.

2. A dignified brief song in free rhythm, typically consisting of five initial lines, two second-part lines and two final lines. It is sung:

    a. By character(s) on entering the stage to *issei* or *shin-no-issei* music. When there are *shite* and *tsure*, they sing together, with the second part or *ni-no-ku* sung by the *tsure* alone. Example: *Yashima*, act two.

    b. Alternately by character(s) and the chorus before *mai* or at a climactic point. Example: *Eguchi* 139--143.

**JI(-UTAI)** 1. The parts in Noh libretto sung by the chorus. 2. The chorus.

**JIDORI** Repetition by *ji* (the chorus) of a *shidai* song after it has been sung by actor(s), or, on rare occasions, by the chorus. (See SHIDAI) *Jidori* is in free rhythm, with the exception of *shin-no-shidai*, which is in regular rhythm, and which occurs in most *waki* (god) Noh. The second line of a *shidai*, which is the same as the first, is not sung in *jidori*.

**JI-UTAI** See JI.

**JŌ-ZA** ("The fixed position") The place to the right of the *shite* pillar in the left back corner of the stage, *shite*'s key position during the whole performance. *Shite* as well as other characters on many occasions, stand there on first entering the main stage. See the Plan of the Noh Stage, page ix.

**KACHI-SHURA** (victorious shura) A *shura*-Noh with a victorious hero.

**KAKARU** In the Noh libretto, this designation is used when certain types of singing or spoken lines change to *sashi* style singing (singing in free rhythm, sung like a musical speech), or when a character first accosts another character or sings to himself in the *sashi* style. Passages which should be marked *kakaru* according to this rule are sometimes marked *sashi*. There are some cases of confusion in librettos in the use of these terms.

**KAKEAI** Alternate singing in free rhythm between two characters, in most cases between *shite* and *waki*, usually ending in a rhythmic song. Sometimes *kakeai* occurs between two or more characters on either side.

**KAKERI** A brief dance accompanied by the flute and two hand drums, performed at a climactic point to represent certain actions, or to express a high-strung emotional state. In *shura*-Noh, a *kakeri* is performed in the fighting scene.

**KARAORI** ("Chinese fabric") A kimono-style robe with comparatively small sleeves, made of rich brocade with colorful, elaborately woven and embroidered patterns. Primarily it is the ordinary attire of female characters.

**KATA** (gesture pattern) A prescribed gesture pattern in Noh with a specific name.

**KATARI** (narrative) Story-telling by *shite* or *waki* to other character(s), spoken all the way, or ending in singing. Often a *katari* is an important feature in the performance. Example: *Yashima* 107--120.

KINAGASHI ("Worn all the way down") Attire without a skirt, consisting of a *kitsuke* (inner kimono) and an upper garment, less formal than attire with a skirt. Examples: ordinary *mae-shite* and *tsure* women in *karaori* robe, such as the *Mae-shite* in *Tomoe* and *Tsure* in *Michimori*; humble persons, such as the *Mae-shite* and *Tsure* in *Yashima*, the fishermen; ordinary traveling monks such as those in *Yashima*.

KIRI (conclusion, finale)

1. In the broader sense, the last section of a Noh. The *kiri* in most *shura*-Noh describes the hero's fight in the battle field or in the Asura Hell.

2. In a narrower sense, a brief section which forms a sort of epilogue. In the Noh libretto, such a section is marked *kiri*. Example: *Michimori*.

KITSUKE A kimono-style basic dress worn with or without an upper robe. When worn as an inner garment, it shows at the wide-open front and from under the large sleeves of the upper robe. There are several kinds of *kitsuke* with different materials and patterns for different types of characters. Sometimes an upper robe is worn as *kitsuke* under a robe.

KOGAKI (special performance) Well over half of the Noh currently performed have one or more variations, or *kogaki*. In a *kogaki* performance, masks, costumes, *kata* or *mai* will change from the standard one. Often there are omissions, the most often omitted part being the *kuse*. The whole atmosphere may change under a *kogaki*. There will be greater accent in singing and action, with increased emphasis on the changing rhythm in performance which Ze-ami referred to as *jo-ha-kyū* (slow/beginning-- > quickening/"breaking" -- > development-- > quick/finale). *Kogaki* literally meaning "in small writing" is so termed because it is indicated in small letters beside the Noh title in the program.

KŌKEN (stage assistant) During performance, two kōken, and three in a few special Noh, sit at *kōken-za* (*kōken*'s place, explained below). They are responsible primarily for *shite*-group actors and take care of their costumes, accessaries and stage properties during performance, and act as prompters. If a *shite*, or a *shite*-group actor, because of sudden illness or some other reason is unable to continue his performance, *kōken* are expected to immediately take his place even during a performance.

KŌKEN-ZA (kōken's place) The place where *kōken* sit, at the left of *ato-za* at the back of the stage.

KURI A high-pitched melodious short song in free rhythm. In the formal structure, *kuri* and *sashi* precede *kuse*, as explained below. The section referred to as *kuri-sashi-kuse* forms the core of Noh.

KUSE A long thematic song in regular rhythm, beginning slowly at a low pitch and ending in an *age-uta*, sung by the chorus, with the exception of short passage in the middle of it which is sung by the *shite*, sometimes by *tsure* or *kokata*, in solo or in duet. In the standard form *kuse* is preceded by *kuri* and *sashi*. *Kuse*, which used to be called *kuse-mai* (*kuse* dance), is an adaptation of a popular song by the same name which Kan-ami first introduced into Noh with great success. Occurring in most Noh, the *kuse* forms the central part of the play. It is often accompanied by a dance. As a rule, a *kuse* that occurs in the first act of a visional Noh is not accompanied by a dance, but the *kuse* in the second act has a dance. However, in a number of *shura-Noh*, the *kuse* in the second act has no dance. Example: *Tomoakira*. A *kuse* with a dance is called *mai-guse* (dancing *kuse*), and one without a dance is called *i-guse* (sitting *kuse*).

MACHI-UTAI ("waiting-song") A brief *age-uta* sung by the *waki* (and *waki-tsure*) at the beginning of the second act of a visional Noh, in expectation of the reappearance of the *shite* as a supernatural being or a ghost. Sometimes a *machi-utai* is preceded by a few lines which are spoken or sung in free rhythm. Example: *Yashima*. Some two-act visional Noh with special structure have no *machi-utai*. Example: when the *mae-shite* in *waki*-(god) Noh makes the interim exit accompanied by music called *raijo*.

MAE-SHITE *Shite* in the first act of a two-act Noh.

MAKE-SHURA (defeated shura) A *shura*-Noh whose hero is the ghost of a warrior of a defeated battle. All but three *shura*-Noh are *make-shura*.

MASUGAMI A young-woman mask with a pair of vertical wrinkles between the eyebrows, expressing the emotional agitation of the character who can be a goddess or a young woman's ghost.

MICHIYUKI (travel song)
1. A type of *age-uta* describing a travel, sung by a character (and his companions) after he has announced his name and traveling intention.
2. A travel song more elaborate and longer than one explained above, forming an important part of a Noh. It is usually indicated as an *age-uta*, *rongi*, etc. according to the occasion.

MIZUGOROMO One of the most widely used upper robes in Noh, worn by travelers or humble characters at work. Examples: traveling *waki* and *waki-tsure* monks, ghosts or spirits appearing as fishermen, or boatmen, such as the *Mae-shite* in *Yashima* and *Kanehira*.

MONDAI, also MONDŌ ("questions and answers") Dialogue spoken as a rule between *shite* and *waki*, especially one that occurs in the early part of a Noh when the *waki* asks questions of the *shite*, a stranger who has appeared before him.

NAKAIRI (interim exit) Exit of a major character who reappears later, typically the exit of the *mae-shite* at the end of the first act.

NANORI (self-introduction or name-telling) Lines spoken by a character on his first entrance onto the stage, addressed to no specific person, telling who he is and what he is going to do. Usually this is done at *jō-za* ("the fixed place"), the key position on the stage for the *shite*, which is also called *nanori-za* ("self-introduction place"). *Nanori* may be preceded by a brief introductory song called *shidai*.

NANORI-BUE ("self-introduction flute") A prelude by the flute played exclusively at the entrance of the *waki* who, on entering the stage, immediately tells his name and intention without a preliminary song. Example: *Michimori*. Sometimes a *waki* who sings no preliminary song may enter without *nanori-bue*.

NANORI-ZA ("self-introduction place") See NANORI.

NASHIUCHI EBOSHI A hat which, when not in use, looks like a bag pressed flat, with an arched top. It is worn with the flat top bent a little to the right or left, by warriors in battle attire, such as the warrior ghosts in *shura*-Noh, and by upper-class samurai in a suit named *hitatare kamishimo*, consisting of a wide-sleeved robe and a pair of long trailing trousers.

NOCHI-SHITE *Shite* in the second act of a two-act Noh.

NORU (in *ō-nori*) A designation in the Noh libretto telling that the rhythm is in *ō-nori*. See Ō-NORI.

NOSHIME *Kitsuke* (inner robe) made of a special kind of silk of the same name. Plain dark-colored *noshime* is for ordinary monks, humble men and women. Examples: *Waki* and *Waki-tsure* monks in *Yashima*, the *Mae-shite* in *Kanehira*. *Noshime* with bold horizontal stripes in white and blue, yellow or brown, is for a samurai or gentleman without a mask. Example: the *Mae-shite* of *Tomoakira*.

NUIHAKU ("embroidered and gilt") A kimono-style silk dress with colorfully dyed, gilt and embroidered elegant patterns, worn by a woman, usually under an upper robe, wrapped about the waist like a skirt in *koshimaki* style. *Nuihaku* is also worn as *kitsuke* by certain types of elegant male characters, such as young warrior ghosts in *shura*-Noh.

ŌKUCHI ("large opening") A type of divided skirt, made of thick silk, plain or colored, wide opening below, worn under *sashinuki* and *suō* trousers; also worn by itself in a costume representing military attire, or in costumes for deities and elegant male and female characters.

Ō-NORI ("large rhythm") In a song in *ō-nori*, the standard eight-beat line has 6--8 syllables, often one beat to one syllable. Because of this, *ō-nori* is slower and more rhythmical than *hira-nori* (ordinary rhythm) which has 12 syllables distributed among eight beats. Example from *Michimori*:

| 1 | 2 | 3 | 4 | 5 | 6 | 7 | 8 |
|---|---|---|---|---|---|---|---|
|   | Mi - chi | - mo | - ri | - fu | - u | - fu |
| u - , | o - kyo | - o | - ni | - hi | - ka | - re |

"Michimori and his wife
To the sutra attracted," Line 129--130

As a rule a song accompanied by the *taiko* is in *ō-nori*, but the converse is not always true, that is, an *ō-nori* song may not be accompanied by the *taiko*.

RONGI ("conversational") A very rhythmical *age-uta* sung alternately between the character(s) and *ji-utai* (chorus), or between characters, ending in chorus. For *rongi* as a working song, see the Introduction to *Matsukaze*, pp. 150--151, "*The Noh*, Vol. 3, Book 2.

SAGE-UTA (low-pitched song) A brief song in *hira-nori* (ordinary rhythm) keyed to the low pitch, often precedes *age-uta*. Example: Line 104--105, *Michimori*.

SANBAN-ME-MONO (third-on-the-program piece) So named because it is the third play on a standard five-Noh program. It is also referred to as *kazura-mono* ("wig play") because its typical heroine is a graceful young woman with a wig bound with a gilt and embroidered colorful *kazura-obi* (wig band).

SASHI A song in free rhythm, sung smoothly like a recitative. It comes in various parts of a Noh. Typically a section made up of *kuri*, *sashi* and *kuse* forms the core of a Noh. See KURI and KUSE.

SHIDAI

1. A brief introductory song in three lines in *hira-nori* (ordinary rhythm) sung by one or more characters on their entrance onto the stage, and repeated by *ji-utai* (the chorus) in free rhythm and without the second line which is the same as the first. This repetition by *ji-utai* is called *jidori*. (See JIDORI.) Sometimes *shidai* comes at a climactic point, or before *kuri-sashi-kuse* as a sort of prelude. The chorus sings it as well as the *jidori*. Example: *Kakitsubata* 113.

2. Music by flute and *daishō* played at the entrance of those characters who sing *shidai* on entering the stage. Example: At the entrance of *Waki* and *Waki-tsure* in *Yashima*.

SHITE ("the performer") The leading role and its performer.

SHURA-NOH (battle Noh) Sixteen (seventeen in the Kanze school) Noh in which a warrior ghost, in all but one instance a Heike or Genji, tells the story of his or her final battle. ("Final," except in victorious *shura*-Noh.) See *The Noh* Vol. 2, Book 1, pp. 1--26.

SHURA-NORI (*shura* rhythm) The quickest of all three rhythms, with more syllables to the eight-beat line, often two syllables to one beat, compared with the *hira-nori* (ordinary rhythm) with twelve syllables to eight beats, or *ō-nori* ("large rhythm") with eight. The quick tempo is fit to describe quick actions. More generally it is called rather illogically *chū-nori* (medium rhythm). The rhythm can occur both in *tsuyo-gin* (strong singing) and *yowa-gin* (gentle singing). Naturally it is in *tsuyo-gin* in a battle scene. The term *shura-nori* is used specifically when it occurs in a fighting scene. Example from *Yorimasa*:

| 1 | | 2 | | 3 | | 4 | | 5 | | 6 | | 7 | | 8 |
|---|---|---|---|---|---|---|---|---|---|---|---|---|---|---|
| ná | ga | ré | n | mú | sha | ní | wa | yú | ha | zú | o | tó | ra | sé |
| ta | ga | i | ni | chi | ka | ra | o | - | a | wa | su | be | shi | to |

"If a man is being swept away, let him seize your bow.
Unite yourselves as one to help each other." Lines 215--216.

**SUMI-BŌSHI** A head covering worn by monks.

**SUŌ** A suit consisting of a finely patterned, large-sleeved robe and a pair of long trailing trousers with the same pattern. Sometimes, as in the case of the *Mae-shite* in *Tomoakira*, the upper robe may be worn with an *ōkuchi* divided skirt. *Suō* is for maskless males such as samurai of lower status, servants or merchants.

**SURIHAKU** A kimono-style dress of satin-type white silk, with fine patterns in gold or silver, worn widely as *kitsuke* (inner robe) by female characters.

**TAIKO** (big drum) One of the three drums used in Noh. It is larger than the other two, and while the other two are beaten with a hand, *taiko* is beaten with sticks. Unlike the other two drums, *taiko* is played only in special pieces, usually in the finale and in certain types of *mai* and musical accompaniment. Songs and music with *taiko* are as a rule in *ō-nori*.

**TAIKO-ZA** (*Taiko* player's seat) The place on the Noh stage where *taiko* player sits. See Plan of Noh Stage, p. ix.

**THIRD PINE** Of the three pines along the *hashigakari* (the bridge stage), the third one from the main stage. When *shite* and *tsure* enter together and sing the first song on the *hashigakari*, the *shite* stands by the third pine and the *tsure* by the first.

**TSUKI-ZERIFU** (arrival speech) Lines spoken by a traveler after a travel song, announcing that he has arrived at his destination.

**TSUKURIMONO** ("Fabricated objects") Stage props so names because they are assembled every time they are used, to be dissembled afterwards, mere frames made of bamboo, wood, cloth etc. representing all sorts of structures and smaller objects placed on the stage floor.

**TSURE** (companion) Short for *shite-tsure* (*shite*'s companion), *tsure* is related to *shite* as a sister, friend, servant and so on. Tsure can be male or female. Examples: the young fisherman accompanying the *Mae-shite* in *Yashima*; *Shite*'s wife in *Michimori*.

**WAKI** The supporting role, second to *shite* in importance, always a male without a mask. *Waki* and *waki-tsure* (*waki*'s companion) roles are played exclusively by *waki-kata* (*waki* players), who never play the part of *shite* and other roles, such as (*shite*-)*tsure*, which belong to *shite-kata* (*shite* players). Many plays have only *shite* and *waki*, and plays without *waki* are exceptionally few.

WAKI-NOH   A genre of Noh having a deity as *shite*, ceremonial and congratulatory in nature, so named because in a formal program, *waki-Noh* meaning "next Noh" is presented immediately after the first piece, *Okina*.   For details see *The Noh*, Vol. 1, God Noh.

# INDEX

Notes: 1. The paged references are read as follows: 42 is page 42; 88 L168 is page 88, Line 168 (a numbered line in a play); 32 n64 is page 32, footnote 64; 8, 43 are pages 8 and 43, etc.

2. "Poet" after a proper name indicates that person is the author of the poem cited, who may also be known as courtier, priest, warrior, etc. as was often the case with authors in anthologies.

# CORNELL EAST ASIA SERIES

For ordering information, please contact:

*Cornell East Asia Series*
East Asia Program
Cornell University
140 Uris Hall
Ithaca, NY 14853-7601
USA
(607) 255-6222.

3-93/.6M/BB